THE EMERGENCE OF CULTURAL STUDIES
ADULT EDUCATION, CULTURAL POLITICS AND THE 'ENGLISH' QUESTION

THE EMERGENCE OF CULTURAL STUDIES
ADULT EDUCATION, CULTURAL POLITICS AND THE 'ENGLISH' QUESTION

TOM STEELE

Lawrence & Wishart Limited
99a Wallis Road
London E9 5LN

First published 1997 by Lawrence and Wishart
© Tom Steele, 1997

ISBN 0 85315 826 6

Photoset by Francesca Hamon
Printed and Bound in Great Britain by Redwood Books, Trowbridge

Contents

Acknowledgements

Introduction

1 A Lost Genealogy:
  Adult Education and the Project of British Cultural Studies   9

2 Class and Nation:
  Working-Class Identity and the 'English' Settlement   33

3 English Studies: an Internal Colonisation   49

4 National Popular: Class Culture or Mass Culture?   72

5 Karl Mannheim:
  the Emigré Intellectual and the 'Sociological Turn'   98

6 Between Cultures:
  Richard Hoggart and Popular Culture   118

7 Edward Thompson and the West Riding:
  Cold War and Cultural Struggle   144

8 Raymond Williams and the Invention of Cultural Politics   176

9 Conclusion:
  Marginal Occupations, Adult Education and Social Renewal   200

Bibliography   211

Index

For
Gertie Roche,
and to the Memory of
Jim Roche

Acknowledgements

This book is an outcome of a research project funded by the former University Funding Council's Continuing Education research budget 1992-94, at the Department of Adult Continuing Education, University of Leeds on which I was the research fellow. My thanks go especially to Prof. Richard Taylor whose unflagging support and perceptive advice have been inestimable. This study has benefited greatly from the comments, corrections and suggestions for sources from my many friends and colleagues in that department whose patience in reading drafts and discussing issues has also been invaluable. It would be hard to find more dedicated, scholarly and generous support. In particular I would like to thank Janet Coles, Andy Croft, Malcolm Chase, David Goodway, Jill Liddington, Rebecca O'Rourke, and Luke Spencer. Professor Stuart Marriott has allowed me to consult the Raybould Papers which he has collected and the collection of *Tutors' Bulletins* and has very helpfully guided my attention to the work of A.D. Lindsay. Chris Sheppard and Anne Farr at the Brotherton Collection also drew my attention to Richard Hoggart's recently acquired correspondence with Bonamy Dobrée and as usual have been more than helpful. M.J. Morgan and Anne Shaughnessy, the Department of Adult Continuing Education librarians, greatly assisted my rummaging through the archives. I'm very grateful to Griselda Pollock and Adrian Rifkin for allowing me the opportunity to try out many of the ideas here on students on the MA in Cultural Studies at Leeds and I've benefited greatly from their feedback and further research.

I am extremely grateful to Richard Hoggart who read earlier drafts of the chapters concerning him and returned them annotated and corrected at a warm afternoon's rendezvous in a café on Waterloo Station. Dorothy Thompson has also very kindly read the chapter on the late Edward Thompson and allowed me to quote from his correspondence with the University of Leeds. I'm grateful to John McIlroy for commenting on my chapter on Raymond Williams, Prof. Roger Fieldhouse for allowing to me use his PhD thesis and commenting on an early draft of chapter one. Prof. Hywel Francis and Rob Humphries at the University College of Swansea gave me a number of helpful suggestions and insights, especially in relation to Raymond Williams. I interviewed a number of former staff of the old extra-mural department including Prof. John Rex, Prof. Bernard Jennings and Tom Caldwell who gave me chapter and verse. Prof. J.F.C. Harrison very kindly let me have an early draft of his chapter about his time in the Leeds department, appropriately called 'Written Work', from his recently published autobiography. I'm very grateful to Sheila Rowbotham for a long interview and for patiently reading back through her early WEA lecture notebooks. Thanks to Ben Knights I was able to interview his father Prof. L. C. Knights who was more than generous with his time and memories. A very nice lunch with Lisa Jardine and Julia Swindells at a café near the British Museum renewed an old acquaintance and provided a fresh perspective on the patriarchal origins of British cultural studies. Jonathan Rée and members of the Radical Philosophy editorial collective made me rethink the chapter on English studies but I'm still not sure they would agree with it. I've benefited greatly from conversations with Dick Leith and Barbara Crowther about these issues and Jim McGuigan has always made the incisive comment. My old friend Ahmed Gurnah commented extensively on chapter two and forced me to revise my ideas on culture. Trevor Griffiths, Harold Best and Gertie Roche have vividly conveyed to me the atmosphere around the beginnings of the New Left. Finally, thanks to Lynne for her love and support. It's almost invidious to name names in this way in what for me has been a cultural interchange lasting many years with many good friends and colleagues. I've been very lucky. I hope those I have not named will know they are in there somewhere. Many thanks also to Vicky Grut at Lawrence and Wishart for such a fine editorial job.

Introduction

The aim of this archaeological study is to attempt to reconstruct a pre-history of British cultural studies, in the work of adult education between the 1930s and the 1960s. It traces the influence of new approaches to working-class history, popular formations, the 'national' culture and socialist politics which were being produced in the work of adult educators in the immediate post-war period. The educational work of E.P. Thompson, Richard Hoggart and Raymond Williams will be of special interest because of their role in the 'founding' both of British cultural studies and the New Left; but they will be contextualised within the broader creative milieu of experiment and re-alignment within adult education. The work of other figures in adult education – such as Thomas Hodgkin, Sidney Raybould, A.D. Lindsay, Karl Mannheim, Karl Polanyi and G.H. Thompson, and their interrelationships – are also significant in constructing what Williams might have called a structure of feeling.

The milieu of adult education in the immediate pre-war and post-war period has been reconstructed by reference to archival searches, articles in the professional, educational and political journals, papers from institutional and professional associations, and private papers and interviews with tutors and students in adult education during this period. The study also examines the founding of English studies in the nineteenth century, and the use of literary and textual criticism as modes of political and social analysis in, for example, the agenda of the Leavises and *Scrutiny* in the 1930s.

The book argues that adult education has, since the nineteenth century, been a critical place of dialogue and negotiation between the forces attempting to modernise the British state and emergent social movements, especially that of the labour or 'working-class' movement. While a revised conception of Englishness which could incorporate the newly enfranchised lower classes was being advocated by liberal intellectuals, the subaltern classes were developing their own forms of collectivist culture. Hardly less important, although until recently relatively neglected, was the space provided by adult education for the education of women. Many were the newly recruited teachers in the board schools created by the 1870 Education Act who had a pivotal role in articulating the new cultures to the rising generations.

The Emergence of Cultural Studies attempts to understand how the practice of interdisciplinary work grew within adult education classes, and to assess the importance of the special circumstances of this work – dialogic democratic practice, mature and experienced students, political commitment and class-consciousness, links with the organised labour movement, the ethic of 'social purpose', resistance to academic compartmentalising of knowledge, and other non-institutional aspects. It argues that interdisciplinary study in adult education was an important precursor of academic British cultural studies; the particular circumstances of cultural studies were focused by arguments over the role and status of the 'literary' and the 'sociological' in adult liberal studies. There is also an examination of the origins of the study of 'popular culture' in adult classes in the early 1930s, and of the increasing importance of sociology, especially in the work of R.H. Tawney and that of Karl Mannheim and other European émigrés who were involved in adult education in the late 1930s. Another important element in the reconstitution of adult liberal studies was the work of socialist and communist historians in the creation of a social history freed from mechanical determinisms, and more open to 'cultural' effects; in this, the Communist Party Historians Group and the work of Tawney and Cole were of central importance.

The study locates the work of Raymond Williams, E.P. Thompson and Richard Hoggart within this innovative pedagogic climate and tracks their preoccupation with the term 'culture' (first noted by Perry Anderson in 1966), which led to the foundation of the Birmingham Centre for Contemporary Cultural Studies, and subsequently the widespread flowering of cultural studies within polytechnics and internal university departments. The strategic importance of the work of Thompson, Williams and their colleagues in adult education in Oxford, Leeds and elsewhere to the formation of the New Left is seen as organically related to their educational project. Finally, the study notes the development of the History Workshop movement from Ruskin College, and the subsequent origins of women's studies in adult education, with, for example, the work of Sheila Rowbotham and feminist critiques of the originating project.

Chapter one takes issue with the assumption that British cultural studies emerged as an offshoot of a university school of English, and documents the work of adult educationalists who were shifting politics into the realm of symbolic values in the immediate post-war period. It argues that, ironically, cultural studies were enabled by the very decline of independent working-class education as a distinct formation, but that they received their radical impulse from this formation. The transition from a class-based to a national popular educational constituency was crucial in relocating the site of ideological contestation. The chapter begins to differentiate the specific contributions of Raymond Williams, E. P. Thompson and Richard Hoggart to this educational project.

Drawing on the work of Eric Hobsbawm and others, chapter two argues that modernised class-based identities and national identities emerged at the same time in the late nineteenth century, and the work of adult education can be seen as attempting to negotiate the contiguities of these identities. The establishment of an English 'settlement' recognised the relative incorporation of the working class into the democratic polity, but also the strength and independence of working-class culture.

Chapter three surveys the rise of English studies as an academic discipline from their colonial roots in India to the Newbolt Report. It suggests that a colonial metaphor of missionary appropriation, which was first tested on the Indian subcontinent, was subsequently applied to the English working class and provincial regions. Thus, as Brian Doyle and others have argued, the development of English studies and the recreation of English identity are interwoven. The chapter also draws on the work of the new generation of radical Indian scholars inspired by Edward Said. However, it is not assumed that this was simply a top-down process of hegemonic imposition and identity erasure, but argues that the marginal space offered by adult education also allowed the contrasting voice to be heard; as a result a dialogic quality was inserted into the English settlement, which recognised difference and diversity.

Chapter four charts the pedagogic wars of the 1930s over the teaching of the arts and culture, and contends that it was possible to see them as constructed between twin polarities. On the one hand were the metropolitan modernisers at the centre of the adult education movement, who wanted to construct the national popular; and on the other the provincial class-warriors bent on maintaining a workers' education based on the needs and experience of the organised labour movement. In many respects this was an (eternally recurrent) argument between the 'literary' and the 'sociological' wings of the movement, the former wanting purity of textual study (and class harmony) and the latter wanting relevance to life (and class struggle). The fecundity and passion of the arguments, it is held, contributed immensely to the emergence and quality of British cultural studies.

It was clear that by the end of the 1930s a different kind of voice was intervening in these debates, that of the European, mostly Jewish, intellectuals who had fled from Nazi persecution to Britain. What they brought was a much more sophisticated sociological reading of Marxism than had been developed in Britain. For many of these intellectuals adult education was the key pedagogical site of intervention. This chapter concentrates on the most active of this group, Karl Mannheim. Mannheim's views on the commitment and autonomy of the intellectual, the

4

need for a totalising sociology or 'science of society', and the centrality of culture in creating social consciousness, were of inestimable importance in shaping the debates to come. The chapter suggests that his importance to the pre-history of British cultural studies has been both seminal and undervalued. Mannheim's ideas are contextualised within his work in adult educational circles in Britain, especially his relationship with A.D. Lindsay, Master of Balliol and chair of the Oxford Delegacy, and his involvement in Christian socialist networks.

The next three chapters analyse the individual contributions of Richard Hoggart, E.P. Thompson and Raymond Williams to the emergence of British cultural studies as an adult educational project. Chapter six attempts to reconstruct Richard Hoggart's epic journey across Leeds from the working-class Hunslet of his childhood to the literary culture of Bonamy Dobrée at the University of Leeds. Hoggart has documented much of this in his recent autobiographies and in his letters to Dobrée. Unlike Williams and Thompson, Hoggart was less interested in the grand political and historical narratives of the working class and the 'common culture', a term of which he was always rather suspicious, and more interested in the detail of everyday life. How was it that a moral culture of resistance to the enfeebling hedonism and triviality of capitalist civilisation had enabled working people to survive with dignity? Could it now survive the onslaught of the mass media? The chapter argues that Hoggart's approach borrowed from a wide variety of sources: Dobrée's style; the Leavises' experiments in applying critical analysis to popular culture; Orwell's journalism which he saw as an antidote to Mrs Leavis's peg on the nose approach; his experiences in ABCA teaching his fellow recruits; and especially in Italy where he set up an Arts Club and came across stimulating Crocean approaches to cultural analysis. His *Uses of Literacy* was the direct outcome of wrestling with his own journey of cultural development, which cannot simply be dismissed as a nostalgic narrative of exile. Necessarily partial, as autobiographical accounts must be, it nevertheless proved a galvanic text in altering Labour's educational and cultural policy. In its use of Leavisite methodology it was the first serious attempt at an academic study of popular culture and the model for the brilliant studies which mark the early years of the Birmingham Centre.

Chapter seven documents Edward Thompson's arrival in the West Riding as a literature and history tutor in the late 1940s, and how, right from the onset of his career, he was forced to mediate his passionate belief in Marxism with the actual needs of working-class students. The fact that he was very nearly an early victim of the onset of the Cold War in academia makes the achievement of his *The Making of the English Working Class* (his 'West Riding book') even more remarkable. As others have since remarked, this was not a book which could have been written in a mainstream university department of history at this time, and it must be seen as the outcome of his extra-mural engagement and political commitment. The chapter goes on to consider Thompson's hatred of American 'mass' culture, his sceptical approach to unhistoricised 'popular' culture, and his belief in the function of education for creating purposeful social consciousness.

Finally, chapter eight ends with Raymond Williams, whose attempts to unite cultural radicalism, left wing politics and adult education were the most ambitious and far-sighted project of the post-war period. This was in large part the original 'old' New Left project. Described by Edward Thompson as 'our best man', Williams's years in adult education contributed some of the most politically incisive and creative commentary on cultural issues yet to be seen. Williams's principal task was to make the study of literature and writing a political activity, and to see it explicitly as an aspect of communications. He was one of the first to grasp the significance of film and television as objects of study, which he pioneered in adult classes. His reconstruction of the Romantic critique of capitalism in the nineteenth century for the first time suggested a way in which the goals and struggles of the working-class movement could be located within a broader struggle for a full, creative and just way of life – the Long Revolution. His pre-occupation with drama, and especially tragedy, provides an ironic counterpoint to this heroic project, and the disillusion he felt on leaving adult education for an internal post in Cambridge may well have foreshadowed the end of 'utopian' socialist politics in Britain.

In one of his last writings Williams criticised the current academic practices of cultural studies as having strayed too far from their radical and grounded origins; he wanted to return them to a more direct concern with political economy and social movements, and to renew the political project of a democratic cultural education. It is hoped that this study will further those aims.

1.

A lost genealogy:
adult education and the project of British cultural studies

A popular misconception about British cultural studies as an academic subject is that it sprang fully-armed from the side of a university department of English. While such a department may have been a midwife, the project of cultural studies more properly belongs to the experimentation, interdisciplinarity and political commitment of adult education immediately before and after the Second World War. The new post-war generation of tutors in adult education, some with engagements with Leavisism, some with European sociology, some with linguistic philosophy, and others with Marxist social history and cultural theory, came into the often newly-founded departments of university adult education at a moment of high promise for popular education, when it seemed that their occupation could be galvanic to the regeneration of a democratic, socially just New Britain. While the pre-war class order seemed fatally crippled, so did the old class politics: the popular front against fascism had suggested a new kind of political struggle not so much at the point of production as at the point of representation. From the embers of the independent workers' education movement arose the phoenix of cultural studies.

By the end of the Second World War, 'independent working-class education' as a vital political formation was virtually moribund. Not only were the Labour Colleges in terminal crisis but the

9

pioneering generation active in the WEA was exhausted. Newly created university extra-mural departments were carving out for themselves areas of adult education that had previously been regarded as the exclusive territory of the WEA. In some places a relatively principled settlement was made, such as in Yorkshire where Sidney Raybould, the director of the newly-founded Department of Extra-Mural Studies at Leeds, declared that the WEA should be concerned specifically with workers' education at a sub-university level, while the university department had responsibilities to a 'wider' public. He revitalised the Extension Committee and initiated professional and vocational education, while allowing the university's Joint Committee to continue to provide 'liberal adult education' with the WEA. Raybould, who had served his apprenticeship under the North Yorkshire WEA District Secretary, George Thompson, became one of the most influential adult educational theorists of the period; Thompson standing, 'somewhat in the relationship of Socrates to Mr. Raybould's Plato', as Tommy Hodgkin the Secretary of the Oxford Delegacy (Oxford University's long-established adult education department) put it. [1] But the department at Leeds was 'sponsored by a small group of professors as part of the university's plans for post-war development', as J.F.C. Harrison noted: 'the new department was intended to supersede, or more accurately perhaps, supplement, the existing organisation (the Joint Committee for Extension Lectures and Tutorial Classes), which was felt to be "too narrow and too rigid" to allow the university to make its full contribution to adult education'. [2] While never quite losing his grip on the reins of his former mount, Raybould skillfully changed horses.

At Oxford, however, the University Delegacy came into direct conflict with Ernest Green, the WEA's National Secretary, for different reasons. Green's concern was not that the Delegacy was undermining the class nature of the WEA's education, but rather that it had imperialist and radically political ambitions beyond the agreed liberal spectrum. Hodgkin was for Green a dangerous subversive who wished to put adult education at the service of partisan politics and so destroy the WEA's claim to objectivity and neutrality (and of course its access to public funding). So things were not as clear cut as they seemed. On the one hand, Raybould in

Leeds was trying to create a proper profession for adult educators, with pay and conditions equivalent to that of internal university staff and 'standards' in classes which would merit the description 'university courses'. On the other hand, Hodgkin saw himself closer to the pioneering conception of workers' education now being abandoned by the WEA itself. According to Raymond Williams, a new member of the Oxford Delegacy:

> Hodgkin ran the department with a very strong and principled conception of how to develop a popular working-class education. He believed that essentially the people to do it were committed socialists. He fought hard to say that tutors had the right, when it was relevant, to declare their position in the class, but to ensure within the open structure of the class that this position was always totally challengeable, naturally subject to opposition and discussion. [3]

When, as Roger Fieldhouse has shown,[4] the Cold War intensified towards the late 1940s and early 1950s, the Delegacy was constantly under suspicion, and when, in 1947, it initiated a remarkable programme of extra-mural education in West Africa with the emergent nationalist leadership, it was seen as not just as 'an internal conspiracy but as subversive externally'.[5]

Other university departments, such as Nottingham under Harold Wiltshire and Hull under Mayfield, took more pragmatic views of their place in the adult educational cosmos but all believed in the need for an expansion of popular education beyond the boundaries of the WEA of a fairly progressive nature. They also embraced the idea of a justifiable university standard without necessarily embracing Raybould's insistence on the three-year tutorial as classically defined in *Oxford and Working-Class Education* (1908).

The idea of popular education, it was clear, had finally gained dominance over the notion of 'workers' education', conceived politically, which had dominated the earlier part of the century. In particular, the sharp debates about the teaching of the arts which raged in the pages of the *Highway*, the *Tutors' Bulletin*, organ of the Tutors' Association, and in the district councils of the WEA during the 1930s, had touched raw nerves at both ends of the political spectrum (see chapter four). From the Labourist left, the arts were the soft subjects of workers' education, stigmatised as 'women's subjects', seen at best as a mere diversion from the class struggle or at worst as the vehicles of bourgeois ideology, clothed in the snake's skin of 'spiritual values'. This was summed up by the WEA Yorkshire (North) District Secretary, George Thompson: 'A distinct word of warning to those who are having so much to say about spiritual values in adult education. The Metaphysical Interpretation of Adult Education may be a song that echoes sweetly in the cloister but it will sound very different in the steel mills, down the pit, in the factories and on the docks'.[6]

But from the liberal establishment the arts and cultural education, especially English studies, were seen as fulfilling a diversity of needs, ranging from T.S. Eliot's belief in culture as consolation in the face of an irredeemably corrupt civilisation, through culture as self improvement, to alternatively, culture as the necessary accompaniment to a new national settlement and 'English' identity.

Believers in workers' education fought a rearguard action. Raymond Williams remembers G.D.H. Cole's outburst at an Oxford Delegacy meeting as: 'I am damn well not interested in adult education, I am interested in workers' education'.[7] Cole had strong words for the 'administratively minded', 'committeemen' and 'bureaucrats' who wanted to reform the voluntary movement because it was untidy and was committed to serve the workers' movement. He argued that the association fell between two stools: trying to provide a general adult education, which was what the modernisers wanted, and providing a class-based education, which he saw as its historic mission.[8] The WEA was healthy, he said, only when it had strong contacts with the local community and the working-class movement. In so far as was possible, especially in the large towns, it should desist from sponsoring classes which had no real connection with the movement for fear of losing its support and independence. He felt that the WEA should vigorously resist the transfer of responsibility for organising its classes to the university departments because they were not capable of responding to the real needs of the movement and would offer instead only a top down provision of what *they* felt was good for workers.

Cole was sensitive to the arguments often asserted against the WEA that its education lacked objectivity and was class-bound (as it happened this objection came not only from the political right but also from the left; the Plebs League, for example, insisted that it was merely the tool of the middle class and expressed its values). But he believed that educators could be committed to the labour movement without becoming party-political or dropping their commitment to objectivity. That was possible, he felt, largely because of the nature of the British working-class movement itself, which was by tendency neither totalitarian nor committed to the class nature of truth, as by implication, were the more orthodox Marxist movements. As Fieldhouse has characterised it, Cole's 'bifocalism' was 'operating at two levels simultaneously' in his support and criticism of both the Labour Colleges movement and the WEA. [9]

Cole offered that fine balance which was to become the focus of the new generation of adult educators to which Raymond Williams and Edward Thompson belonged. The working-class movement, he said, 'does not believe that because Britain is a capitalist country, there can be nothing in it that is good or worth preserving. It does believe in the real value and certain cultural qualities of British society, and wishes to help in their diffusion and in the carrying of them over intact into the new society that lies ahead of us.' [10]

Despite the defeat of the Labour government in 1951 and the weakness of the wider movement, Cole believed that if the workers' educational movement was to allow itself to be 'merged in the general movement of adult education' it would 'commit suicide'. By this time, however, the modernisers at the centre were well advanced in their project of converting the WEA from the educational arm of the workers' movement into a more general provider of liberal studies for adults.

Nevertheless, it was Cole's creative working of the libertarian-Marxist tradition, Fieldhouse argues, that enabled it to be taken up by the New Left after the break with communism in 1956. [11] Those who were to become the leaders of this new movement were only now entering the institutions of university adult education, for whom the 'new society that lies ahead', in Cole's words, shaped their thinking . This was the moment at which

Williams, Thompson, Hoggart and the many other adult education tutors associated with the development of the interdisciplinary approach to the arts, involving Marxist sociology, social history, close textual analysis and Leavis's approach to literary criticism, which later came to be inscribed into the mainstream as 'cultural studies', began their work in earnest. The seminal texts such as *The Making of the English Working Class*, *The Uses of Literacy*, *Culture and Society* and *The Long Revolution*, together with the scholarly but less well-known works like J.F.C. Harrison's *Learning and Living* (1961) were all written over the following ten to fifteen years, while their authors were university adult educators. It is important to emphasise that these works were not isolated events but were nested in a widespread culture of experiment in adult education which had begun with the debates over arts and literature teaching in the mid- to late-1930s. Much debated had been the idea of a 'sociological approach' to the arts, which benefited largely from the pre-war influx of European émigré intellectuals. Karl Mannheim, for example, originally a member of Georg Lukács's circle in Budapest, brought a 'totalising' cultural orientation to the subject. In addition to establishing the path-breaking 'Arts and Society' series for Routledge, Mannheim was actively involved in adult education and had argued in the *Tutors' Bulletin* before the war for the radical need for the holistic study of society, as we shall see in chapter five.

Even otherwise well-informed accounts of the origins of British cultural studies have tended to omit this prehistory in adult education and to assume that the subject began as an outcrop of a department of English. Michael Green, for example, notes that what became known as 'the founding texts were ambitious brave, but lonely ventures, whose premises were largely given by their common foundation in Left-Leavisism'. [12] None of the texts he mentions were written in English departments but in extra-mural departments and Left-Leavisism was in reality only one of many 'foundations'. Subsequently Stuart Laing, Graeme Turner and Ioan Davies have offered much fuller accounts which properly recognises this prehistory. [13]

In one of his last attempts at putting the record straight, Raymond Williams noted:

> when I moved into internal university teaching, when at about the same time Richard Hoggart did the same, we started teaching in ways that had been absolutely familiar in Extra Mural and WEA classes, relating history to art and literature, including contemporary culture, and suddenly so strange was this to the Universities they said 'My God, here is a new subject called Cultural Studies'. But we are beginning I am afraid, to see encyclopaedia articles dating the birth of Cultural Studies from this or that book in the late 'fifties. Don't believe a word of it. That shift of perspective about the teaching of arts and literature and their relation to history and to contemporary society began in Adult Education, it didn't happen anywhere else. [14]

He saw what he and others were doing was quite definitely not founding a new academic subject area but contributing to the process of social change itself. It was clear from those who originated these ideas that cultural studies began as a *political project of popular education amongst adults.*

Stuart Hall has also corrected the balance, noting that cultural studies in the 1950s emerged from the centre of the political debate about how British society was changing and 'was at this time identified with the first New Left'. [15] He notes that this New Left was founded on the books of Hoggart, Williams and Thompson who, he is at extreme pains to point out, were all extra-mural teachers. Moreover, he adds, 'I myself was working as an extra-mural teacher, once I left the university of Oxford, in and around London'.

> We thus came from a tradition entirely marginal to the centers of English academic life, and out of an engagement in the questions of cultural change – how to understand them, how to describe them, and how to theorise them, what their impact and consequences were to be, socially – were first reckoned within the dirty outside world. [16]

Edward Thompson also located the pioneering of new intellectual currents in adult education. He noted that many outstanding historians – Tawney, Cole, Beales and Briggs, for example – had been closely tied to the adult education movement, which had allowed the new social history to fill out areas wholly neglected by university departments of history. Furthermore, the experience of adult education had been able at times to modify subtly and radically the whole educational process:

> Areas of study long neglected, and, in some places, still neglected – in university history schools were explored over several decades in university tutorial classes: and today one may still see new offshoots of social history – in local history, in industrial archaeology, in the history of industrial relations, and in that area of cultural studies pioneered in this country by Richard Hoggart – the initiatives for which have often come 'from below', from the adult class and the adult tutor, and not from the academic schools. [17]

Richard Hoggart also confirmed the general tenor of these observations, but unlike Thompson and Williams his own involvement in adult education was less politically motivated. Coming from a working-class family in Hunslet, his concerns had been more closely tied to anxieties about the decline of community, the family and working-class values, and more significantly about his own alienation from the community he was raised in. The attention of this 'scholarship boy' was always more centred on the mystery of his own difference than on the long march of labour or the formation of a common culture, a term of which he was always rather suspicious. In a sense literature both released him from some of the narrowness of this life but also contained him in a world of symbolic values. He became more concerned with reading the signs of the times, which he saw as a logical extension of Leavis's work, than with Williams's work of cultural materialism or Thompson's theorised social history. He focused particularly on popular culture: 'I'd been teaching, for about five or six years, WEA and extension classes. Anyone who was serious about that sort of work – and there were a great number of us at that time who were engaged in the writings of Leavis and the *Scrutiny* group and Denys Thompson and Mrs. Leavis – had a special interest in popular culture. It was more than that, it was also mass culture.' [18] For him the peculiarity of adult students was the fact that, unlike the undergraduates of his day, they lived in the world outside universities composed of newspapers, radio and pop song. There was he said, 'a side interest in making sense of that among extra-mural tutors'. [19]

It is clear, however, from Hoggart's description that the teaching of English had been a key site for adult education tutors who were concerned with the social relevance of their work. In fact it was a location of intense ideological conflict throughout the immediate pre-war years and in important ways one's stance over English teaching was a sign of political commitment. Undoubtedly the Leavises had brought to the subject a number of elements that adult education tutors could find congenial. Close reading of texts, a moral stance, contextual relevance, scorn of dilettante literary history and biographic detail and, of course, dangerous D.H. Lawrence, conspired with the all-important combative tone of Leavisism to create an oppositional climate for those convinced that culture had a political value. Moreover, Leavis's attack on metropolitan literary fashion as well the loathed Bloomsbury hegemony, enhanced the feeling of the marginal vitality of adult education, the feeling that cultural renewal would come from 'below' and from the 'border country', be it Wales or Yorkshire, rather than the London élites. 'Leavis' was a sign for the shock troops of English studies, much as 'deconstruction' is today (or possibly was yesterday).

The debate about teaching English and the social relevance of the arts was not confined to the tutors, and indeed the intervention of members of the adult education movement into the debate in the 1930s gave it a quality which grounded it in the needs of the working-class student. George Thompson wrote a number of articles in the *Highway* as well as a celebrated pamphlet for the WEA called 'The Field of Study in WEA Classes' in which he campaigned for this grounded approach. He argued firstly that the working-class student did not require an overly abstract approach to any subject. Whatever was taught had to first of all relate to the student's life and experience, and only when that contact had been established could more abstract matters be broached. Secondly, the approach should be 'sociological'; it should enable the student to see how his or her life related to social conditions, not in a simply determined sense but in an activist sense to see how social conditions could be changed in line with justice and equity. Lastly, and perhaps most importantly, Thompson was quite impatient of conventional academic divisions of knowledge:

Whatever the purpose of study elsewhere, it seems to me that in the WEA the study of one subject should not only give an understanding of that subject but be a gateway through which a vista should be glimpsed of the importance of other subjects. A subject encased within the high walls of specialisation whether of subject matter or of theory – economic, scientific, aesthetic – leads I believe, up a blind alley. [20]

Interdisciplinarity, as this was later to be called, was thus a key feature of the WEA approach for Thompson, as it was subsequently to be of academic cultural studies.

It is tempting to see another even more direct link between George Thompson's prescriptions and those of Richard Hoggart, then undergoing his higher education in Leeds less than half a mile from the WEA offices. Thompson's WEA was unashamedly for the working-class élite, whom he described as the 'socially effective' and 'the salt of our democratic order, for it is they who make it work and give it stability which neither the worst blunders of the high ups nor the deficiencies and failings of the mass can undermine'. [21] Popular education is a term which would not have much appeal for him and he was fond of remarking that if the people were flocking to hear St Patrick when he was converting the Irish then St Patrick was most definitely not teaching the gospel. But the phrase 'socially effective' and the general sentiments have resonance with something Richard Hoggart says later about WEA students in *The Uses of Literacy*. These, he calls, not the 'socially effective' but 'the earnest minority', who have 'an influence on their group out of all proportion to their numbers ... I have in mind people such as those who take up voluntary trade union activities, and those who seek adult education, through for instance the classes run by the Workers' Educational Association'. [22] Hoggart is speaking of the movement a decade on from Thompson and registers it not so much a 'political' as a 'voluntary' movement, which reflects how successful the transformation had been in the intervening period. At the metropolitan centre, the WEA had become increasingly embarrassed by the class-warriors of the provinces and in important ways Hoggart, although less overtly political in his intentions, had rescued the provincial voice and the importance of local activity.

18

Although he was a working-class hero of almost biblical proportions – a carpenter by trade – George Thompson was remarkably blind to the power of cultural study, which he took to be a woman's occupation. As far as he was concerned the health of a good WEA branch was judged by the number of male manual workers it could attract to tutorial classes in politics and economics, social history and social philosophy. These 'controversial subjects' he held to be the core of the WEA programme and the 'cultural subjects' such as literature, art and music were secondary. During the 1930s he took great pride in Yorkshire's high level of provision of the core subjects for manual workers, but tragically for him this provision collapsed with the outbreak of war and in their absence the cultural subjects came to dominate. Thus for Thompson the growth of literature and the arts in place of politics and economics represented the defeat of his project, and shortly after the war he retired. However, this 'feminisation' of the WEA appears to have been critically important for the development of cultural studies and with the demise of the male-dominated working-class movement they steadily took over from the political-economic curriculum.

The educational practices which came to be called 'cultural studies', then, seem to emerge at a critical juncture after the Second World War. To summarise: the arguments over literature and arts teaching in the inter-war period signalled that these subjects were a politically sensitive arena within which notions of Englishness and class were being fought out. In the literary critical academy, English studies was the place where 'Englishness' itself was being consecrated. [23] Leavis and his followers saw themselves as being at the centre of the humanising mission, in opposition to official Cambridge notions of literature and metropolitan literary culture. It was well understood by adult education tutors that successful teaching began with the life experiences of their students and not abstract theory or general attempts at promoting notions of spirituality. The sociological attitude was strongly encouraged and the interdisciplinarity, which was largely due to starting from the needs of the students rather than the formalities of the subject, allowed tutors the space to indulge in constructing different kinds of relationships between academic subjects and learners.

The political imperative of adult education work had sharpened before the war when the popular-front, anti-fascist struggle took over from specifically class-based politics. From this time, the late 1930s, the concept of the 'people' and the popular vies with 'the working class' as the subject of the political struggle. For many tutors, as for Edward Thompson, it had been an extraordinary formative moment, 'a particular political struggle which was at the same time a popular struggle' in which he lost his personal sense of isolation. [24] From the time of the Popular Front onward, Cole, who wrote a book for the Left Book Club on the subject, had argued strongly that Labour and Communist Party intellectuals should engage in fraternal educational activity rather than ideological sniping. The defeat of fascism in 1945 and the subsequent election of the Labour government produced a climate of intoxication on the left about the potential for a genuine socialism for a few brief years, before the Cold War intensified and once more erected an iron curtain through intellectual life.

Many of those who became sensitive to the possibilities offered by the new cultural struggle were recruited within a few years of each other to university adult education departments: Williams to the Oxford Delegacy in 1945, Hoggart to Hull in 1946 and Thompson to Leeds in 1948. The Leeds department also included the sociologist John Rex, the literary critic Walter Stein, the social historian John Harrison, the philosopher J. M. Cameron and the future Secretary General of the Arts Council, Roy Shaw, all of whom were experimenting with different interdisciplinary approaches and who taught not just their own subject but a range of non-specialist subjects such as international relations and trade-union studies. It was, however, significant that Williams, Hoggart and Thompson had studied English literature at university and were recruited as English tutors. Thompson and Williams were both at Cambridge and had been to Leavis's lectures but were never a part of his circle. Thompson read history for the first part of his tripos but had decided on free-wheeling English study for his part two. Richard Hoggart studied English at Leeds, where Bonamy Dobrée, the Professor of English, picked him out as one of his bright hopes. [25]

At Oxford's extra-mural department a similar galaxy of talent included Henry Collins, Laurence Lerner, Tony Maclean, Lalage Bown and many others. At Hull, Hoggart was friendly with the Marxist art historian Francis Klingender with whom he engaged in comradely disputes. Although it is somewhat invidious to pick out the work of the three celebrated 'founders' of cultural studies from what was generally agreed to be a common pursuit, the widespread influence of their publications and spokesman qualities may well justify it. There are also important differences in their approaches.

E.P. Thompson, a poet in the Labour archives

When Edward Thompson applied for a post in the newly formed extra-mural department in Leeds in 1948, his membership of the Communist Party nearly cost him the job (chapter seven). He immediately immersed himself in life in the West Riding but taught as far afield as Harrogate and Middlesbrough. Though for some years he taught nothing but English literature, increasingly his courses, which had always emphasised historical context especially the Romantics and the industrial revolution, turned towards social history. For Thompson, education was always against the grain of the academy. His membership of the Communist Party Historian's Group with Christopher Hill, John Saville and Eric Hobsbawm was, he said, more vital in shaping his historical approach than anything he learned at university. Dorothy Thompson, too, was a celebrated social historian, whose work on the working-class movement of the nineteenth century very much complemented his own. While at Leeds Thompson divided himself more or less equally between his educational work and his party activities, which centred on the anti-nuclear campaign and the Korean war. As made plain in his celebrated controversy with Louis Althusser, one of his key conceptual categories was that of 'experience', which, he held, offered the necessary corrective to academic systems of knowledge, which, because of their class nature, regularly suppressed the experience of working people. In this respect, because it denied popular experience, education was not always to be taken simply as a good:

For a century and more, most middle-class educationalists could not distinguish the work of education from that of social control: and this entailed too often, a repression or denial of the validity of the life experience of their pupils as expressed in uncouth dialect or in traditional cultural forms. Hence education and received experience were at odds with each other. And those working men who by their own efforts broke into the educated culture found themselves at once in the same place of tension, in which education brought with it the danger of the rejection of their fellows and self-distrust. [26]

Because of this, the self-educated man was expected to doubt the experience of his fellow workers and to disavow his own: 'the educated universe was so saturated with class responses that it demanded an active rejection and despisal of the language, customs and traditions of received popular culture'. [27]

Thompson's cultural studies project then was to retrieve radical and popular movements neglected in academic accounts and to reveal another untold history from the 'bottom up'. Out of this work, and that of many other historians in adult education such as Raphael Samuel at Ruskin, grew the History Workshop movement, which has been responsible for fundamentally shifting the approach to social history towards the fine archival evidence of popular and labour movement activity. Thompson was, however, unsentimental about the current political situation in which what he called 'the old parochial popular culture' had long since crumbled and the 'more politically articulated working-class class culture which succeeded it in the industrial centres' had been waning in vitality since the latter 1940s – precisely, of course, when he began its study. [28] In his concern with the disjunction between education and customary experience Thompson coincided with Raymond Williams. But unlike Williams, Thompson had never experienced this disjunction from the inside. The son of a railway signalman from the Welsh borders, it has become received wisdom to see the 'Border Country' as a place Williams occupied throughout his lifetime.

Raymond Williams: a cultural politics

Like Thompson, Williams studied at Cambridge and then saw active service in the army during the war. His contact with the Leavises, though influential, was mostly secondary through his friend Wolf Mankowitz who attended Leavis's seminars.

With Mankowitz and Collins, Williams started a journal in the late 1940s called *Politics and Letters* which intended to extend and politicise the Leavisite critique. Although Williams had joined the Communist Party just before the war he did not renew his membership because the party line now recommended a period of social unity and reconstruction. [29] Williams was also not happy with party's 'intellectual errors' and anyway, in a mood of avant-gardism, he and the group of Left-Leavisites at Cambridge felt that *they* were the most radical elements in the culture. Williams did not know Thompson, who was in a different year at Cambridge, but was connected to Eric Hobsbawm. He then became the Oxford Delegacy's staff tutor on the south east coast where his courses included English classes with housewives and public expression classes with trade-unionists from local trades councils. Because of his relative isolation from Oxford he had considerable scope for autonomous development in his work. It was in these classes that the elements of *Culture and Society* took shape, in the same way as Thompson's *Making* and Hoggart's *Uses* came out of an active dialogue with adult and working-class students.

Although the three of them were critically aware of each other during this period, through the Tutors' Association for example, little actual collaboration took place. What is important is that there was what Williams might have called a *structure of feeling* which included argument and experiment in adult education and around cultural matters, which was continuously active in the seminars and journals of the movement. In this crucible tutors were constantly being challenged to consider their methods and approaches and their relationship to students and progress. The exhaustive documenting of Williams's work by John McIlroy can leave no doubt about their centrality in his own political and theoretical formation. [30]

Williams's own short lived journal, *Politics and Letters*, and a companion volume called *The Critic*, were attempts to engage in that arena which Williams increasingly saw as the 'decisive' world for his political work: 'Virtually every WEA tutor was a Socialist of one colour or another. We were all doing adult education ourselves. So we saw the journals as linked to this very hopeful formation with a national network of connection to the working-class movement. If there was a group to which *Politics and Letters* referred, it was the adult education tutors and their students.' [31]

It was significant that Williams saw the adult education universe as a 'formation', a term he later defined in his book *Culture* as having a specific sociological meaning. A 'formation' was capable of having a distinct politics and ideological perspective. Williams later acknowledged, however, that the journal failed because it was in effect *too* cultural and had failed to develop a properly economic critique. He was also unhappy that those involved had not made contact with Communist Party intellectuals like Thompson whose understanding of economics could have been invaluable, in an organised way. The marriage of Leavisism and left politics had failed because it had not taken into account that Leavisism, despite its oppositional standpoint, was unhappily also hostile to socialism. Williams later said: 'The correct perspective was to try to help to build a very strong cultural mobilisation to take part in a battle inside the Labour movement. But we still shared one illusion with precisely the position we were attacking. We thought we could do so simply by literary argument, by cultural discourse. That was the influence of Leavis...' [32]

So although Thompson, albeit increasingly impatient of its refusal to criticise Soviet politics or democratise itself, was still wedded to the Communist Party, Williams saw adult education as a relatively autonomous space within the labour movement where independent socialists like himself could develop an alternative cultural politics. Their respective positions nevertheless overlapped significantly and indeed they came increasingly to reference each other, the key moment being Thompson's review of Williams's *Long Revolution* in *New Left Review*, (nos. 9 and 10 and a page in no. 11) which, although critical of its lack of engagement, clearly held the book in deep respect. Thompson was, however, still working within internationalist protocols while Williams had more locally defined objectives which centred on popular education. He believed that the Labour government should have made a priority of funding institutions of 'popular education and popular culture that could have withstood the political campaigns in the bourgeois press'. [33]

Later he believed that the failure to do this was a key factor of the disintegration of Labour's position in the 1950s, and it was because of this that he and Thompson opted for a new politics to the left of Labour and independent of the Communist Party:

> I don't think you can understand the projects of the New Left in the late 'fifties unless you realise that people like Edward Thompson and myself, for all our differences were positing the re-creation of that kind of union. In part the problem was that CP intellectuals did not actively share in the project until the break with the party post-1956. [34]

Had this happened a decade earlier Williams felt that the New Left project would have gained much more stability and chance of success.

Thus for Williams adult education, at its best, was actually a part of the process of social change and not merely, as it was ironically characterised by Cobbett in the nineteenth century, 'taking learning to a class seen in deficit'. By the time he joined the Oxford Delegacy, Williams perceived it as shifting subtly from workers' education to popular education. Although there was much to be lost in jettisoning the class-character of this education, Williams felt there was always much to be gained by taking on the 'common' non class-specific identity. However, he was very concerned that the move towards popular education would merely be assimilated into university needs because the university was a peculiarly middle-class institution and not a popular one. Like Thompson, he drew attention to the deficit in the academy, but while Thompson emphasised the neglect and abuse of common experience and popular cultures, Williams pointed to its more structured exclusions. The academy, he said, was defined to exist for potentially academic persons, a formula which, of course, excludes the bulk of working people.

In adult education, by contrast, a relatively open-ended space existed for dialogue between intellectually motivated working people and radical intellectuals. During the 1930s, Williams argues, a significant change had taken place in which many intellectuals went into adult education, not so much with a missionary sense of social conscience as in an earlier period, but with the intention of helping to build a social consciousness to meet the crises of a modern capitalist society. Unfortunately, many had a kind of 'message in a bottle' approach, which failed to recognise the subtle nature of adult education, namely: that adults wanted not the conclusions of arguments already reached but the actual process of arguing, through which to reach their own conclusions. [35] This, as we have seen, was also George Thompson's and Cole's point of view.

The post-war period thus saw a decisive shift in and broadening of the material and subjects of adult education away from the subjects based in politics and economics towards what Williams called, 'thinking about symbolic values', or how social consciousness is made. While, previously, left tutors had somehow thought themselves second class if they were teaching literature or the arts rather than politics and economics, now their colleagues came increasingly to see the political value of this kind of work. Williams wryly remarked that a curious change took place in the 1950s which shocked 'the really virgin innocence of those who thought themselves hard, mature, political analysts', when close reading of newspapers and advertisements became a form of political education. [36] In his own case he noted how his classes on international relations gradually turned into 'literature' classes, reading amongst other things newspapers and adverts.

In a complementary movement Thompson's literature classes in Yorkshire were turning increasingly historical and sociological (with colleagues like Arnold Kettle and Kenneth Muir making guest appearances), but he was not interested in the kind of statistics-led economic history which had characterised conventional approaches. Instead, his focus too had shifted to the formation of social consciousness and beyond that, heretically for a Marxist, to the effect that consciousness had on shaping class. Thompson now turned towards a history writing which heavily referenced literary texts and popular writing in ways which were dramatically innovative. One major outcome of this experimental work was the heightened importance given to the realm of the symbolic, rescuing it from relative obscurity behind the facticity of the 'material'.

Thus both Thompson and Williams were converging on the critical conjunctural moments of the formation of class and social consciousness. For Thompson the convergence of his politically centred interests in the literary and the historical now rested on

William Morris, as a way not only of retrieving a lost contributor to the radical tradition but also of making a coded criticism of Communist Party policy. His massive work on Morris (1955) expresses a joyful irreverence towards the jealous boundaries of academic knowledge and represents an important innovation in cultural historiography. Williams, too, was reconstructing the nineteenth-century Romantic critique of capitalism, of which Morris was one of the last, and most radical, representatives. 'William Morris' for some considerable time then came to signify a fecund marriage of the British romantic critique of capitalism and the non-Soviet Marxist tradition. Thompson especially insisted that he was not trying to inscribe Morris within Marxism but on the contrary to see what Marxism could learn from Morris.[37] 'Morris' then functioned as a sign for the unpartied left for whom communism had become identical with Soviet foreign policy, Trotskyism, however prescient its critique of communism, a kind of theological maximalism, and Labourism, after the collapse of the Atlee government, an unprincipled vehicle for career politicians.

Richard Hoggart and popular culture

Richard Hoggart was less interested in this grand political project and, convinced that the schism between the educated minority and the undereducated mass was perhaps unbridged, was rather wary of the idea of a 'common culture'. [38] Instead he focused down onto 'popular culture', in particular those forms already investigated by the Leavises, the popular press and advertising. This kind of enquiry had in fact been pursued in the WEA from the early 1930s by no less than the founder of *Scrutiny*, Lionel Knights, when he worked as a part-time tutor in Bethnal Green and Manchester. Knights used *Culture and Environment* by Q.D. Leavis and Denys Thompson and G. C. Fields's *Prejudice and Impartiality* in his classes to analyse examples of propagandist writing current in the popular press and advertisements. He was, moreover, ticked off for so doing by the local HMI in Bethnal Green because the class was 'supposed to be the study of literature'. [39] Knights subsequently taught Roy Shaw and Walter Stein, who later became members of the Leeds extra-mural department, as undergraduates at Manchester University.

Hoggart was, however, disquieted by the patrician tone adopted by Mrs Leavis in relation to working-class readers of 'popular', or as she preferred to call it 'mass' culture. From his own intimate experience of being raised in a working-class family he was convinced that working people were not the kind of *tabula rasa* upon which the popular press merely imprinted its views, but were, on the contrary, capable of making critical and ironic readings of the material and absorbing what they needed into their own local cultures. He insisted that, historically, there had been a strength in working-class culture which had enabled it to resist the tinsel and glitter of the sirens of capitalism, but he now felt that in the era of the new mass communications industry, that capacity was being seriously eroded.

Hoggart believed that the 'peg on the nose' approach of Mrs Leavis could be counteracted with ideas from the non-academic arena of serious journalism, as exemplified by the essays of George Orwell. He was particularly impressed by Orwell's study on the postcards of Donald McGill and boys' weeklies where, in a phrase of C.S. Lewis's, 'people could bring good instincts to bad literature'. Hoggart was more interested therefore in the private and personal strengths of working-class culture and paid little attention to the public domain of working-class organisations or to the realm of the political. A Marxist colleague at Hull, F.D. Klingender, complained that in *Uses*, Hoggart presented the working class as far too passive, and certainly socialists generally have not found in Hoggart's work the heroic class of myth.

The Uses of Literacy is not this kind of a work. As much as *Culture and Society* and *The Making of the English Working Class* are centred in enquiries into public discourses, so *Uses* is about the inwardness of feeling and response from the perspective of one whose relation to the working class of politics and organisation was profoundly troubled. In a characteristically honest admission of his differences, in conversation with Raymond Williams, Hoggart reflected:

> At any rate I felt from your book [*Culture and Society*] that you were surer, sooner than I was, of your relationship to your working-class background. With me, I remember, it was long and troublesome effort. It was difficult to escape a kind of patronage, even when one felt one was understanding the virtues of working-class life one had been

brought up in – one seemed to be insisting on these strengths *in spite* of all sorts of doubts in one's attitudes. One tried consciously, in the light of day, to make genuine connections, to see deeply and not just to feel sentimentally ... but it was a running argument. [40]

Uses was not a conventionally academic text, as Hoggart would be the first to affirm, but a product of teaching adults who come with different agenda. This was a new kind of work in which the ethnological study of a known community and theoretical considerations were juxtaposed (a form which later became quite familiar in the Birmingham Centre for Contemporary Cultural Studies, cf. Paul Willis's *Learning to Labour*). Hoggart insisted that, 'I was recreating the working-class life I knew and that was a woman-centred life'. [41] His work is much more revealing of himself than either Thompson's or Williams's, and much more centred in the everyday life of the working class. Although *Uses* is undoubtedly a lyrical celebration of aspects of this rather than a pure sociological study, he is not afraid to show his own doubts about the current health of that culture.

Moreover, although not *feminist*, his work is more feminised than that of his contemporaries, in the sense that women and subjectivity occupy a more central space. For the sensitive working-class boy it has often been mothers, aunts and older sisters who have opened the doors to varieties of experience not constrained by class. Women, who make a fairly restrained showing in the work of Thompson and Williams, are for Hoggart structurally important. In a recent interview with the Leeds-born poet, Tony Harrison, for example, he celebrates Harrison's use of the word 'mam' rather than 'mum', which 'captures something of the close mother-centred world of a working-class childhood, a world which for a sensitive child the women are usually much more important than the men'. [42] Furthermore, it is axiomatic that 'for children who might go further academically it's almost always in working-class life the women who see to it.' [43]

Like D.H. Lawrence, whom he so staunchly defended at the *Lady Chatterley* trial a few years later, Hoggart has little reticence in exposing the imperfections of working-class life but it is done without bitterness, and moreover he continues that vein of puzzled reflection of the potentially emancipating role of women in working-class life without Lawrence's pusillanimity. Leavis had rehabilitated Lawrence for a new post-war educated class which read their own lives through the Lawrentian filter. Until the impact of the feminist movement was felt in the 1970s, Lawrence was one of adult education's most popular authors. Although 'Lawrence' meant two fingers to the class system it was unhappily also inimical to the means of changing it, a retreat into passionate individualism for those sceptical of collective solutions.

The Flight of the Pelican

All three authors had an enormous influence over the way class, culture and community came to be revalued in the 1960s when, courtesy of Pelican Books, their ideas gained a vast audience among the lower professional classes, many of whom were employed in the educational system. Many were likely to have been members of adult education classes, part of a passionate democracy impatient with the blunderings of what E. P. Thompson has called 'the New Corruption'. The 'scholarship boys' of the inter-war years were now replaced by a (relative) flood of children from working-class backgrounds benefiting from Butler's 1944 Education Act and subsequently the Robbins Report on universities of 1963. While the New Left took strength from the work of Thompson and Williams and their colleagues, there emerged what could be called a new cultural politics. Hoggart inaugurated the Birmingham Centre for Contemporary Cultural Studies in the mid 1960s and from its work, the sustained study of popular culture. The assault on conventional literary studies was probably not as fatal as has been argued by Anthony Easthope since departments of English literature continue to flourish, but no area of what used to be called the Humanities has remained unaffected. [44] Nevertheless, the revolution looked in danger of devouring its own and the popular political intentions of the founding fathers were also almost drowned by the inundation of continental structuralist and post-structuralist theory unleashed by their unruly and somewhat Oedipal offspring. Now that the glaciation of theory has melted back up the mountain a little – leaving behind much of interest and correction – it might be possible to examine what is left of that initial project of popular education when independent workers' education was receiving its fond farewells.

A lost genealogy

Notes

1 Thomas Hodgkin, 'University Standards', *Tutors' Bulletin*, Autumn, 1948; Janet Coles, 'S. G. Raybould and the Development of Extra-Mural Studies at the University of Leeds, 1946-69', unpublished M.Ed. thesis, University of Leeds, 1992.

2 J.F.C. Harrison, *Learning and Living 1790-1960*, Routledge Kegan Paul, London 1961, p341.

3 Raymond Williams, *Politics and Letters*, Verso, London 1979, p80.

4 Roger Fieldhouse, *Adult Education and the Cold War*, Leeds Studies in the Education of Adults, Leeds 1985, pp29-54.

5 Williams, *Politics and Letters, op cit*, p80; Fieldhouse, *Adult Education and the Cold War, op cit*, pp55-68.

6 G.H. Thompson, 'Progress and Aims in Adult Education', *Tutors' Bulletin*, April, 1945, p9; see also Tom Steele, 'Class Consciousness to Cultural Studies: the WEA in West Yorkshire, 1914-1950' in *Studies in the Education of Adults*, vol. 19, no 2, Autumn, 1987, pp109-126.

7 Williams, *Politics and Letters, op cit*, p78.

8 G.D.H. Cole, 'What Workers' Education Means', the *Highway*, October, 1952, p11.

9 Roger Fieldhouse, 'The Ideology of English Responsible Body Adult Education 1925-50', unpublished Ph.D. thesis, University of Leeds, 1984, pp74-6.

10 Cole, 'What Workers' Education Means', *op cit*, p10.

11 Fieldhouse, 'The Ideology of English Responsible Body Adult Education 1925-50', *op cit*, pp74-5.

12 Michael Green, 'The Centre for Contemporary Cultural Studies' in Peter Widdowson (ed), *Re-Reading English*, Methuen, London 1982, pp77-90.

13 Stuart Laing, *Representations of Working-Class Life 1957-1964*, Macmillan, London 1986; Graeme Turner, *British Cultural Studies an Introduction*, Routledge, London 1990; Ioan Davies, 'Cultural Theory in Britain: Narrative and Episteme' in *Theory Culture & Society*, Vol. 10, No. 3, August 1993, pp115-154 and *Cultural Studies and Beyond*, Routledge, London 1995.

14 Raymond Williams, 'The Future of Cultural Studies', in *The Politics of Modernism*, Verso, London 1989, p162.

15 Stuart Hall, 'The Emergence of Cultural Studies and the Crisis of the Humanities', *October*, 53, 1990, pp11-23, p12.

16 *Ibid*.

17 E.P. Thompson, 'Education and Experience', University of Leeds, Department of Adult Continuing Education, Albert Mansbridge Lecture, 1968, p1.

18 John Corner, 'Studying Culture: reflections and assessments. An interview with Richard Hoggart', *Media Culture and Society*, Vol. 13, 1991, pp137-151, p139.

19 *Ibid*.

20 G.H. Thompson, 'Views on Literature' York's North Record supplement to the *Highway*, April, 1939, n.p.

21 G.H. Thompson, 'Progress and Aims in Adult Education', *Tutors' Bulletin*, April, 1945, p9.

22 Richard Hoggart, *The Uses of Literacy*, Pelican, London 1957, p318.

23 Brian Doyle, *English and Englishness*, Methuen, London 1989.

24 Henry Abelove *et al*. (eds), *Visions of History*, Manchester University Press, Manchester 1983, p10.

25 Richard Hoggart, 'Teaching with Style on Bonamy Dobrée', in *Speaking to Each Other*, Pelican, London, 1973. Dobrée had a signally powerful effect on the life of the university in his Michael Sadler-like role of cultural promotion. He encouraged interdisciplinary activities such as making English students study Fine Art and was himself largely responsible for the appointment of Arnold Hauser, the Marxist art historian, to Leeds in 1951. He also persuaded a local businessman named Gregory to sponsor poetry, painting and sculpture fellowships on campus so that students could become actively involved with creative artists.

26 E.P. Thompson, 'Education and Experience', *op cit*, p16.

27 *Ibid*, p14.

28 *Ibid*, p19.

29 Raymond Williams, *Politics and Letters*, Verso, London 1979, p65.

30 John McIlroy and Sallie Westwood (eds), *Border Country: Raymond Williams in Adult Education*, NIACE, London 1993.

31 Williams, *Politics and Letters*, *op cit*, p69.

32 *Ibid*, p75.

33 *Ibid*, p73.

34 *Ibid*.

35 Williams, 'The Future of Cultural Studies', *op cit*, p165.

36 *Ibid*.

37 E.P. Thompson, *William Morris: Romantic to Revolutionary*, (second edition), Merlin, London 1977, p792.

38 Corner, 'Studying Culture: reflections and assessments. An interview with Richard Hoggart', *op cit*, p150.

39 Author's interview with L.C. Knights, 1993.

40 Richard Hoggart and Raymond Williams, 'Working-Class Attitudes', *New Left Review*, No. 1, Jan./Feb. 1960, pp26-30, p26.

41 Corner, 'Studying Culture: reflections and assessments. An interview with Richard Hoggart', *op cit*, p142.

42 Richard Hoggart, 'In Conversation with Tony Harrison', in Neil Astley (ed), *Tony Harrison*, Bloodaxe Books, Newcastle 1991, p36.

43 Corner, 'Studying Culture: reflections and assessments. An interview with Richard Hoggart', *op cit*, p142.

44 Anthony Easthope, *Literary into Cultural Studies*, Routledge, London 1991.

2.

Class and Nation:
working-class identity and the
'English' settlement

How did it happen that by the beginning of the twentieth century working people in this country appeared not only to have established a decent and humane culture of their own, which denied the claims to moral superiority of the capitalist order, but also that they identified with some notion of 'Englishness' which appeared to fuse elements of that same working-class culture with a common, national, identity? I want to suggest here that this can only be understood if we see the 'culture' of working people not simply as a set of attitudes and rituals laid down in some traditional past, but as a complex of purposive activities designed to improve their individual and collective lot in the face of a clearly understood class oppression. I also want to suggest that through educational activities two significant changes took place. Firstly, that, through their educational contact with liberal intellectuals, working people constructed and were constructed by a notion of a *common culture* which transcended class and, secondly, that these negotiations contributed to a modernised version of the nation which inscribed the working classes into 'Englishness'.

E.J. Hobsbawm's compelling account of the formation of working-class culture in the second half of the nineteenth century takes over from where E.P. Thompson's *The Making of the English Working Class* left off. [1] Hobsbawm focused on the three decades following the defeat of Chartism in 1848, which he saw as consolidating the patterns of working-class culture first identified by Thompson, who limited his inquiry to the period of activism which led up to the emergence of Chartism in the 1830s. Hobsbawm argues that by the 1880s this culture had developed a relatively permanent shape and remained more or less intact until the 1960s. The high point of this culture coincided with the period of Attlee's's post-war Labour government, 1945-1951. During the period of Attlee's government both trade union membership and the electoral strength of the Labour Party peaked. Similarly attendance at football matches and cinemas and the consumption of mass circulation newspapers aimed at a proletarian audience also reached their zenith. Hobsbawm makes the point that by this time working-class culture seemed so firmly established that it was easy to forget it had specific chronological origins in the mid to late nineteenth century. Many traditional signs of working-class culture first make their appearance then: fish and chips first appeared in Lancashire in 1865; football became professionalised in the 1880s; and tea was first mass-packaged in 1884. Subsequently, high wages, full employment and the new consumer society of the 1950s and 60s substantially transformed the material life of the working classes. Despite the improved conditions of working people, many then felt the intense sense of loss of community and betrayal of principle that was to result in those nostalgic narratives which signalled both the decline of the culture and the break up of the settlement.

The factors which, for Hobsbawm, crystallised working-class culture centred on the emergence and rapid consolidation of the mass labour movement in the 1880s. The rediscovery of socialism, the new unionism which organised the unskilled workers and the formation of an independent party of labour were central to this process. This culture presupposed a number of elements. Between 1848 and 1880 the working class understood that capitalism was not a mere historical aberration but a relatively permanent and a *national* feature. Workers could not escape it by moving to some other city or region as its writ ran constantly before them. The pattern of industrial development which had first appeared as a regional phenomenon of the Northern English hill towns had become dominant. By 1880, however, it was clear that the working class was itself stratified and a clearly defined labour aristocracy of skilled artisans had emerged. Betraying the archaic form of British industrialisation, its members saw themselves as distinguished by their craft, ideally learned in apprenticeship. This stratum, however, persisted doggedly in maintaining a working-class identity and saw itself as the natural leader of manual workers as a whole. Finally, working people created many voluntary organisations of a co-operative nature through which they saw to their own provision of goods and services. This form of consumer co-operation was indeed one of the most significant legacies of the period and widely copied throughout emerging industrial and developing nations.

What clearly marked this period was the strong sense of class-consciousness exhibited by the British working class which clearly distinguished between 'us' and 'them'. 'They', as Hobsbawm points out, were not just the capitalist class and aristocracy, but the new stratum of white-collar workers, which aped the middle class in style and manners and, ably courted by Disraeli's populism, tended to vote Tory. The sense of difference already implicit in the associations and organisations of the working class was intensified by their political rupture from the Liberalism of the older ruling party and their adoption of socialism as a galvanising idea. 'Socialism' as Göran Therborn wrote recently, 'has existed as a culture of identity, primarily in terms of class – the working class'. [2] But socialism as a culture also spread beyond the English and European working class through identification with 'the people' and oppressed groups until it became a global phenomenon of opposition to capitalist imperialism. But socialism, as a theory, was not the creation of the working class alone and was always implicitly 'a strand of high culture'. That is to say, middle-class intellectuals have almost always been implicated in the development of socialism even though its 'bearers' have historically been seen as working-class and subaltern ethnic and national groups. Therborn also argues a second important point, that although the values espoused by socialism can be found in various historical periods

35

'socialist culture as such forms a major part of one particular epoch, that of *modernity*'. [3] In the account that follows I want to show that a related form of working-class culture developed in Britain which, although clearly socialist in many of its manifestations, still bore the traces of its own separate national development. The role of both formal and informal adult education in this development seems to me to have been crucial.

The modern historical compromise and political settlement between the classes which resulted in the modernised British state were, of course, the product of complex negotiations at many levels. Much of this, I believe, was shadowed informally in adult education classes of various kinds between the working-class men of intelligence and curiosity who came to form the leadership of the labour movement, and liberal and socialist intellectuals for whom adult education was a political, and almost religious, commitment.

There was also a third group, which was in many respects just as important to the settlement but is often left out of the picture, that of lower-middle class women, especially schoolteachers and those involved in welfare work. They formed perhaps the biggest single group in university extension classes in the late nineteenth century and many were pioneers in the women's suffrage movement. This group was the most persistent in demands for courses in English and history, as against science or economics or other more overtly political courses. For many of them university extension became a kind of in-service training in the 'national culture', and the benefits of their new understanding were quickly passed on to their pupils. In many respects they acted as key intermediaries between the ideological demands of the modernising state and the by now crystallising working-class culture.

Many liberal and radical reformers, perhaps conditioned by the narratives of poverty and degradation generated by the many 'inquiries into the state of the poor', especially the London poor, had failed to register much of this remarkable self-development of working-class culture. They were genuinely amazed when they experienced it at first hand. For example, when the young Beatrice Webb visited Bacup, in Derbyshire, in

1883, she found much to her surprise that ordinary working people had created what amounted to a different order of life based on attending to their own needs as a class rather than focusing on individual enrichment. 'How had this class' she asked, 'without administrative training or literary culture, managed to initiate and maintain the network of non-conformist chapels, the far-flung friendly societies, the much-abused trade unions, and that queer type of shop, the co-operative store?' [4]

What Beatrice Webb discovered was not the dangerous mob familiar to metropolitan high culture, but a different and appealing kind of culture. Not as lettered or refined in table manners as she would have liked but dignified, self-ordered and purposeful. It was co-operative rather than communalist, the modest and well-founded arrangement of activities and organisations for the common benefit. It was not a product of nature but of society, that is of jointly agreed activity based on thought and deliberation. Perhaps more importantly, although the outcome was without doubt the product of working-class activity, it was not that of the intellectual and cultural isolation of the working class as she may have supposed. For by the time she made this observation working people had for more than a half century, been engaged in various forms of education, both self-education and education from 'external' sources. Although the non-conformist chapels were one important axis of this education others included the Mechanics Institutes, the corresponding societies and the membership education of the co-ops and trade unions. The formation she encountered in Derbyshire was the product of the merging of their routine culture of self-preservation and the enlightened search for a decent and humane life, which brought them into contact with elements of 'bourgeois' culture.

It is clear that working people and other subordinate groups have always placed a high value on education, both for individual enlightenment and social progress. Jonathan Rée follows Jacques Rancière in suggesting that thoughtful proletarians have always desired the 'secrets' of middle-class intellectuals, not so much to explain their own exploitation as to escape from it to something better. But more than this, 'proletarian desires for education and high culture have been vital to socialist movements, and not merely, if at all, distractions from some wished-for (but by whom?) pure proletarian socialism'. [5]

If this sounds as if it is offering too many hostages to bourgeois fortune, it is worth noting that Gramsci himself, while imprisoned by the Fascist authorities, softened his earlier hostility to the value of bourgeois intellectuals. He accepted that the Italian Popular Universities, which were loosely modelled on British university extension and the French *universités populaires*, enjoyed a certain success in that 'they demonstrated on the part of the "simple" a genuine enthusiasm and a strong determination to attain a higher cultural level and a higher conception of the world'. [6] The significance of this lies in the fact that Gramsci had shifted from a belief in a purely proletarian culture of his earlier 'ultra-leftist' *Avanti!* phase to a concept of a 'common' cultural inheritance with the middle class. Nevertheless, he continued to believe that Italian intellectuals involved in the popular universities had betrayed the Italian people by not wholly identifying with their class interests. They could only have become 'organic intellectuals' if 'they had worked out and made coherent the principles and the problems raised by the masses in their practical activity'. [7] Interestingly, he believed that this kind of process had been much further advanced in Britain, particularly through the work of the Fabian Society. But Gramsci may have erred in undervaluing the co-operative and associationist side of British working-class culture which he labelled economico-corporative, or essentially defensive.

Gramsci, then, one of the subtlest Marxist thinkers on the matter of culture, swung between his earlier Bolshevik view of culture as wholly class bound and the more liberal idea of a common culture inspired by radical bourgeois thinkers. But, as Williams, Hoggart and Thompson in various ways have shown, working-class culture and high culture have occasionally combined to produce a new synthesis which has set a common marker for progress. In the late nineteenth century the political groups which adopted socialism arguably produced such a moment. It was not therefore a one-way process of the lower class borrowing from higher culture, since the 'simple', in Gramsci's phrase, already possessed a valuable communal culture of their own which allowed them valuable critical distance. The model is more that of cross-cultural borrowing and re-interpretation such that a new cultural entity was postulated between and beyond the existing boundaries. As a consequence, middle-class radical culture lost much of its individualistic and property-based assumptions, while the political working class discovered the virtues of systematic thought, and the possibility of a 'common humanity' in selected aspects of high culture.

British working-class culture was then notable in at least two important aspects, namely, the intelligent creation of institutions and associations for the maintenance of a distinct way of life different from and owing nothing to the middle class, but also the active appropriation of education and 'higher' culture for individual and class advancement. For many working people the desire for education rested on belief in the *common* inheritance of enlightenment ideas. While the women were drawn to the humanities, scientific rationalism was of obvious use to the skilled worker, both in his trade and, by extension, his view of society. Hobsbawm is again very illuminating on this:

> self-education and self-improvement was one of the major functions of
> the new working-class movements and one of the major attractions for
> its militants. And what the masses of newly educated lay persons
> absorbed, and welcomed if they were politically on the democratic or
> socialist left, were the rational certainties of nineteenth-century science,
> enemy of superstition and privilege, presiding spirit of education and
> enlightenment, proof and guarantee of progress and the emancipation
> of the lowly. [8]

The gifts of culture and enlightenment were, however, bought dear by individual workers who were often regarded with fear and suspicion by their fellows. In the last two decades of the nineteenth century Carl Levy has suggested,

A growing stratum of highly literate workers appeared. They were shaped by the older institutions of the dying artisan culture and by the educational networks maintained by the churches. But the self-educated worker seemed anomalous in a world of mass organisation. He or she could be considered 'queer' by colleagues and in turn, might well nurse a grudge against others he or she thought illiterate bigots. Self-education allowed workers to articulate the demands of the confused and apathetic, but it also distanced them from much of ordinary working-class life. [9]

Education for many was, therefore, acquired only at the cost of alienation from the very people they wanted to represent: access to the abstract model of culture, 'the highest and the best', often meant separation from and loss of 'traditional' or customary culture in order to create a new cultural formation. This seems to have been a tragic narrative threading biographies of the educated working class from Tom Maguire to Richard Hoggart. Culture as a tool both of personal development and of political struggle could be used often only through profound dislocation of identity.

The sense of excitement as well as the distress of this cultural alienation through education is caught by Sheila Rowbotham in her study of working-class students in the university extension movement at this time, 'Travellers in a strange country'. As one Cleveland miner wrote after attending his first geology class, 'I have lived in Cleveland about eighteen years of my life, but find it true that I am now in a strange country. I mean however to know it.' [10] And a Hull working joiner said 'I cannot tell how much I owe to these lectures. They have worked a revolution in my life. I am able to take broader views of questions and my interests are widened. My life is altogether brighter and happier'. [11]

As for the university extension lecturers themselves, they often burned with missionary zeal to bring enlightenment to the working class, but it would be crude to represent their work simply as an imposition of a bourgeois world view on simple proletarians. Indeed these lecturers were themselves often the object of the ridicule of other Oxbridge guardians of the culture for vulgarising the learning they offered. John Ruskin, who inspired the university extension movement, was regarded as little more than a 'showman' by his academic colleagues, because he cheapened art through his numerous and well-attended popular lectures and newspaper articles. Ruskin was exceptional in his ambition to open a dialogue with the working men of West Yorkshire, whom he addressed in his *Fors Clavigera* letters as 'My Dear Friends…'. It was from him, rather than Marx or Marxists, that many in the working-class movement traced the origins of British socialism. Kier Hardie wrote on his death, 'Thus disappears from earthly view last of the giants who made the modern British Socialist movement possible. We may not always agree with Ruskin's words, but the innermost thought of the man was sound, and his influence ever pure and wholesome'. [12] Ruskin's strength lay precisely in his ability to recognise the great cultural achievements *already* made by the working class, and his least desire was to incorporate the working class into a bourgeois hegemony, which he despised. The *Fors Clavigera* letters begin with the confession that 'certain things which I knew positively must soon be openly debated' namely, 'the transference of power out of the hands of the upper classes so called, into yours'. [13]

Central to this process was to be education, not conceived of as the transferring of bourgeois values and attitudes to artisans but as the critical interrogation of their own experience and understanding. Ruskin asked: 'Whose fault is it that through all your furrowed England, children are dying of famine?' and answered, 'Primarily of course it is your clergymen's and masters' fault: but it is also your own, that you never educate any of your children with the earnest object of enabling them to see their way out this, not by rising above their father's business, but by setting in order what was amiss in it'. [14] Ruskin's advice was to strengthen and develop their own organisations to enable the working class ultimately to shape a new civilisation which would be superior ethically and artistically to that under which they suffered. He was not interested in education that enabled the individual to rise out of his or her class but precisely in finding ways of 'setting in order what was amiss in it'. However, Ruskin was no democrat and his model of a future society was both medieval and hierarchical. To this extent, although it might be argued that he remained true to his own class interest and did little more than prepare the educated working class for peace and incorporation, this is not the whole story. His own class conceded considerable political power (although not economic) and were forced to accept the idea of the growth of the political state to encompass the welfare of all its newly created 'citizens'.

Following Ruskin's example many young men such as Michael Sadler and Edward Carpenter found their vocation in the university extension movement. In this movement, established by the Scottish radical James Stuart in 1873, the universities of Cambridge, Oxford and then London paid for itinerant lecturers to give courses of lectures for adults. These were held mostly in northern towns. In thinking about the early motivation for this movement it is hard to avoid the comparison with the colonialists' dream of 'civilising' Africa, but it nevertheless attracted radicals who found in it the opportunity for a genuinely popular education. [15] University extension flourished nationally and had considerable influence both in Europe and America. Thousands who had never before had access to higher education came to the courses of lectures and for the first time had the opportunity to engage and debate with university learning. The annual summer schools held in Oxford and Cambridge became international festivals of learning and sociability where men and women from Britain, Europe and America met together as citizens in the republic of knowledge. As a result of extension a New Universities movement began, which led to the founding of University Colleges in many of the industrial towns, as well as modernising elements of the ancient universities. This movement consciously avoided emulating Oxbridge's ivory tower image by insisting on the new universities' duty to serve the needs of their own locality. Many extension lecturers, like Arthur Grant and Frederic Moorman at Leeds, subsequently became professors of newly established history and English departments. During the 1890s university extension activities on the British model mushroomed across Europe, embracing and signifying radical, democratic and nationalist movements. [16]

With the advantage of historical distance the limitations of university extension may seem obvious. Charges of paternalism, national chauvinism and opposition to revolutionary socialist activity are not without substance. Nevertheless, whatever the intended ideological instruction within extension classes, they were viewed with intense suspicion by more traditional guardians of the national culture and the net effect on the working people who attended them was not to make them more content with their political lot but to excite them to demand more. Arguably, the reluctance by the British state to accede to these demands in the 1880s and 1890s led to the foundation of the Independent Labour Party, with its own agenda of social and welfare reform.

Would this advance in the political consciousness of the working class have been possible without a popular education movement, or was it, on the contrary, bought at the expense of revolutionary consciousness? After the surge of militant socialism and trade unionism in industrial areas in the 1880s, it is by no means obvious there was widespread popular demand for revolution. Only a small proportion was interested in any form of politics and, as Stedman Jones has maintained, in London at least, once the day's work was done, the majority of working people were interested only in popular culture of a different sort. [17] Those who actually became engaged in politics and education (usually the same people) were what Richard Hoggart called 'the earnest minority' or what George Thompson, the Yorkshire WEA District Secretary called 'the socially effective'.

What kinds of issues were raised in adult education classes at this time? Undoubtedly one of the most important was the question of citizenship and the shape of the modern democratised British state. As might be expected, much of this went on in classes in history, philosophy, political economy and social science, disciplines usually dominated by men. These men were also usually active in the co-operative movement, trade-unions or local politics, where insights gained in the classroom were rapidly turned into policy initiatives at the local WEA, trade union, co-op or Labour Party branch.

But important as this was for the advancement of working-class economic and local political interests, a key discipline for the cultural settlement reached was English studies. What had to be established was: What did it mean to be English? In some sections of the hegemonic order this was seen as the crucial debate and English literature was seen as *the* vehicle of the 'civilising process'. In his pioneering but rather uninflected account Chris Baldick writes:

> [Matthew] Arnold had often spoken of the need for a softening and humanizing influence to be exerted upon the masses in Britain to wean them from class-conflict and intellectual turmoil, and had offered poetry as a means to that end. The introduction of literary study among the middle and working classes through Mechanics Institutes, Working Men's Colleges and extension lecturing was already taking place with this aim in mind. [18]

In support Baldick quotes from Lord Playfair, who said: 'The main purpose is not to educate the masses but to permeate them with the desire for intellectual improvement, and to show them methods by which they can attain this desire. Every man who acquires a taste for learning and is imbued with the desire to acquire more of it becomes more valuable as a citizen, because he is more intelligent and perceptive'. [19]

There can be little doubt of the sobering effect of literature on inflamed minds intended by Playfair and others, and it is possible that the 'vulgar' minds so readily conjured up by the cultural elite were cowed by contact with the creative genius of the race. But it is clear that there were unintended consequences of this process of indoctrination. Students found radical heroes and impressively free-thinking women in the pages of George Eliot, theological subversion in Milton, moving descriptions of the inhumanities of capitalism in Dickens, and weak and frivolous aristocrats and monarchs in Shakespeare. By the end of the century when translations of European literature became more freely available in cheap editions, they discovered the powerful heroines of Ibsen, the communalist idealism of Tolstoy and the radical humanism of Heinrich Heine. Literacy, in the end, although it may have bought off the more extreme moment of revolution, could not be made unequivocally to bow to the voice of the dominant class interest.

More important perhaps is that it did not leave the dominant order unscathed. By bearing the torch of humanism which was to achieve class harmony to 'the masses', literature also suggested modes in which they could voice their own oppression and offered glimpses of the pre-capitalist past which might inform alternative futures. The utopian imagination on which Blatchford and William Morris drew was read in vast numbers by working people, and the works of Morris, Shaw, Whitman and other reformers were regularly included on university extension and WEA English course syllabi.

A New English

Hobsbawm notes that, in the late nineteenth century in Europe, national identity becomes 'a sort of general substratum of politics' which embraces appeals for social liberation and political reform. [20] Nationalist movements, however, were noticeably absent from the English scene during the same period and indeed England might seem to be an exception to the general rule. But as Ellen Meiksins Wood argues, the pressure for a nationalist ideology was mercifully weak in England precisely because the *actuality* of the nation was stronger: 'A conception of the "nation" associated with the dominance of English law and culture, was already present in the sixteenth century; but thereafter there were no strong demands upon the unitary state to reaffirm a national identity against the forces of parcellized sovereignty'. [21] Nor were there militant groups of English exiles plotting insurrection since most of the last generation of radical exiles such as Tom Paine had, in effect, founded a new democratic order elsewhere. However, the ideas of the New Age and 'New Life' were widespread in Britain, and over the century from Paine, Blake, Burns and Shelley to Edward Carpenter and William Morris, dissenters of all kinds had re-imagined England itself as the site of the New Jerusalem.

The subtle process of modernising English identity took great strength, in fact, from the expansion of the political and bureaucratic state, which now became the country's largest employer. The thousands of new jobs the state now created to run its vast commercial and educational concerns greatly expanded the new white collar stratum already mentioned. But as Hobsbawm notes, the idea of 'the nation' was held out as a kind of civic religion which transcended both religion and class, and as an employer the state insisted on a personal oath of loyalty to the nation itself. But in offering its subjects the new national identity the state could not avoid the implications of citizenship, which in effect required new rights.

For the working class to be inscribed in Englishness meant expanding the notion of 'English' to include the working class, just as the political franchise was expanded to include working-class men in the 1880s. But it was not simply a one-way process of absorbing this class into an already complete totality. The strength of existing working-class culture and values had a significant impact on English political culture, which led, by stages, to the founding and development of the welfare state and eventually the enfranchising of women. Nevertheless, the newly negotiated polity, which saw the Labour Party gradually assume the role of representing the working class was incomplete. By 1950 a settlement between the classes had been reached in which the dominant order still maintained its overall hegemony but at the expense of significant concessions to the 'social wage' and to the 'common culture' that the organised working class was demanding.

It could be argued that the late nineteenth and early twentieth century was then a conjunctural moment at which three developing cultural formations converged to crystallise in what became the British settlement, namely: an established industrial working-class culture, a modernist sensibility and an articulation of 'Englishness'. Thus as Hobsbawm argues both 'modern' working-class identity and English identity were born on the same ground, where the newly democratised state recognised the existence of a separate (but subordinate) working class with its own 'culture' and where working people could identify themselves both as 'working-class' and 'English'. [22] Working people then, could identify with *both* class and nationality, sometimes in harmony as in the First World War, sometimes in bitter conflict, as in the General Strike.

As we shall argue in the next chapter it was partly through the English studies that were first taught in university extension classes that modern English-ness was recognised and given cultural substance, not as a function of the all powerful state to which obedience had to be given, but as a complex and rich network of civil life which in many key aspects was relatively self-governing, working-class institutions being but one aspect of this. Because it was not achieved as the result of a nationalist struggle for independence but by a process of internal colonialism, class negotiations and compromises based on a share of imperialist fortunes, it had only an ambiguous appeal for its regional and ethnic minorities, which did not win something from the original settlement. Not only did Irish, Scots and Welsh identities refuse to lie down under 'Englishness' but, by the turn of the century, had developed militant minority nationalist movements and persistent campaigns for national sovereignty. These movements rudely unmasked the secret of the older identity of 'Britishness', that it concealed an English hegemony, in which, it came to be seen, the English working class was partly complicit.

Notes

1 E.J. Hobsbawm, 'The Formation of British Working Class Culture' in *Worlds of Labour*, Weidenfeld and Nicolson, London 1984, pp176-193.

2 Göran Therborn, 'The Life and Times of Socialism', *New Left Review*, 194, July/August, 1992, pp17-32, p18.

3 *Ibid*, p19.

4 Quoted in Stephen Yeo, 1987 'Notes on three socialisms – collectivism, statism, associationism – mainly in late-nineteenth- and early-twentieth century Britain' in Carl Levy (ed), *Socialism and the Intelligentsia 1880-1914*, Routledge Kegan Paul, London 1987, p229.

5 Jonathan Rée, 'Socialism and the Educated Working Class' in Carl Levy, *Socialism and the Intelligentsia*, 1987, *op cit*, pp211-18, p217.

6 Antonio Gramsci, *Prison Notebooks*, (eds) Q. Hoare and G. Nowell Smith, Lawrence and Wishart, London 1971, pp329-330. In 1916 Gramsci several times attacked the popular university movement as having no understanding of the different needs and backgrounds of people who had not been through secondary school; they merely aped the curricula of existing bourgeois universities. In an article in the Socialist newspaper, *Avanti!* considering the need for a workers' cultural association, Gramsci dismissed the popular university in Turin with savagery,

> It is best not to speak of the Popular University. It has never been alive, it has never functioned so as to respond to a real need. Its origin is bourgeois and it is based on a vague and confused criterion of spiritual humanitarianism. It has the same effectiveness as charitable institutions which believe that with a bowl of soup they can satisfy the physical

47

needs of wretches who cannot appease their hunger and who move the tender hearts of their superiors to pity. (Antonio Gramsci, *Selections from Cultural Writings*, (eds) D. Forgacs and G. Nowell-Smith, London Lawrence and Wishart, 1985, p21n.).

Gramsci, then at the extreme moment of his refusal of bourgeois culture, claimed that the Turin proletariat, at the highest point of its development, should dispense with all bourgeois cultural props and agenda and create its own specifically proletarian institution for its own class ends. It was, he felt, a world historical moment when the proletariat recognises 'that the complexity of its life lacks a necessary organ and creates it, with its strength, with its good will, for its own ends'. Compared with Italy's backwardness, he claimed that both England and Germany had contained powerful organs of proletarian and socialist culture and curiously, in the light of domestic criticism, named the Fabian Society, when it belonged to the Second International, as its exemplar. For Gramsci the value of the Fabian Society was that it offered a forum for thorough and popular discussion of the moral and economic problems affecting the working-class. But just as important was the fact that it had moved a large part of the English intellectual and university world into this work. It was unfortunate that Gramsci did not comment on how far he felt university extension was involved in this work, because it would seem a necessary corollary to his argument.

7 *Ibid*.

8 E.J. Hobsbawm, *The Age of Empire*, Cardinal, London 1987, p263.

9 Carl Levy, 'Education and self-education: staffing the early ILP' in Carl Levy, ed. *Socialism and the Intelligentsia, op cit*, pp135-210, p166.

10 Quoted in Sheila Rowbotham, 'Travellers in a strange country: responses of working-class students to the University Extension Movement – 1873 -1910', *History Workshop Journal* 12, Autumn, 1981, p73.

11 *Ibid*.

12 Quoted in Malcolm Hardman, *Ruskin and Bradford*, Manchester University Press, Manchester 1986, p317.

13 Quoted in *Ibid*, p315.

14 Quoted in *Ibid*, p316.

15 Edward Carpenter, for example, frequently used his visits to places like Leeds on extension business to also lecture to socialist and other militant groups.

16 See Tom Steele, 'A Science for Democracy: The Growth of University Extension in Europe 1890-1920' in *Adult Education Between Cultures, Encounters and identities in European adult education since 1890*, (eds) Barry J. Hake and Stuart Marriott, Leeds Studies in Adult Education, 1993, pp61-85.

17 Gareth Stedman Jones, *Languages of Class*, Routledge, London 1980.

18 Chris Baldick, *The Social Mission of English Criticism 1848 -1932*, Oxford University Press, Oxford 1987, p63.

19 Quoted in *Ibid*, p64.

20 Hobsbawm, 1987, *op cit*, p144.

21 Ellen Meiksins Wood, *The Pristine Culture of Capitalism*, Verso, London 1991, p32.

22 Hobsbawm, 1987, *op cit*.

3.

English studies – an internal colonisation

'English' functions as a contradictory sign in contemporary culture, over which fierce ideological dogfights are mounted. Few other fields of academic activity have witnessed quite the degree of bitterness unleashed, for example, over Cambridge's 'sacking' of Colin McCabe in the late 1970s, or during the methodological controversies of the 1980s. As a field of study, English has been a peculiarly contested area, from the recent arguments over structuralism and post-structuralism, through to the sectarian divisions over Leavisism in the decades before and after the Second World War, and other divisions before that. As a discipline, English studies is currently in the process of being reconstructed in the light of the claims from what some might describe as its bastard offspring, cultural studies. Indeed, the conjunction of the formulations 'English' and 'culture' appears to be implicit in the very origins of the newer subject. Could it be that cultural studies is, in effect, the 'truth' of English studies? Is what has impelled the institutional study of English literature not so much the desire to encourage the disciplined study of written texts, but rather the desire to evoke and disseminate an ideal of a unifying culture?

English arrives on the academic scene, as Terry Eagleton has argued, as a radical deconstruction of the late nineteenth century, when both the universities and the institutions of political life were fracturing in the face of radical and popular demands for democratisation: '"English" as an academic subject was first institutionalized not in the universities but in the Mechanics' Institutes, working men's colleges and extension lecturing circuits'. [1]

The debate over the origins of English studies is of special interest here because as an academic subject it appears to have developed within adult education, a practice whose very marginality enabled it to be an experimental site. Many of those like Churton Collins, who pioneered English within the universities, were primarily active in university extension, where by the 1890s English had become one of the most popular subjects. English was subsequently established as a discipline in the new civic universities of the industrial towns such as Birmingham, Manchester, Sheffield, Liverpool and Leeds. The establishment of the civics themselves, many of which began life as university colleges, owed a great deal to the activities of university extension in the industrial towns and in particular to the missionary activities of the extension lecturers.

As Ian Hunter argues, the modern debate over the origins of English studies begins in the 1960s when John Dixon and others celebrate them as the triumph of the Arnoldian humanistic vision over the utilitarian philistinism, or Gradgrindery, of the early school system. English studies was regarded as the most important key to a fully humanised society in which individual creative potential could be allowed to flower in line with a maturing democracy. This celebratory view was subsequently contested by Terry Eagleton, Chris Baldick and Brian Doyle in the 1980s, from a broadly cultural materialist perspective. The central tenet of their approach was that, during the nineteenth century, English studies was the product of the struggle of the industrial middle class for hegemony over the emerging political strength of the working class. Through the development of English studies a powerfully ideological veil could be thrown over the real needs and experience of the working class, who would come to identify their interests with those of their political masters. Developing on the work of Gareth Stedman Jones and Brian Simon, Brian Doyle went so far as to situate the development of English studies within a strategy of 'classification, pacification and cultivation' in order to create a new authoritative collectivity. [2] The trick was to separate off the respectable working class from the rougher elements and make the leaders of the class, through 'humane' education, fit for a limited role in government. Such a view, although highly conspiratorial, was certainly shared by the more militant leaders of working-class education between the wars.

In turn, this view has been strongly challenged from Foucaldian perspectives by James Donald and Ian Hunter, supported by considerable close examination of the original documents. [3] For Hunter in particular, literary education occupies a special place in the development of the educational system in the nineteenth century. His focus is largely on schools and universities and he pays little attention to popular adult education. He argues that the idea of 'culture' effectively takes over from the panoptical surveillance technology of popular schooling during the late nineteenth century, to create 'a machinery of moral training'. By introducing the notion of culture, the morally managed environment of the school is fortified by the ethic of self-cultivation developed by a relatively dissident cultural aristocracy during the earlier part of the century which disseminated its views largely by means of cultural journalism, as in, for example, the work of Carlyle and Ruskin, or in the morally didactic novels of Charles Dickens. Hunter argues that through English study this ethic of self-cultivation becomes a method for advancing the general cultural growth of society. The expectation is that children in school learn to police themselves in line with social expectations and thus that the need for external surveillance and policing is minimised. The human products of the school system, in theory, internalise the needs of the social order and identify them as their own spontaneous desires. This is the real meaning of culture.

Cultural materialism, Hunter argues, understands the hegemonic project involved but mistakenly assumes that the vehicle of English studies is simply the embodiment of Arnold's class version of literary criticism and that culture was supposed to trickle down from the universities. Hunter insists that, in fact,

English is the literary form of a special pedagogy which involves aesthetic and psychologistic elements drawn from other progressive practices which foreground ideas of natural growth and imagination. Margaret McMillan, for example, believed that through the encouragement of art and the imagination, the havoc wrought by the outside world – and the family – on the working-class child could be 'corrected' in the schoolroom.

The special virtue of English literature was its proclaimed 'closeness to life'. In fact, the identification of the student with the life represented in the text, according to Hunter, was a function of a number of elements, including supervisory techniques employed in the pedagogical space of the classroom and the special teacher-student relationship developed in the field of English studies. The new subject involved the study of texts which contained moral exemplars and moral narratives to be unravelled under the guidance of the teacher. The ideal teacher would, in turn, become such a moral exemplar to the student by creating a space 'where the student could talk in order to be corrected while the teacher could listen in order to correct'. As such, the strategy culminated in the Newbolt Report of 1920 on the teaching of English where the training of English teachers was identified as a priority in order to produce what the report called the lever with which to raise the mass.

It seems that the distant origins of English studies did in fact reflect this imperative but a dimension which Hunter appears to neglect, although Doyle draws attention to it, is that of colonialism and empire. The idea of English as an object of systematic study appears to have begun as a technique of colonising the identity of the Other, in particular of Anglicising the Oriental subject. As Macaulay's famous Minute of 1834 had it: 'We must do our best to form a class who may be interpreters between us and the millions we govern … a class of persons, Indian in blood and colour, but English in tastes, in opinions, in morals, and in intellect'. [4]

Key to this, as we shall see, was the teaching of English, first as the administrative language of empire, which produced a linguistic rupture between the elite and the mass population of the country, and secondly, as literature, the repository of the ideal

Englishman, as opposed to the unsavoury actually existing Englishman who represented the East India Company. Macaulay's brother in law, Charles Trevelyan, unlike most Victorian imperialists, understood from the beginning that India would not be held as a colony indefinitely, therefore a strategy was needed which tied India to Britain commercially even while inevitably she moved towards independence:

> No effort of policy can prevent the nations from ultimately regaining their independence. English education will achieve by gradual reform what any other method will do by revolution. The nations will not rise against us because we shall stoop to raise them ... We shall exchange profitable subjects for still more profitable allies ... and establish a strict commercial union between the first manufacturing and the first producing country in the world. [5]

The form of education envisaged in this strategy was not one that produced a deep grasp of principles but rather relied on an aping and recital of English literature and philosophy, the function of which was, firstly, to impart a vocabulary of administration and governance. Secondly, the aim was to instil an awe for English aristocratic virtues and a corresponding disdain for the indigenous culture. It created, in effect, a reformed Brahmin intellectual class, indifferent to science and technology, with an exaggerated respect for literary culture. From this élite, it was hoped, the culture so achieved would 'trickle down' to the masses below, a policy which had the incidental advantage of freeing the administration from any further expense on education.

The relative success of this policy in imposing a cultural hegemony over the Indian educated élite was studied closely by the governing class in Britain and at the time, lessons were drawn from it. In a recent account of the history and function of English studies in India, one of India's new generation of critical scholars, Gauri Viswanathan, suggests that, in the nineteenth century, India was regarded as an experimental pitch for processes of cultural control through education. [6] Crucial to this experimentation was the development of the specialist area of English studies, a subject which was not then seriously regarded in British universities. Viswanathan argues that English as a discipline is coterminous with the process of colonialism and from being the occasional diversion of the middle classes in their leisure time, 'literature' appears to undergo a profound transformation into an instrument of ideology 'for the insertion of individuals into the perceptual and symbolic forms of the dominant ideological formation'. [7]

The discipline of English literary study in India begins as a strategy of containment. With the Charter Act of 1813 came the assumption of new responsibilities for native education and a relaxation of the controls over missionary activity. Since a straightforward Christian mission amongst historically well-entrenched religions had been tried and failed, 'English' studies appeared to offer a secular solution to some of these problems. Moreover, the initial object of reform was not simply native 'immorality' but the representatives of civilisation themselves, as Viswanathan notes: 'It is impossible not to be struck by the peculiar irony of a history in which England's initial involvement with the education of the natives derived less from a conviction of native immorality, as the later discourse might lead one to believe, than from the depravity of their own administrators and merchants'. [8] Edmund Burke's speech to the Commons supporting the Bill demanded, 'a strong and solid security for the natives against the wrongs and oppressions of British subjects resident in Bengal'. The subtext of English studies was, therefore, the construction of an ideal type of Englishman, or moral exemplar, against which the actual representatives of the race might be measured and eventually erased from memory. Instead of the real merchant adventurers making a fast buck, the 'Englishman' would come to be realised as a fateful invention of the great literary tradition. English studies and the construction of Englishness, as Brian Doyle says, are not in the end separable. English, he argues, 'is best seen as an invented or constructed cultural form which was a culmination of attempts to produce a truly "English" theory of society and a prospectus for cultural renewal'. [9]

English studies also represented the triumph of the policy of Anglicism over Orientalism, although it was the careful toleration of certain aspects of Orientalism that won for Anglicism a softening of its boundaries, a fluidity which encouraged a degree of incorporation. The policy of Orientalism, which had been introduced by Warren Hastings in the late eighteenth century as a pragmatically liberal response to the need for native administrators, argued that good government required a responsiveness to Indian culture rather than a refusal of it, a reaction which in itself demonstrated just how unfixed and relatively open the definition of Englishness was before the high point of imperialism: 'they do not understand our character and we do not penetrate theirs ... we have no hold on their sympathies, no seat in their affections'. [10] Thus, rather than intensifying the force of a national English identity as yet not fully achieved, Hastings suggested a kind of 'reverse acculturation' in which Indian culture should be studied and respected, a policy which produced the great scholars of Orientalism, Jones, Colebrooke and Wilson. The liberal imperialist function of Orientalism envisaged at this stage ranged from, 'the initiation of the West to the vast literary treasures of the East, to the reintroduction of the natives to their own cultural heritage'. [11] This is recognisably the language of multiculturalism and incorporation rather than orthodoxy and exclusion that reflects a greater confidence in the hegemonic colonialist culture's ability to absorb and enrich itself from the Eastern 'treasure-house' while yet allowing the 'natives' the dignity of their own inheritance.

However, because of political and financial scandal, Hastings was forced to retire and the policy of Orientalism was abandoned. His successor, Lord Cornwallis (1786-1793), was not slow in blaming the 'deteriorating standards', as he saw it, 'on the earlier policy of accommodation to the native culture. In his view the official indulgence towards Oriental forms of social organisation, especially government, was directly responsible for the lax morals of the Company servants'. [12] Cornwallis immediately reversed the policy in favour of red-blooded Anglicisation, the policy of 'Anglicism'. So, in abandoning Hastings's policy of liberal Orientalism and replacing it by a more assertive English nationalism, English studies swiftly came to have a key support role.

The teaching of English studies was pioneered, almost against his will, by the Christian evangelist, Alexander Duff, in his Free Church Institution. Duff was very suspicious of the official educational policy of secularism which he rightly perceived had been instituted in India in a spirit of experimentation. India was used, he said, as 'a fair and open field for testing the non-religion theory of education'. [13] His own response was to adapt secularism to the evangelical mission by sleight of hand, choosing curricular texts for their 'Christian' values. Milton and Cowper were included in the curriculum, as might be expected; more surprisingly, so were Bacon and even Schlegel. However, probably the bulk of the reading matter comprised of texts such as Pollock's *Selection from English Verse* and Macaulay's *Lays*.

English literary study's founding moment, therefore, already included an elaborate agenda which involved on the one hand a secular programme of acculturation to British business and administrative needs and on the other a deeply coded subtext of 'spiritual values'. English literature, more than any other 'national' literature, was seen as the repository of the word of God. Shakespeare, according to Duff, was 'full of religion'; only Christians, however, could recognise it.

For the evangelists, this balancing act was always a dangerous strategy. Interpreting the complex coding of the curriculum required an initiated mentor, and in the absence of a literary critical profession, colonial teachers could not always be relied on to give a canonical reading. Thus it was not long before complaints were made about the outcomes. Shakespeare, for example, was for some full of religion but it was not necessarily Christian: his excessively *pagan* vocabulary contained words like 'fortune', 'fate', 'muse' and worst of all 'nature'. While many educated Indians made their way to an orthodox Christianity and Anglo-Indian identity, a minority discovered not only the noble ideal that was intended but the cunning and subversive anti-hero of *Paradise Lost*, Satan, and made their own comparisons between divine and secular imperialisms. This minority ultimately fuelled the growing Indian nationalist and anti-imperialist movement. [14]

For the secular administration, however, Christianity was a side-issue to the central project of constructing an ideal of Englishness. Trevelyan wrote that through the study of English literature, '[The Indians who] daily converse with the best and wisest Englishmen through the medium of their works, perhaps gain higher ideas of our nation than if their intercourse were of a more personal kind'. [15] Becoming English was inscribed within a larger discourse of the necessary development of 'civilisation' which sufficiently obscured the elision between the notion of Englishness and that of civilisation, such that the two became identical. Studying English was to study the growth from barbarism to civilisation, of which the British empire was the shining and inevitable example. To become English was to become human. By 1855 the East India Company had successfully incorporated English studies into its educational requirement and had outlined plans under the India Act of 1853 for competitive examinations in which English literature and history were the most important aspects. [16]

There were lessons to be learned here. Quite early in the process the Marquise of Tweedale had 'observed' the same characteristics in the English working class as she had seen in Muslims and Hindus: immorality, sensuality, self-indulgence, corruption and depravity. She compared the situation in India with England, even mobilising the colonial metaphor of 'those living in the dark recesses of our great cities at home'. [17] The problem was that, even in the heart of the metropolitan power, the Church of England had manifestly failed in its appeal to the members of the working class to take their allotted positions 'at the gate', while the dissenting chapels, in truth, attracted only the artisan stratum. As in India, some more effective means of incorporation and control had to developed.

It was inevitably the liberal intellectuals who first recognised the potential of the experiments in India, men such as Michael Sadler, the Secretary of the Oxford Delegacy in the 1880s, who in other circumstances might have found their vocation in the Indian Civil Service. Sadler, indeed, had briefly considered a Professorship in the Moslem College of Aligarh, which was suggested to him by his friend D.S. MacColl who considered him 'the most missionary spirit he knew'. [18] Sadler kept up a passionate involvement with the subcontinent, which he regarded as an experimental crucible for educational policy. He chaired the influential Calcutta University Commission in 1919, which proposed the modernisation of the university system, and became an admiring friend of Rabindranath Tagore, whose educational work he celebrated. By no means wholly an Orientalist, Sadler was, however, convinced that India possessed a spiritual aspect sadly absent from industrialised Britain. As Secretary of the Oxford Delegacy, Sadler's evangelism was focused on the working class and women nearer to home, for whom the question of a secular education was his highest priority. 'Our work' he said, 'lies among those who have hitherto lain outside the influence of University life and our task is to win them ... to a new appreciation of the worth of knowledge and a new respect for the dignity of laborious self-culture'. [19] The educational experience of English studies in India encouraged him in 1907 to establish a Bureau of Education for the British Empire the aims of which were: 'the accurate study of the methods of teaching and educational administration in the different parts of the British empire, not forgetting those parts where the experience of persons engaged in the training of native races and of non-English speaking peoples throws light upon methods of teaching English as part of a character-forming course of education'. [20] This identification of English studies with 'character-formation' strongly echoes the rhetoric of the debates on colonial education, except that now the Other to be formed is not the Hindu or Muslim but the manual labourer.

Sadler also believed there was an exemplary Englishman to be discovered in the texts of English literature. As late as 1917, in his address on 'The Educational Movement in India and Britain', he drew a portrait of the noble dissenter who embodied for England 'the most valued of her possessions': the right to express 'discordant and often inconveniently trenchant opinions on fundamental questions of politics, ethics and religious belief'. [21] As an example he cited the contrasting politics of Wordsworth, Johnson, Milton and Shakespeare and approved the 'shrewd judge of English character and political thought' who said that if you bound together in one cover Tom Paine's *Rights of Man* and Burke's *Reflexions on the French Revolution*, (sic, *Reflections on the Revolution in France*) you would have a good book; 'Mix Milton, Johnson and Wordsworth and you get England'. If literary England was characterised by internal difference as well as identity, it follows that Englishness inhered in a plurality of opinion mysteriously bound together.

What Sadler may have had in mind is something like Sorel's enabling myth, which he might well have come across recently in the pages of Orage's *New Age*. Certainly he imagined that the idea of a national English literature could create an idealised unity out of the actual diversity and real contradictions of English social life. Indeed, elsewhere Sadler specifically refers to the break up of social tradition under the pressure of economic change as an evil to be addressed by education. In Britain and America, under modern conditions of displaced and immigrant communities, school now had to bear the burden left by the destruction of social tradition 'where pits and factories had drawn together a medley of new-comers for whom nothing had been prepared in the way of organised community life'.[22] So while diversity is a virtue in the ranks of the literary English, among the lower orders it is a vice which education has to cement into some sort of organic whole called 'community'.

By the 1880s English studies had taken root in university extension classes run by the Oxford Delegacy (of which Sadler was secretary) together with Cambridge and London universities; it became a missionary cause for many of their idealistic lecturers. The first university departments of English did not appear until later in the century and not at all in Oxford and Cambridge until the twentieth century. In many cases departments of English had been fostered by extension's itinerant lecturers, augmented by an almost messianic desire for 'national' cultural renewal. Many of the founding chairs in English were given to men, like Charles Vaughan and Frederic Moorman, who began their careers as extension lecturers.

As in India, there was a perceived relationship with Christian ideals and in some cases literary studies in university extension were an almost direct outgrowth of bible studies. Charles Moulton, for example, regularly mixed biblical and secular material in his lectures. A report in one of the university extension journals of 1894 describes how in a course on Ancient Classical Drama held in Newcastle, which attracted an audience of 700-800, 'His suggestive treatment of Shakespeare and the poetry of the Old Testament turned scores of attendants at his lectures into students of literature'. [23] But because of dissenting opinion, gradually, overtly religious texts and references were excluded from classes and a more humanist approach taken. The process of secularising literary studies was also influenced by utilitarian considerations such as the need for technical education. The debate occasioned by the Technical Education Act of 1889, came to characterise English studies as the spiritual complement of technical training, or in other words the character forming aspect that, as we have seen, Sadler emphasised. [24] What the new approach required was a humanist interpretation of spirituality removed from any overtly religious reference, with Christian ideals seen as implicit in the text.

One of the most insistent campaigners for the establishment of literary studies against the resistant Oxbridge establishment was John Churton Collins, later Professor of English at Birmingham. For his pains he was labelled a 'louse on the locks of literature' by the poet laureate, Alfred Lord Tennyson. Like many others, Collins had become a university extension lecturer in 1889 without any qualification in literature, because at this stage there were virtually none to be had, but with a burning zeal to spread the news: 'What they lacked in term of special expertise in particular areas of English studies they made up for with their range of literary knowledge and, above all, with their quasi-religious sense of cultural mission'. [25] Collins, who also coached students for the East India Company examinations, placed literary studies at the centre of the newly conceptualised policy of 'citizenship' education:

the ideal of the university extension system is ... the liberal
education of the citizen – the dissemination of aesthetic instruction
by the liberal interpretation of poetry, rhetoric and criticism; of
ethical and spiritual instruction by the interpretation in this spirit, of
the great masterpieces of poetry ... By not including the study of
literature in its courses, a [Technical Education] Centre is closing the
door to all this side, this most important side, of popular education.[26]

In his article of 1887 'Can English Literature be Taught ?' he
also argued for the need to see literature as an organic whole in
which national idiosyncrasies expressed themselves under
various conditions. This was a deliberately historical approach
because Collins was less in favour of theorising literary studies
than of having a sound knowledge of particular periods. As
Kearney remarks, the notions of uplift and inspiration familiar
from the writings of Arnold and Carlyle were subordinated to a
systematic syllabus. [27]

Like most other extension lecturers of this period, Collins did
not see English studies as informing a narrow national
chauvinism but, on the contrary, as placing English literature
within the broader prospect of European literature. This
accorded with the classical emphasis of Benjamin Jowett and
Matthew Arnold and, with Charles Moulton, Collins took a
leading role in trying to develop classical courses in university
extension in the 1890s. Although this policy was only fitfully
successful, and dwarfed by the success of English studies, Collins
was celebrated within the profession as having done more than
anyone else to waken and nourish the new 'Humanist Revival'.

But although the new 'discipline' of English was gathering
many hitherto separated elements, such as English History and
Literature, to itself, it was clear that the subject was bifurcated
between the study of philology, which was its older academic
parent and that of literature, which was the firm emphasis taken
in university extension. For Collins this was yet another element
of the Humanist Revival. He campaigned vigorously against the
'barren drudgery' of Anglo-Saxon and celebrated the cause of
'modern literature' (which for most dons was no more than an
entertaining diversion). Charles Moulton declared in 1890 that,
through their extra-mural work throughout the country,

extension lecturers were showing the universities 'there is a world outside their charmed circle which is being influenced and moulded by that which they regard so lightly as literature.' [28] When Oxford at length recognised that there was a world outside and, in 1895, established the new Merton Chair in English Language and Literature at Oxford, Collins was, perhaps not surprisingly, passed over. He subsequently became Professor of English at Birmingham.

Another pioneering figure in the establishment of English studies from university extension was Frederic Moorman. He never lost his attachment to adult education, and while he was Professor of English Language at Leeds was instrumental in enabling the Yorkshire District of the WEA to gain its independence in 1914. Although nominally on the side of philology, his greatest interest was in dialect studies and he was in fact responsible for making some of the first sound recordings. He wrote a number of dialect plays and encouraged his students, one of whom was Herbert Read, to do the same – he is also the man who gave 'Ilkla Moor b'aht 'at' to the world. He characterised literary studies as the contemplation not just of style but 'of an author's thoughts, and, above all, of the great ideals into which his thoughts crystallise'. Literature for him was the transparent medium through which the exemplary character and within that, spiritual harmony, is revealed, 'the study of literature is above all the study of ideals – ideals of truth and beauty'. [29]

While Moorman thought that the function of literature was not so much to teach as delight the reader, others craved more discipline. P. H. Wicksteed, another extension lecturer, believed that tutors must forge the 'minds of their students into instruments of greater precision than before, to whatever subject they apply them, and at cultivating such habits of work and thought as will make them intellectually trustworthy, and give them a deeper sense of responsibility and a higher standard of accuracy'. [30]

But, like Moorman, he also distinguished the non-literary function of literary studies, which he called the 'vital' criticism, as being more important than the linguistic or rhetorical function. He uses an interestingly spatial metaphor: 'the strange regions of metaphysical and social speculation into which [the author] leads us will reveal themselves to us in living connection with thoughts and principles that are still active in our lives'. [31] Here the author acts as Virgil to the reader's Dante, roaming through unexplored territory. This is a return to the colonial/mapping metaphor, the function of study being to familiarise the reader with the estranged literary origins of his own sensibility. The effect of this approach is to appropriate the reader's own deeply held beliefs, luring them into the open only to reveal them as a product of literary culture, the reader being merely the unconscious and unwitting parchment upon which a culture has stamped its images. Thus, to study culture is to reveal a debt to its élite, who have provided the reader with what they naively believed to be their own thoughts and principles.

There was, therefore, a powerful current in university extension concerned with constructing and cementing in place through the study of literature, an ideal and authoritative culture to which the student would come to see that he or she belonged. The culture itself was not of their creation but the product of great men, an élite to whom he or she should pay homage. Studying literature revealed the debt the humble student owed to them and the greater collectivity which nurtured them, a collectivity which went by the name of nation rather than class.

With the publication of the Newbolt Report, *The Teaching of English in England*, the colonial metaphor reached its apogee. Most significant is the report's acknowledgement of the importance of adult education in pioneering the founding of English studies, and its continued importance in furthering the subject. Not surprisingly perhaps, a number of the committee's members had been actively involved in the extension movement or were strongly sympathetic to it. One of them, the Shakespeare scholar, John Dover Wilson, had also been an HMI (His Majesty's Inspector of Schools) with responsibility for adult education and in 1914 had kept an official eye on the formation of the Yorkshire District of the WEA. He took great relish in teaching classes in Shakespeare to 'heavy iron workers' in Middlesbrough, which he regarded as some of his most rewarding work. He knew both

Moorman and Sadler in Leeds and deeply respected 'the genius' of George Thompson 'whose memory I revere above that of most of these early apostles'. [32] Perhaps surprisingly, he was wholly in sympathy with Thompson's commitment to raising the intellectual standard of the working class as a whole rather than merely elevating a few of its members.

The pressure to set up the Newbolt committee came from the English Association, in which former extension lecturers like Moorman were well-represented, and it was very much as a reaction to the horrific consequences of the First World War. The committee's aim was 'to promote the due recognition of English as an essential element in the national renewal'. [33] Under the slogan of 'Culture unites classes', the Newbolt Report held that a liberal education based on English 'would form a new element of national unity, linking together the mental life of all classes'. [34]

The language of the report, especially its section on adult education, is replete with references to territorial conquest, colonisation and missionary activity. Much of this, to be fair, was borrowed from the adult education movement itself, the university settlement movement being a key example. Both Toynbee Hall and Keble College's Oxford House had been founded in the "darkest" East End in 1884 by Christian Socialists in a frankly missionary spirit. Oxford House's first annual report, for example, related baldly that 'Colonisation by the well-to-do seems indeed the true solution to the East End question, for the problem is, how to make the masses realise their spiritual and social solidarity with the rest of the capital and the kingdom'. [35] The task of the settlement was not so much to enquire into the causes of distress but to incorporate 'the masses' into a semblance of national unity, through a process of internal colonisation.

After the double trauma of the First World War and the Bolshevik Revolution in Russia, the Newbolt Report seems at one level to reflect the beleaguered consciousness of the home counties and the middle classes. Consequently, the committee saw its task as that of national renewal in which Britain's own hearts of darkness – the 'great cities' and their swarming millions – could be incorporated into the new national polity. The instrument with which to bring about this new settlement was to be English studies. Brian Doyle notes that, 'In presenting English culture as a transcendental essence inhering within an "organic" national language and a humanistic literary tradition, the goal was to establish for the study of English at the universities a status equivalent to Oxford's *Literae Humaniores*'. [36]

English was not intended to supplant the study of classics, which was still implicitly assumed to be the appropriate education for the ruling élite, but it was seen as part of a much wider mission of cultural renewal, with the task of co-opting the lower classes into the national settlement. The newly founded departments of English studies were important, consequently, not so much for their internal university role, but in 'leading, co-ordinating, and sustaining extra-mural initiatives'. [37] The report signalled the importance it accorded to existing adult education: 'In view of the growth of the tutorial classes movement and of adult education generally, which carries with it an increasing demand for courses in English literature, the influence and responsibilities for English departments at universities, especially in the provinces, are likely to be extended considerably in the near future'. [38] It went on to make clear that all work done with adult students should be regarded as university work and carried out at the highest standard. The Professor of English should make it part of his duties to keep in close touch with tutors and 'in short that the extension and tutorial classes should be regarded as an integral part of the English Department'. [39]

Doyle notes the tone of anxiety that pervades such passages in the report, betraying the fear that anarchy lurks beyond the university walls, in the form of shiftless men awaiting the false prophets who will no doubt lead them into the ways of Bolshevism and bloody revolution should their courses in Shakespeare not be delivered on time. Continuing in this vein, the report ascends a register of imperialist and messianic imagery until it culminates in a cataclysmic prophesy. If literature is, 'a fellowship which "binds together by passion and knowledge the vast empire of human society, as it spreads over the whole earth, and over all time" then a nation of which a considerable portion rejects this means of grace, and despises this great spiritual influence, must assuredly be heading to disaster'. [40]

As we have seen this is not mere rhetoric, since English studies were consciously promoted, at least in the Indian part of Britain's 'vast empire', precisely to bind its subjects more closely to their imperial master. Doyle also notes how the section on adult education in the report is the most political in its aims but the most transcendental in terms of language. Literature is claimed to be above politics, yet, suitably wrapped in the discourse of high moral calling, is employed as a political instrument. It is perhaps appropriate that when the report discusses the social crisis which has brought about the need for English studies, it employs its most surreal of colonial images, the poet militant, 'who will invade this vast new territory, and so once more bring sanctification and joy into the sphere of common life'. [41]

The key to the social crisis is a version of the 'dissociation of sensibility' thesis, which held that a rupture occurred in English social life in the sixteenth century and, greatly accentuated by the Industrial Revolution, created a gulf between what the report calls, 'the world of poetry and the world of everyday life'. This created an indifference and even hostility to literature among the people at large. However, other parts of the report reveal a subtext to this statement which suggests that it was driven by more specific anxieties. For the authors of the report, the 'hostility towards the "culture of capitalism" now prevalent in Bolshevist Russia' [42] was closely related to the antipathy to literature expressed by the working classes, especially those belonging to organised labour movements: 'Literature, in fact, seems to be classed by a large number of thinking working men with antimacassars, fish-knives and other unintelligible and futile trivialities of "middle-class culture" and, as a subject of instruction, is suspect as an attempt "to side-track the working-class movement".' [43]

Such patently erroneous beliefs, the report concluded, pointed to 'a morbid condition of the body politic which if not taken in hand may be followed by lamentable consequences', notably, Bolshevism. But it was a liberal imperialism rather than authoritarian repression, that was advocated, much in the spirit of Warren Hastings's orientalist approach in India the previous century: 'The ambassadors of poetry must be humble, they must learn to call nothing common or unclean – not even the local dialect, the clatter of the factory, or the smoky pall of our industrial centres.' [44]

Moreover the report recommended that the instruments for this missionary work were already to hand in the shape of the university extension movement, the WEA and the evening classes arranged by Local Education Authorities. Thus, rather than new state apparatuses, the educational machinery already in place within adult education was seen as the key agency of the new policy.

The 'political, economic and social implications are clearly spelled out in the Newbolt Report, and most clearly in those parts of the report which we know were written by Dover Wilson', notes Terence Hawkes. [45] One man cannot, of course, be singled out to account for a whole ideological tendency, but there is something emblematic about Dover Wilson's contribution to the report, to which Terence Hawkes draws attention. We have already seen how extraordinarily positive Dover Wilson was about adult education and the WEA in Yorkshire in particular. Hawkes argues that as a Fabian Russian specialist in 1906 he had spectacularly misread contemporary Russian politics and had backed the Social Revolutionary Party against the Social Democrats, whom he dismissed out of hand. He appears to have been so dumbfounded by the arrival of Lenin in April 1917 and the Bolshevik Revolution that nowhere in his writings does he mention them. Hawkes suggests that the revolution's existence did in fact (neurotically) work its way out in his writings on *Hamlet* or *Telmah* as he was to call it. That is to say that, like Hamlet's father, the Bolshevik Revolution hovered spectrally over his passions and haunted his writing. This was perhaps nowhere more evident than in his contributions to the Newbolt Report. His staunch advocacy of an English crusade through the provinces of the homeland was precisely to exorcise the spectre of revolution haunting England.

English studies, and by extension Englishness, were to be a solution to social disharmony and an antidote to Red Revolution. But it was by no means a flight into an authoritarian orthodoxy. There are passages in the Newbolt Report which, as we have seen, suggest an open Englishness which reflects regional difference and dialect, and the 'diversity within unity' approach advocated by Sadler. However, this is more often than not masked by an appeal to an essential or spiritual unity which is the mystery at the heart of culture. Both the terminology and the practice of this kind of education drew on the experimental work of British colonialism's administrators and educators in far flung corners of the empire, whose practice was constructed by the language of territoriality and notions of a 'civilising' mission. As a project it was both integrative and divisory, both incorporative and alienating, since the recipients of that education were allowed membership of the imperial or national polity only after torturous separations from the cultures of their birth.

Ian Hunter argues that the report in the end did little more than advocate the establishment of 'language and literature' departments – which characterised the structure of university training in English until the appearance of I. A. Richards. [46] His magisterial summary of the founding moment of English studies in Britain is worth considering:

> In the first decades of this century 'English' did not name a single subject, but a loose ensemble consisting of a literary pedagogy supporting the tactics of a supervised freedom embodied in the popular school; the minority caste practice of self-culture carried out through the ethical dialectics of criticism; and, on the margins, the knowledge of language and literature made available by historical philology. It should now be clear that the gradual emergence of English at the centre of a national curriculum was not the result of the delayed institutionalisation of Arnoldian culture and criticism. Neither did it occur at the behest of a culture promising the 'full' development of human capacities or an ideology threatening to withhold this development in the interests of a particular class. [47]

While this admirably, if rather abstractly, characterises the larger picture, some additional commentary is needed to be made, for it was not in effect so clear cut. The margins did not just passively submit to this Grand Plan of Englishness, but were, in effect, spaces of complex negotiation. Revolution may well have been bought off and the production of the 'persona of the cultivated man' or moral exemplar have become an element of government educational policy – Matthew Arnold was, of course, the father of the Newbolt Report, as Hawkes notes, and F.R. Leavis the son, (with Dover Wilson acting as midwife) – but there was a force operating at the margins of society with which both national policymakers and missionary tutors had to reckon. This was, precisely, that much derided social force, the organised labour movement, or 'working-class movement' as it was known from the inside.

As we shall see in the next chapter, although by no means unitary, the labour movement possessed residual strengths which enabled it to resist the family settlement that the English ideologues had in mind, and to argue for a pedagogical practice which reflected its own needs. No doubt it made concessions by opting for reform rather than revolution, but in the name of national unity the dominant order was forced to make important concessions to the organised working class. To belittle these reforms as 'welfarism' is not adequate, and to assume that in the name of 'culture' the whole movement was splintered into self-policing individuals is also to misread the nature of the compromise that was agreed, and ultimately implemented by the 1945 Labour government. Such was the distrust of 'middle-class culture' in the labour movement that it all but rejected an aesthetic education, *tout court*. Thus the notion of Englishness had to be adapted to embrace many of the working class' own puritan values, including the collective institutions it created in the nineteenth century.

It was not, of course, a permanent settlement; it fell apart under the pressures of left- and subsequently right-wing libertarianism, which demanded difference and individualism from the 1960s onward. But the margins have to be seen as important negotiation space which were never entirely incorporated and which, it is the burden of this book to prove, prevented the necessary ideological closure. English studies and the notion of Englishness appear to be historically relative phenomena, now no longer capable of offering hegemonic identity or the necessary powers of self-cultivation. Indeed, the subject's own academic offspring, cultural studies, may even have contributed to subverting the ideological and institutional efficacy of English studies and may ultimately erect tombstones for the discipline and its vision of a united identity.

Notes

1 Terry Eagleton, *Literary Theory: An Introduction*, Blackwell, Oxford 1983, p27.

2 Brian Doyle, 'The Invention of Englishness' in Robert Colls and Philip Dodds (eds), *Englishness: Politics and Culture 1880-1920*, Croom Helm, Beckenham 1986, pp89-115, p90.

3 James Donald, *A Sentimental Education*, Verso, London, 1989; Ian Hunter, *Culture and Government, The Emergence of Literary Education*, Macmillan, London 1986.

4 Quoted in Martin Carnoy, *Education as Cultural Imperialism*, Longmans, New York 1974, p100.

5 Quoted in *Ibid*, p101.

6 Gauri Viswanathan, *Masks of Conquest*, Columbia University Press, New York 1990.

7 *Ibid*, p4.

8 *Ibid*, p27.

9 Doyle, 'The Invention of Englishness', *op cit*, p102; see also Brian Doyle, *English and Englishness*, Methuen, London 1989.

10 Quoted in Viswanathan, *op cit*, p28. Viswanathan notes that Hastings's 'Orientalism' was indeed a policy and not merely an approach: 'Orientalism was adopted as an official policy partly out of expediency and caution and partly out of an emergent political sense that an efficient Indian administration rested on an understanding of "Indian culture"'. (Ibid.)

11 Quoted in *Ibid*.

12 *Ibid*, p30.

13 Quoted in Viswanathan, *op cit*, p65.

14 B. T. McCully, *English Education and the Origins of Indian Nationalism*, Peter Smith, London 1966.

15 C. E. Trevelyan, *On the Education of the People of India*, London 1838, p152.

16 Chris Baldick, *The Social Mission of English Criticism 1848 -1932*, Oxford University Press, Oxford, 1987, p70. At this stage English studies included the study of both literature and history because a separate literary critical discipline had not yet been developed. Historicism was weeded out only later.

17 Quoted in Viswanathan, *op cit*, p71.

18 Linda Grier, *Achievement in Education*, Constable, London 1952, p4.

19 *Ibid*, p21.

20 Michael Ernest Sadler, *Selections from Michael Sadler, Studies in World Citizenship*, compiled by Dr. J.H. Higginson, Leeds University Press, Leeds 1979, p79.

21 *Ibid*, p134.

22 *Ibid*, p147.

23 Janet Coles, '"With Fire and Faith": R. G. Moulton's university extension mission to the United States', in Stuart Marriott and Barry J. Hake (eds), *Cultural and Intercultural Experiences in European Adult Education, Essays on Popular Education since 1890*, Leeds Studies in Adult Education, Leeds 1994, pp52-69, p55.

24 Norman A. Jepson, *The Beginnings of English University Adult Education – Policy and Problems*, Michael Joseph, London 1973, p225.

25 Anthony Kearney, *John Churton Collins, The Louse on the Locks of Literature*, Edinburgh, Scottish Academic Press Ltd., Edinburgh 1986, pp37-8.

26 *University Extension Journal*, vol. 1, pp69-70, quoted in Jepson, *The Beginnings of English University Adult Education, op cit*, p238.

27 Kearney, *John Churton Collins, op cit*, p42.

28 Quoted in *Ibid*, p45.

29 *University Extension Journal*, vol. III, pp107-8, quoted in Jepson, *The Beginnings of English University Adult Education, op cit*, p239.

30 Quoted in *Ibid*, p237.

31 *Ibid*, p239.

32 John Dover Wilson, *Milestones on the Dover Road*, Faber, London 1969, p83.

33 Quoted in Baldick, *The Social Mission of English Criticism, op cit*, p93.

34 Quoted in *Ibid*, p95.

35 Quoted in Doyle, *English and Englishness, op cit*, p30.

36 *Ibid*, p59.

37 *Ibid*.

38 Board of Education, *The Teaching of English in England, Being the Report of the Departmental Committee appointed by the President of the Board of Education to Enquire into the Position of English in the Educational System of England* [chair: Sir Henry Newbolt] H.M.S.O., London 1921, pp248-9.

39 Doyle, *English and Englishness, op cit*, p60.

40 *The Teaching of English in England, op cit*, p253.

41 *Ibid*, p258.

42 *Ibid*, p254.

43 *Ibid*, p252.

44 *Ibid*, p260.

45 Terence Hawkes, *That Shakespeherian Rag, essays on a critical process*, Methuen, London, 1987, p114.

46 Hunter, *Culture and Government, op cit*, p139.

47 *Ibid*, pp139-40.

4.

National Popular – Class versus mass culture

The subtext of the debates about the meanings of culture in the WEA was the struggle over the spiritual heart of the movement. The debates were waged at a variety of levels, from the classroom to the national conference, as befitted a democratic organisation proud of its traditions of tolerance and eloquence; many of its members were lay preachers and well versed in public speaking.

Inevitably, little evidence of these passionate verbal debates remains, but some of the original fire is reflected in the debates held in two of the most important of the adult education movement's journals. These were the *Tutors' Bulletin*, which was the journal of the professional body of the adult educators, the Tutors' Association, and the journal of the WEA, the *Highway*. The first was a small A5 journal of relatively few pages, while the latter was a quarto sized volume edited for many years from London by W.E. Williams. During the 1930s and 1940s the *Highway*, under Williams's editorship, was a model of radical cultural exchange and featured many of the major writers on culture of the period, including Storm Jameson, Herbert Read, George Orwell and W.H. Auden. There were also regular articles by R.H. Tawney, G.D.H. Cole, Harold Laski, Ivor Brown and Guy Chapman on cultural themes.

The *Tutors' Bulletin*, which for some of this period was edited by Thomas Hodgkin, contained for the most part shorter position papers and replies from what was reluctantly becoming a 'professional' body of tutors. Occasionally there were significant interventions by non-tutors, of whom George Thompson, the District Secretary of the Yorkshire (North) District of the WEA, was the most notable. These two journals are the main sources for understanding how the idea of 'cultural studies' emerged as a new site of contest between conflicting ideologies of popular education in the years before, during and just after Second World War, until ultimately the Cold War radically shifted the terms of debate.

The debates were, roughly speaking, polarised between two main positions which could be called 'class' versus 'mass'. An example of eternal recurrence in some ways, it was one of the major re-enactments of the traditionalist–modernising dialectic. Each pole was occupied by a major individual voice that signified, for observers and for the other camp, a whole set of related positions. 'Mass' was Williams, who represented the voice of metropolitan radical taste, a moderniser, publisher, academic and back-room fixer, whose project was to shift adult education away from its 'archaic' concern with the working class and class struggle towards a more popular educational style centred on the arts and closer to the universities.

Williams was a remarkable figure, described in his obituary in *The Times* (1 April 1977) as 'one of the greatest and most effective mass educators of his time'. The son of a Welsh carpenter, he won a scholarship to Manchester University, which he regarded as his 'intellectual seed-bed'. He was a staff tutor in the University of London Extra-Mural Department, 1928-34, Secretary of the British Institute of Adult Education, 1934-40, Director of the Army Bureau of Current Affairs (ABCA), which he founded, 1941-45 and Director of the Bureau for Current Affairs, 1946-51. From this pivotal role in adult education he exercised an enormous influence over the cultural debate as was manifest in his promotion of actual cultural institutions.

Williams was a strong supporter of the forerunner of the Arts Council, the Council for the Encouragement of Music and Drama (CEMA), which amongst other things organised touring art exhibitions and concerts for mainly working-class audiences. When CEMA metamorphosed into the Arts Council in 1946, he became the first director of the Art Section. Five years later he became its Secretary General and was knighted for his work in 1955, remaining in post for 12 years in all. As if this were not enough, he crowned all these achievements by his collaboration with Allen Lane in creating the vast Penguin and Pelican library of popular editions. As a director of Penguin Books and Editor in Chief, his publishing mission outstripped even that of Joseph Dent's *Everyman* editions. Penguin and Pelican published and popularised the arts, sciences, classics, politics and sociology throughout the English-speaking world. It could be seen as a major achievement in public education, perhaps unsurpassed this century.

Perhaps what most distinguished Williams from his colleagues in the adult education movement at this time was his unqualified commitment to art and the aesthetic. He was convinced that Art was a Good Thing, that it could touch ordinary people's lives and that without it no civilisation of the future could be desirable. This stood in direct contrast to the views of Thompson and those seen by metropolitan figures like Williams as the 'puritan' element in the movement. Williams's commitment to Art was again consolidated in institutional positions. He was a trustee of the National Gallery, 1949-56, secretary of the National Arts Collection Fund, 1963-70 and Arts Adviser to the Institute of Directors. He was a trustee of Shakespeare's birthplace in the heart of the heart of the country from 1953 to 1968, (from the year of the coronation to the year of *les événements*, from the year of national unity to the year of the student international). Like Michael Sadler, his friend and occasional collaborator, the cultural movements and ruptures of the times were reflected in his life. His role in persuading Allen Lane to back Richard Hoggart's request for funds for his new-fangled Birmingham Centre for Contemporary Cultural Studies was, in Hoggart's view, crucial to its success (see chapter six).

W. E. Williams's journey to the centre of the national culture from the borderlands, for which Art was the guiding star, seemed not to involve the painful negotiations of class and culture of other writers we are considering here, most notably Richard Hoggart and Raymond Williams. The transitional media for all three were of course the grammar school and the university, but for the latter pair the transformation was marked by a strong sense of their own regional as well as class difference, and for each of them the 'centre' turned out to be a relative absence, evacuated of the vitality that had held in context their early lives.

In contrast to W. E. Williams, what marked out many of the staunch defenders of what we have termed the 'class' argument was their provinciality, their strong ties to their region expressed by Thompson, for instance, as a commitment to 'district chauvinism', and their celebration of the secular puritan values of the working-class movement so ably characterised by J.F.C. Harrison. [1] Thompson, although coincidentally also the son of a carpenter, was from the generation before Williams's. Thompson's youth in the West Riding of Yorkshire was marked by the last flaming of the ethical socialist movement which had witnessed within a few miles the birth of the Independent Labour Party, the election of Victor Grayson, the first and last independent socialist MP, Edward Carpenter's New Life movement, the Guild Socialism of Arthur Penty and the Nietzscheanism of Alfred Orage. [2] The West Riding at this time was crossed by powerful currents of contending ideologies anxious to bring forward the New Jerusalem. The dominant tradition was non-conformism, which carried the puritan message into the heart of the Labour movement, but this was challenged by the revival of a semi-mystical Anglo-Catholicism, which desired a new relationship between the Anglican church and labour, and sent a newly militant clergy into the battle (among whom was Neville Figgis, G. D. H. Cole's tutor at Balliol). Beyond the established churches lay a plethora of occultist and spiritualist organisations such as the Golden Dawn, the Order of the Knights Geruda and the Rosicrucians. [3] The most politically influential of these, Theosophy, to which Carpenter and Annie Besant were affiliated – she briefly became its leader – held great appeal for both socialist New Lifers and the nascent feminist movement. Gandhi himself was at this time greatly in sympathy with it.

'Yorkshire' for Thompson then, signified a militantly (male) industrial working class straining to bring about a New Order of society in its own image, for which the WEA was the principal educational vehicle. In 1914, Thompson was largely responsible, with Arthur Greenwood (later deputy leader of the Labour Party), Harold Clay and others for creating the new Yorkshire District of the WEA in what was something of an insurrection from the WEA nationally. Worried about the consequences of this potentially dangerous turn, the Board of Education gave the task of overseeing the new district to its regional HMI, John Dover Wilson. His reservations were soon overcome and he declared the new district under Thompson 'the greatest instrument for the development of adult education that this country has yet seen'. [4] As we have seen, Wilson had a growing cultural influence, not just through his work as a publisher – his New Cambridge edition of Shakespeare and his new edition of Arnold's *Culture and Anarchy* brought the work of these writers to a mass audience for the first time – but also for his persuasive role on the Newbolt Committee on the function of English teaching. Thompson maintained that the core of WEA tutorial classes should be the 'controversial' subjects of economics, politics and philosophy; he regarded the arts as secondary or significantly 'women's' subjects. Wilson was not at all concerned by Thompson's lack of interest in what he called the 'cultural' subjects and was content that these subjects would follow in their own good time and should not be forced.

Except for two periods when he returned to work as a carpenter, Thompson occupied no other position than District Secretary in his whole working life. He appears to have had no other political ambitions (apart from being a Labour councillor) and remained a stubborn opponent of all deviations from what he saw as the WEA's fundamental purpose: the emancipation of the working class. His main contribution to adult education, which was so admired by Dover Wilson, was the formidable development of three year tutorial classes throughout the Yorkshire (North) region, the largest and most demanding programme in the country. A consequence of this was that he could argue successfully throughout the 1930s, against strong professorial opposition, that there was no need for a department of extra-mural studies to be established at the University of Leeds. Despite being nominally co-secretary with the university registrar, Thompson effectively controlled the university's joint committee programme and appointed staff tutors, one of whom was Sidney Raybould (who was to become the first director of the university's extra-mural department when it was eventually established in 1946). In terms of evaluating the 'outcomes' of good tutorial classes, Thompson looked not at individual qualifications but at how many WEA students took up public positions and exercised influence within the community; the number probably ran into several thousands from local councillors and JPs to MPs.

This single-mindedness increasingly brought him into conflict with his own staff tutors, whom he regarded as missionaries rather than professionals. James Cameron, who was recruited as a staff tutor by Thompson in 1943, but who had taught courses for the district in the early 1930s, succinctly summed up the balance of power:

> The love-hate relationship between the tutors and George Thompson was an important determinant of the atmosphere of the time ... it makes clear one of the decisive things about liberal adult education at the tutorial level in the pre-Raybould period: that it was an entirely WEA affair; Thompson was everything; the part played by the university was purely formal. Tutors rarely thought of themselves as part of the (then) rather small university community. They were WEA tutors, carriers of the word according to Tawney, not university teachers who happened to have chosen adult education rather than undergraduate education. Their ambitions and their interests were identified with those of the WEA, they were not much concerned with professional advancement. [5]

I have deliberately elected to focus on these two iconic figures, Williams and Thompson, because their contrasting views on the question of 'culture' clearly reflect the main dilemma confronting the WEA in the inter-war period. It was undoubtedly the key debate within the adult educational movement, one in which the various notations of culture, so ably summarised by Raymond Williams two decades later, were first generated. If, on the one hand, W.E. Williams viewed culture as something akin to the Arts and the cultivation of sensibilities in the light of the best creations of society, then Thompson was distinctly on the other side. For him culture was unequivocally to be found in the way of life of a people, in its institutions and habitual activities. In a judgement which foreshadowed that of Raymond Williams, he noted that what marked the cultural creativity of the working class was its collective organisations of the trade unions, the co-operative movement and the Labour Party against which, he added, the creations of the middle class were insignificant.

A symbolic engagement between W. E. Williams, as signalling the modernising metropolitan element wanting to popularise the WEA's provision to a wider social public, and Thompson, as a provincial Yorkshire traditionalist atavistically bent on class warfare, occurred in the *Highway* in December 1939. This particular issue was dedicated to the Arts, with articles by Anthony Bertram on some principles of interior design for the home, descriptions of Art courses in the WEA, Elizabeth Denby on the need for Civic Arts to regenerate industrial towns and Guy Chapman on war-time reading. Thompson's intervention was in the form of a letter protesting about the editorial comment in the previous issue that the WEA should offer more popular classes in the arts to attract the masses who were not already coming. Clearly at boiling point over what he saw as a pitiful dilution of the WEA's project by those at the centre, Thompson fumed that those who wanted cultural diversion could go to the theatre, the cinema or the pub and leave those who wanted a more solid use of their leisure time to the WEA. [6] Williams used his editorial privilege to reply, with obvious exasperation, that Thompson never let an opportunity pass to foster the illusion that literature and the arts were soft options. 'We can't have it both ways: either we are merely an austere student body, or we are a cadre of leaders for civic life' (by which Williams did not mean merely service on public bodies). He concluded: 'Mr Thompson wants this movement to be a nice little aristocracy of the book-learned. I want it to be a democracy, where there is

78

room for every capacity and every taste; and I don't fear contamination of the "serious" by the "simple".' [7]

Williams allowed Thompson to reply at length in the following *Highway* which resulted in a classic piece entitled 'What Sails shall be Set?' Here Thompson rehearsed his argument that the distinctiveness of the WEA's provision was that through the 'tutorial class' system it gave to the working class a quality of higher education not available to them elsewhere. The WEA's greatest achievement was to 'bring to those active in the working-class movement education specially designed to illuminate the questions that face them socially and to assist them to serve the working-class movement more effectively either in their organisations or on public bodies'. [8] It was in this article that Thompson gave his clearest interpretation of the term 'culture':

> It provides opportunities for study designed to help workers to recognise that culture is of real and permanent value to them as individuals and as members of society. By culture I do not mean the snobbish notion of intellectual and artistic polish with which a section of the nineteenth century industrial and commercial middle-class coated itself as a defence against the charge of vulgarity made by "high society", and as a proof of superiority over the common herd on whose backs it had climbed. I mean the older concept of culture as that quality of mind and understanding which comes through effort to extend and improve the range of knowledge and by undergoing mental and moral discipline. [9]

Although he may have found the plain, undecorated language of class struggle distasteful, Williams would have found little to disagree with here, certainly where the notion of 'quality of mind' was concerned, but what was undoubtedly at issue was the role of 'the Arts', significantly absent from Thompson's definition of education. The Arts were, for him, simply not in the frame; walking around an art gallery or sitting down to read a good novel were pleasant diversions only, not to be confused with cultural seriousness. Beauty, he held, with William Morris, was inherent in design and use, while everything you wanted from a good read could be found in Tawney. Music, on the other hand, was something different, this was for everyone to enjoy in full but by passionate involvement rather than passive enjoyment. Where, by implication, Williams and the modernising tendency wanted to provide a mass educational system with no particular end in view except democratic participation in some abstract notion of 'culture', the WEA had the specific purpose of 'liberating working-class capacity', which Thompson argued, if fully developed 'would revolutionise society and human relations'. [10]

Thompson then moved on to outline his objections to the way literature was taught, making clear that he was not against literature as such. Elsewhere he was at pains to point out that it was in fact literature classes that had been responsible for the successful establishment of WEA classes among the miners of the South Yorkshire coalfield. Thompson objected to the 'spiritual values' approach, which for him was little more than bourgeois ideology designed to give workers a superficial polish while placing literature on the pedestal of Art. Against this he opposed what he called the 'sociological approach', which by contrast saw value in a work only in so far as it illuminated the lives of working people and enabled them to clarify their objectives. He went so far as to deconstruct altogether the notion of 'literature' as a discrete subject of study. Taught properly, it would become 'the gateway through which the value of other WEA subjects may be glimpsed by marginal contacts with politics, economics and philosophy'. [11]

This demonstrates clearly how the notion of interdisciplinarity could become such a linchpin of the post-war cultural studies project and why the sociological turn of the 1930s in adult education was such an important marker. Thompson here articulates, however haltingly, the sense that the truth of literary study lies in its imbrication with what is *not* literature, specifically the social science subjects – the 'truth' of English studies was cultural studies. The conflict between the so-called sociological approach, as outlined by Thompson and others, and advocates of text-centred literary study was at the heart of the style wars through the 1930s. The debate engaged such eminent figures as Ivor Brown and L.C. Knights, and brought Thompson rancorous abuse from one of his own staff tutors, yet another Williams, J.R.

Both J.R. and W.E. Williams regarded the sociological approach to literature teaching as anti-art, which in a sense it was. Their most astute criticism, one that was subsequently levelled at the early cultural studies movement, was that this approach missed the specificity of literary study, which was in truth the use of language, the materiality of words, and the fact that they were not a transparent film through which reality could be seen. However, the debate was overdetermined by another issue in the pedagogy of English, that of 'Leavisism'.

The impact of Leavisism

Leavis and his followers (particularly those involved in the journal *Scrutiny*) impressed adult education teaching, perhaps, more profoundly than in any other sphere. This was possibly because such early and enthusiastic interest was taken in his publications and because notable Scrutineers including the editor L.C. Knights, himself, were actively engaged in teaching WEA courses. The review by Storm Jameson of Leavis and Denys Thompson's *Culture and Environment* in 1932 was one of two highly enthusiastic notices in the *Highway*. [12] W.E. Williams was one of the first to recommend it as essential reading for WEA literature classes in 1933. The close reading of selected texts as opposed to the historical survey course became the *cause célèbre* of the Leavisite avant-garde and the issue was fiercely debated. The abuse of language, especially in advertisements and the popular press, and the phenomenon of the 'stock response' became objects of study in the Leavisite mode. But more than this it was Leavis's moral crusade on the impieties of the modern age and commercial civilisation which appealed to tutors in an association that historically saw itself as oppositional.

W.E. Williams's promotion of *Culture and Environment* in the *Tutors' Bulletin* of April 1933 was part of a broader plea for a redefinition of literature teaching in the WEA. His argument was that the problems of modern life were so complex that 'the plain man' could not possibly cope with them 'intellectually'. Thus, since emotion was the ultimate arbiter, the need was for 'more *cultivation* of emotion and less training of mass-opinion'. He recommended in passing D. H. Lawrence's essay, 'Insouciance', J. C. Powys's *The Meaning of Culture*, Aldous Huxley's *Brave New*

81

World and I. A. Richards's *Practical Criticism,* but the most timely book was *Culture and Environment.* This was an interesting list for the time since Lawrence was regarded as barely house-trained by the literary establishment and Huxley was an unknown quantity. Although he was for many years a popular university extension lecturer for London University, Powys was seen as a mystical eccentric, and Richards was definitely not playing the gentleman's game. Leavis himself was regarded by the Cambridge establishment as little more than a provincial upstart.

Williams's regard for Leavis's book was remarkably measured and elements of his critique can be seen in more recent works. [13] For example, he immediately took the book to task for its nostalgic view of the lost rural golden age of the craftsmen, and ticked off both Chesterton and Eliot for subscribing to the same myths. Instead he took the robust line that the sensibility characteristic of that period should be recreated within the new industrial and urban conditions. He argued for the development of a new educational method which could repair the damage of the industrial process, and suggested that 'the recovery of that basis of an emotional identity is a primary purpose of education'; he cited the reorientation of social purposes which seemed to give Russian factory workers a sense of identity as the kind of goal he was seeking – clearly no-one is exempt from the cultural myths of their time. Despite his reservations he was convinced of the real value of *Culture and Environment* and its relevance to the adult education class.

> Leavis's book is a manual of defensive exercises against the strategy of publicity and pseudo-education. He devises problems which help the average man to develop and sustain a critical and discriminating habit – not a habit of mental reaction but of emotional judgement. It is a book which ought to be immensely valuable on our particular work, and its method is evidently capable of considerable extension. [14]

This ringing endorsement of Leavis set the agenda for the next decade and possibly the one following that, and can be seen as presenting a set of problematics that the post-war generation – especially Raymond Williams, Richard Hoggart and, to an extent, Edward Thompson – had to confront and ultimately come to terms with in their own ways. As well as concentrating the class's attention on the text in front of it, the Leavisite approach had the further virtue, insisted on by adult education, of relating that activity to 'life' outside the classroom.

Such was its importance that the subject of literature teaching became the cause of a major report for the WEA by H.E. Poole, entitled 'Teaching of Literature in the WEA' (1938). On its publication a conference was held jointly between the WEA and the Tutors' Association, a conference judged by H. C. Sherwood of the national WEA leadership, to have been dominated by the shadow of Leavis. [15] Not only had *Culture and Environment* and *Reading and Discrimination* both been highly recommended to the conference but three contributions, those of H.E. Poole, H.L. Elvin and L.C. Knights were, he said, so deeply imbued with Leavis's approach that it had not even occurred to them to acknowledge their indebtedness.

The central question was, should the severely analytic approach of Dr. Leavis be recommended for adult classes? There was complete agreement that the older 'survey of literature approach' was entirely inappropriate and smacked of nineteenth-century paternalism reminiscent of the worse kinds of university extension. But was the study of literature really the 'discipline' that the Leavisites imagined or should it be more concerned with enjoyment? Sherwood insisted that the last thing a WEA class should be was a forcing house for parlour critics and that one honest philistine was worth more than ten art prigs. His summary of the dilemma facing the literature tutor confronted with, on the one hand Leavisite rigour and on the other hand the intelligent but relatively unlettered WEA student was acute:

> Consider the reading habits of the familiar type of student. He reads the *Daily Mail* or the *Daily Herald*. He knows something of Galsworthy and perhaps Dickens. He is vaguely interested in good books and joins a literature class. What is the tutor's prime duty? Is it to encourage him to wider reading and the enjoyment of work of good quality or is it to make him conscious of the vulgarity of popular taste? Is it not a wiser course to prepare him for the time when confident in his discovery of new values he will be able to appreciate the limitations of the old? Once he is capable of enjoying writing of good quality he will be able to apply himself to a more severe critical method without any sense of

inferiority or of false superiority that a premature knocking away of his reading foundations may bring about. In matters of taste it is dangerous to force the pace in the hope of quick returns. However acutely a tutor may analyze advertisements and newspaper leading articles, he will not be able to argue his students into an interest in Shakespeare or Tolstoy.

It is indisputable that the approach to a literary study suggested by *Culture and Environment* is a useful one. Very few teachers of literature in the present can be completely happy in their approach to their subject. Dr. Leavis and his followers mark the extremity of the reaction to the gush and platitude, 'Eng. Lit.' approach. Their attempts at accurate analysis, the importance that they attach to detailed examination of selected texts, and their concern with the decline in public taste are healthy signs. I do not doubt that there is a place, and an important place, in the study of literature for the kind of approach that is to be found in *Culture and Environment*. But it was with some concern that we saw at the conference on the teaching of literature so much that Dr. Leavis had already suggested in his work reduced to a formula, a kind of universal cure-all, and useful phrases, valuable in the context of his own criticism, turned into a solemn jargon. A new 'Eng. Lit.' is already coming into circulation. [16]

This commentary is remarkable for the way it summarises both the strengths and weaknesses of Leavisism and also for the assumptions it makes about the exercise of literature teaching itself. Absolutely no value is placed on the student's own cultural habits of reading and every value, implicitly, placed on those to which he should aspire – Shakespeare and Tolstoy, for example. The assumption is that literature teaching provides a ladder which the student will climb, ascending from the poor taste and narrow limitations of the uninitiated to the exalted levels permeated by Culture as such. The actual experience, judgement and taste of the student are valued at nothing; he or she is seen as little more than the victim of the siren voices of the commercial press, from which the literature tutor will liberate him by virtue of close textual analysis.

It was precisely just such assumptions that rankled with George Thompson and made him profoundly suspicious of the aims of literature teaching. It was why he took such pains to point out that the WEA student was not just an adjunct of the 'mass', which was how she or he was positioned by the teachers of literature, but part of the collective that created those enduring institutions of working-class life and which signified *its* culture. For Thompson the student was not merely the victim of commercial exploitation awaiting the rescue of the Leavisite knight errant but the potential agent of her or his own liberation by more directly political means. This in a nutshell was the dilemma.

Evidence that a creative approach to the special kind of student found in WEA classes was being developed comes from a variety of sources. A very interesting example is from a tutor commenting on his approach to teaching modern poetry to an adult class. The group he comments on belongs to the kind of class-conscious worker that Thompson saw as the core of the association. This group is 'best described as essentially Marxist':

> It is interested in contemporary society and contemporary social problems. It is concerned to reform that society and solve the problems in the light of a revealed politico-economic dogma. It is very unimpressed by art and aesthetics and it would be inclined to reply to any generalisation about the contemporary consciousness that, although it might be true of the bourgeoisie, it was not true of the proletariat. It is a group with defined and limited but strong interests. And it is very fond of more or less abstract argument if that argument can be related to its existing interests. A mere historical survey of English literature, however well done, would be useless to such a group. Criticisms and comparisons of technique would mean nothing to it. [17]

This group is interested only in what will advance working-class consciousness and is rather dismissive of any other approach. But, says the author of the article, 'a conception of tradition in Society and in Literature which could be debated and analysed would at least be given a hearing'. [18] Instead of dismissing this as workerist philistinism, as many of his more purist colleagues might have done, this tutor takes a creative approach. He suggests that the conception of 'tradition in society and literature' would be given a hearing because in this way literature could be used as a clue to the functioning of specific historical traditions, and in this way the class could be persuaded to view literature as an avenue to otherwise unattainable experiences. Although this has obvious affinities to Thompson's idea of literature as a window through which other subjects can be glimpsed, it also maintains the integrity of literature as subject of study. Such an approach could then be applied to the current situation in which they lived, which, by implication, would first require an interrogation of the contemporary cultural position in its broadest terms, especially the background of physical and biological science, of psychology, anthropology and political disillusionment.

This begins to look like the agenda for an early cultural studies course, although modern cultural studies tutors would no doubt be surprised to find the physical sciences on board. Barrett suggests that the focus of this kind of study should be the modernist poetry of Eliot and Pound, where the objective for the class would be to discover 'a culture active and valuable for all who like to approach it'. [19] Here we can see quite clearly a transitional moment in which the study of literature becomes the study of 'culture', envisaged in both the symbolic and anthropological usages of the term, through interdisciplinary work.

It cannot be assumed that the term 'culture' enjoyed the kind of currency prior to this period that it did subsequently. Certainly 'working-class culture' and 'popular culture' were not terms in widespread use. They were in a sense interpellated or called into being by such debates and given substance because 'culture' as a term was still much more closely associated with its nineteenth-century usage, denoting the highest forms of achievement in art and thought of the period.

For Matthew Arnold 'culture' was the binary opposite of 'anarchy' or that state of being among the masses which had succeeded the break up of the old craft culture celebrated by the Romantic critics of industrialism. An important publishing event of the early 1930s was the reissuing of Arnold's *Culture and Anarchy* by Cambridge University Press, edited and introduced by John Dover Wilson. This was the first relatively popular edition and it made the work accessible to an informed reading public which had not existed at the time of its original publication or subsequent editions. As may be expected, Dover Wilson's introduction regarded the work of the former schools' inspector as 'the finest apology for education in the English language'. [20] More significantly it also introduced Arnold as a contemporary whose view of culture needed scarcely less emphasis than it did on its original publication in 1869 but, Dover Wilson argued, it needed to be read in conjunction with William Morris's *Hopes and Fears for Art*. The addition of Morris gave the critique an important shift in the direction of the labour movement and made its relevance to adult education even more acute. Its publication in the same year as *Culture and Environment* foregrounded the idea of culture as a subject of theoretical analysis.

At this time there was a strand of thought which saw culture as a whole way of life, emerging in the relatively new discipline of anthropology. Frazer's *Golden Bough* and Jessie L. Weston's *From Ritual to Romance* had been signposted for the literary élite in Eliot's *The Wasteland* in 1922, but the radical approach of the Russian anthropologist Malinowski and the more accessible work of Ruth Benedict and Margaret Mead were now receiving public notice. Pointing the way to a new form of cultural studies, the historian Constance Dyson recommended the study of anthropology for those who wanted to see *cultural patterns* in history, drawing particular attention to 'man's symbolic activities'. Dyson believed that tutorial classes too often fell into the trap of modelling themselves on the teaching in university history departments. She noted that, in developing a new approach to history teaching, 'some tutors might find simple anthropology useful – a study of primitive societies where the pattern of culture can be seen as a whole and the interdependence of social and economic institutions, religion, morals, art, are obvious'. [21] She had great hopes for a revitalised adult education sector after the war and she proposed a three year tutorial class course structure which would integrate the study of history, art, psychology and literature. This was a significant step in the direction of structured, interdisciplinary cultural study, but her argument – that if the post-war reconstruction was to create a more humane society, there was an urgent need to foster a life-centred as opposed to the contemporary death-centred culture with its crass neglect of human personality – belonged wholly to adult education's tradition of social purposiveness.

Although the immanent object of anthropological studies was the so called primitive societies, the notion of culture as a way of life with symbolic properties gained currency. Did the British working class possess a culture that could be defined in this way? By the late 1930s, articles which talked in terms of working-class culture or, more importantly, the active creation of that culture, became more common. Two University of Leeds joint committee tutors, both strongly committed to Thompson's approach, Dryden Brook who taught history and H.D. Dickinson in economics, developed this usage but centred it in a discourse of class struggle.

Brook's contribution to the debate was in response to earlier *Highway* articles supporting, and presumably placed by, W.E. Williams and he rose to attack the move against political commitment in the WEA. Unequivocally, Brook declared that the purpose of the WEA was 'the creation of a type of adult education and popular culture that will be a tool in the hands of the working class in forging a new social order'. [22] This is an early example of the usage of the term 'popular culture' to indicate an element of working-class struggle rather than mass, commercial culture, and it implies the idea of conscious agency. Brook developed this idea further. He quoted from the WEA's national 'Report on Policy and Organisation' of 1934, which stated that the WEA was a working-class body whose aim was to awaken the desire for education amongst working people in the belief that education was central to the cause of emancipation. He pointed out the that the term 'working-class' should not be interpreted in a static sense, as a conglomeration of separate units, but in a dynamic way as 'a movement which has a historical development and a conscious purpose'. This growth of conscious purpose was, he went on to say, one of the most fundamental facts of working-class history and one to which the work of the adult education movement had contributed significantly. With this, Brook underlined the connection between the idea of cultural study and the growth of social and political consciousness. This was important in the work of many later academics, for example Edward Thompson, whose *The Making of the English Working Class* develops the idea that social class, particularly the working class, is something *made* rather than found, a process in which education has played a central role.

Dickinson, a lecturer in Economics (who had also been a member of Orage's Leeds Arts Club) made a slightly different point. His was that the primary demand for adult education came not from the 'masses' but from the socially-conscious workers who sought to redress the disabilities of their class, through collective action. [23] For this core group the acquisition of cultural values, in the older sense of the term, was merely a by-product. What had to be grasped was that adult education originated as a distinct *social movement* and, because here 'culture' meant a different thing, it should not take over the university's standards uncritically. Unlike the classical economists, for example, who were *not* university men, current university courses seldom made trenchant analysis or rigorous criticism to existing institutions of the kind required by the working-class movement. Nevertheless, the manner of university teaching was worth adopting in classes because of its thoroughness, clarity, consistency and, at its best, intellectual honesty. But impartiality, he argued, was not required. On the contrary, WEA tutors should believe in democracy and working-class emancipation – although they must, in the interests of objectivity, also present the case against. His conclusion, like Brook's, again insisted on the radical viewpoint that culture was the construction of an active movement, not merely the residue of an artistic activity. The working class had to create a new culture worthy of free men in a classless society but in doing so it must inherit all that was of value from 'bourgeois' society, including the intellectual habits of study and scholarship.

Although the contest over the nature and meanings of culture were conducted along a largely provincial–metropolitan axis with the voices for the 'mass' approach (meaning a more popular educational style which privileged the notion of 'the people' over that of social class) coming from the centre and those for the 'class' approach from the provinces (in truth, mostly from Yorkshire), there were also attempts to create a middle way. The most vociferous supporter of what Thompson saw as the traditional purposes of the WEA – serving a working-class movement – was G.D.H. Cole, who as we saw earlier, strongly equated adult education with workers' education. Cole, and to some extent Tawney himself, was more than a little concerned at the direction they saw Williams as taking the WEA, and more than once voiced his doubts. But on the broader plane of politics, he was not convinced that mobilising around the banner of 'class'was sufficient to rally the nation against the menace of fascism; he became wholly committed to the policy of a popular front. In his book *The People's Front*, published by the Left Book Club in 1937, he argued that the Labour Party should overcome its hostility to the communists and create an anti-fascist front. He took a similar line in the *Highway* of March 1939, maintaining that 'democracy' could win the trust of the mass of the people only if it was led by a movement for social and structural reform at home. [24] He envisaged the educational work of the WEA as playing a leading role in educating the broader democratic movement but doing so without abandoning its class position, which Cole regarded as its primary strength. [25] He was, however, trying to construct a notion of the 'popular' which recognised the force of the idea of class-within-nation rather nation-before-class. His assertion that the workers' movement was the only possible rallying point for a left majority lay in the belief that, 'The groups in the middle will rally far more to a working-class movement which looks formidable, competent and united, than to one which is constantly engaged in internal bickering'. [26]

The appearance of Cole and Postgate's book, *The Common People, 1746-1938*, in 1938 was a significant step in the production of this new version of the popular. Although A.L. Morton's monumental *A People's History of England* had been published the year before, pioneering the idea of a popular history reaching back to earliest times, Cole and Postgate's book was the most signal attempt thus far to construct a modern history of the 'British People' centred on the history of the working classes. It was a bold strategy to put the workers' movement at the heart of a people's history but one that was quickly censured by the reviewer in the *Highway*.

This was none other than Guy Chapman, who lectured in history at the University of Leeds, in George Thompson's parish. [27] Chapman found *The Common People* to be 'a noble and impressive work' which deserved to be on the shelves of every WEA student of economics, history, sociology and literature. [28] But it was flawed precisely by its political project in representing the Common Man as a manual worker. Chapman introduced what was subsequently to become one of the most pertinent critiques of theories of class, namely the theory of 'stratification': 'To be frank I feel that the authors are still looking from the viewpoint of the immediate post-War generation. They are still thinking in terms of the Class War, whereas the society we live in is the most socially stratified in the world. They do not explain satisfactorily why the Labour Movement has failed so signally to establish its obviously dominant power in the country.' [29] Here was an interesting example of a 'provincial' intellectual speaking with a 'metropolitan' voice against a 'metropolitan' intellectual speaking with a 'provincial' voice. (What gave the criticism added piquancy was the fact that Chapman was a close friend of Edward Thompson senior, an Oxford colleague of Cole's, and it was Chapman who suggested that the young Edward should apply for the staff tutor's job in Raybould's new extra-mural department.) Chapman's distancing of models of class conflict in favour of stratified differentiation may well have contributed more to the cross-class concept of the 'popular' than was possible for Marxist models.

Another academic who attempted to find a centre ground was Ifor Evans, Professor of English Literature at Queen Mary College, London. Evans tried to modify the Leavisite position by suggesting that literature could make a definite contribution to the social sciences – rather than being swallowed up by them – through the study of popular forms, for example the study of advertisements. He proposed that literature become more scientific in its methods, and he initiated 'a new study of words from a scientific point of view which should lead to conclusions worth publishing' [30] (which sounds like a precursor of Raymond Williams's, *Keywords* project). Evans joined with W.E. Williams in the view that adult education should not simply remain the interchange of ideas and information among a minority but must produce leaders 'who will attempt the education of the inert mass'.[31] This was of course not dissimilar from what Cole was suggesting, except that for Cole the Leavisite rhetoric of the 'inert mass' would have been politically unacceptable. Cole, too, emphasised the class specific nature of this leadership, which in turn would almost certainly have been unacceptable to Evans.

Thus both sides of the mass/class dialectic could share some common ground around the notion of the popular but it was obvious that different and perhaps irreconcilable sociological models were in play. What united them, however, was their belief in the importance of the grounded nature of cultural study, and the belief that interdisciplinary techniques in the social sciences and literature could contribute not only to an understanding of social consciousness but actually contribute to its growth. It was in the context of these arguments, and the growing conviction of an understanding that 'culture' could refer to anthropological or sociological phenomena, that a series of remarkable cultural interventions created a radical shift of perspective.

The impact of émigré intellectuals

The arrival of Karl Mannheim, Adolph Löwe, Karl Polanyi, Arnold Hauser, Norbert Elias and many other émigré intellectuals as refugees from Nazi-dominated Europe made a considerable impact on British educational debates. It was through these groups that the first attempts at a 'sociology of culture' and a 'science of society' were made. Indeed, the totalising sociology of the Weberian, Lukácsian and Frankfurt schools of thought seems to have been a necessary pre-condition for the foundation of British cultural studies. Many found their way into adult education by default because university posts were not available to them. However, both Mannheim and Polanyi made deliberate interventions into adult education, which they saw as the avant garde for both democratic social reform and also the restructuring of higher education. The resonances of these debates lasted well into the post-war period and positions articulated at this time – particularly on questions like the base and superstructure debate, the creation of class-consciousness, the need for a total science of society and the foregrounding of interdisciplinary study – echo through the founding texts of British cultural studies.

What this group and other radical intellectuals found attractive about adult education was that in many areas it was genuinely controlled by working-class student bodies organically linked to the organised labour movement and committed to interdisciplinary study methods. They were impressed by its democratic nature and emphasis on social purpose. Further, in some areas, especially in the industrial north, the WEA seemed to embrace a form of class-conscious pedagogy which could challenge traditional academic approaches.[32] They strongly disapproved of conventional academic approaches which encouraged the working-class student to reject and transcend his or her background and enter 'the world of culture'. Such was the influence of Karl Mannheim that he will be considered separately in the next chapter. But the case of Karl Polanyi is resonant of the explosive thinking of this group.

Polanyi became a staff tutor in the Oxford Delegacy around 1935. He was unequivocal both in his support for the existing achievements of working-class education and in the need to free it from rigid orthodoxies – both Marxist and academic. At the end of the war he wrote in the *Leeds Weekly Citizen*:

> It is true that thousands of workers have been advanced in their calling by the help of adult education; that many more have experienced the joy of a broadening flow of knowledge and beauty; that numerous badly needed functionaries of the working-class movement owed their competence to this source; and that the life of the British people would be the poorer for its absence.
>
> Nor do I believe that any purely Marxist education could better this achievement. Unless socialism is unhampered by rigid orthodoxies it must prove a fetter to the emancipation of the working class. Socialist consciousness should not be cramped by dogmas ... To fight his battles, the socialist needs undogmatic instruction. What we must guard against is the infiltration of the capitalist outlook under the guise of 'objectivity'.[33]

Consequently Polanyi opposed the notion of a 'cultural' education in favour of one that made the working-class student more effective *as a worker* and intensified his own class culture. Such an education would adopt the worker's approach rather than that of the university, abandoning its nineteenth-century divisions of knowledge, conceptions of culture 'for leisure' and basing itself on the workers' own experience. Already in the adult education movement, Polanyi noted:

> A vast amount of imaginative experimenting was done by tutors, who spared not time or effort to produce new solutions. Without their creative endeavours in the realm of presentation, dramatisation, and dialectical treatment, tutorial classes could never have attained their present success, while maintaining standards ... Yet in one decisive respect these experiments were fatally limited. The subjects themselves were set by the academic tradition. [34]

The key to interdisciplinary teaching, as he saw it, was *not* to respect the conventional academic divisions of knowledge but to begin with the workers' own needs and create new categories of knowledge related to them; as he noted, one of the newest of these subjects was the 'Industrial Revolution' (a subject foreign to the academy then, and still resented by conservative historians). Universities would then cease to reproduce middle-class perspectives and reflect those of the working class, which he believed were essential if the social problems of the inter-war years were to be solved peacefully.

What was so remarkable about Polanyi's intervention was the boldness of his utopian vision compared with inhibitions of domestic perspectives. He took for granted that the Labour Party would win the post-war election and that the future was socialist – which was 'beyond' politics. That being the case, there would be a vast increase in the responsibilities of working people as they struggled to build a new kind of society. Central to this new civilisation would be the security of the home, useful employment, liberty and status, and for this the worker needed to be able to see society as a whole in which the interdependence of the state, industry, government and business were made clear and not artificially separated by what he called 'the authority of academic thinking'. [35]

The social and historical sciences, because they were fundamentally skewed towards the problems of the bourgeoisie as the emergent class in the previous centuries and were consequently

94

archaic, would have to shift their emphasis in line with the perspective of the emergent social class: 'the disciplines and sub-disciplines of the human sciences crystallised around other problems, more directly in the line of vision of the social classes whose orientations of life higher education was hitherto designed to serve'. Now, however, a number of 'illegitimate' subjects, offensive to the boundaries set by the academic tradition had found their way into the adult curriculum. Apart from the Industrial Revolution, these included International Affairs, Contemporary Political and Economic Problems, Fascism and Communism, to which Reconstruction and Social and Political Institutions had been added. Polanyi doubted that such new subjects would have emerged had the academic framework of the 'old' subjects not been so inelastic.

The time had now come, Polanyi continued, for what had been done more or less unconsciously in adult education to be made conscious. Development towards a re-arrangement of subject matter without strict regards for the traditional limits of the subject such as 'Politics and Economics' and 'Government and Industry' should be now be formalised and in effect treating it as a study of society *'from a definite angle'*.[36] The boldness of Polanyi's conclusion showed his confidence in the project: 'This is the manner in which new disciplines are born. Even within the self-imposed limits of our tutorial work, the tendency should not be discouraged but rather made conscious of itself and brought under pedagogic control'. [37]

Thus interdisciplinary study took on a radical new impulse, the object of which was to abolish traditional academic subject areas and construct wholly new ones from the perspective of the soon-to-be-hegemonic working class. The stage was set by these debates and interventions for the study of culture in a radically revitalised way. Although hotly debated, Polanyi's revolutionary vision was never introduced in practice, but the impulse behind it, to restructure academic subjects by a transgressive study of society as a cultural totality from the perspective of the working class, produced a new confidence among adult educators, and encouraged them to pursue what had previously been more or less experimental subjects with a more theorised and radical sense of purpose.

Notes

1 J.F.C. Harrison, *Learning and Living 1790-1960*, Routledge Kegan Paul, London 1961.

2 See Tom Steele, *Alfred Orage and the Leeds Arts Club, 1893-1923*, Scolar, Aldershot 1990.

3 Logie Barrow, *Independent Spirits: Spiritualism and English Plebeians, 1850-1890*, Routledge Kegan Paul, London 1986.

4 John Dover Wilson, 'Adult Education in North Yorkshire', *Journal of Adult Education*, vol. III, October 1928, p49; Tom Steele, 'Class Consciousness to Cultural Studies: the WEA in West Yorkshire, 1914-1950', *Studies in the Education of Adults*, vol. 19, no. 2, Autumn, 1987, pp109-126, p111.

5 James Cameron, 'Education for Freedom', The Raybould Memorial Lecture, University of Leeds Department of Adult Education and Extra-Mural Studies, 1979, p2.

6 G. H. Thompson, 'Beehive Incident', *Highway*, Dec. 1939, p55.

7 W.E. Williams, 'Reply', *Highway*, Dec. 1939, p55.

8 G.H. Thompson, 'What Sails shall be Set?', *Highway*, Feb. 1940, p111-12.

9 *Ibid*.

10 *Ibid*, p112.

11 *Ibid*, p113.

12 Francis Mulhern, *The Moment of Scrutiny*, Verso, London 1979, p315.

13 See especially Raymond Williams, *The Country and the City*, Chatto & Windus, London 1973.

14 W.E. Williams, 'The Limitations of Literacy', *Tutors' Bulletin*, no. 8, April 1933, p4.

15 H. C. Sherwood, 'The Teaching of Literature' *Tutors' Bulletin*, No. 22, April 1939, p23.

16 *Ibid*, pp26-7. Remarkably similar comments now circulate over deconstruction and post-structuralist theory suggesting a new orthodoxy has arrived – is this another example of the cyclic function of the avant-garde?

17 T. K. Barrett, 'The Adult Class and Modernist Verse', *Tutors' Bulletin*, no. 7, January, 1933, p14.

18 *Ibid*.

19 *Ibid*, p17.

20 Reviewed in R. E. Brettle, 'Reviews', *Tutors' Bulletin*, no. 4, May, 1932, p32.

21 Constance Dyson, 'The Approach to History', *Tutors' Bulletin*, July 1946, p6.

22 Dryden Brook, 'Where are we Going?', *Highway*, Nov. 1938, pp14-15.

23 H .D. Dickinson, 'Academic Standards in Adult Education', *Tutors' Bulletin*, No. 20, Feb. 1938, pp35-7.

24 G.D.H. Cole, 'The Lesson for Democracy', *Highway*, March 1939, p155.

25 'Experience of fascism did much to strengthen Coles' belief that the working-class movement should actively seek class allies (particularly from critical sections of the middle class), yet he always linked this prescription for strategy with an insistence that it involved no 'dilution' of socialist policy', A.W. Wright, *G.D.H. Cole and Socialist Democracy*, Clarendon Press, Oxford 1979, p245.

26 G.D.H. Cole, *The People's Front*, Gollancz, London 1937, p79.

27 Guy Chapman was the husband of the novelist and feminist Storm Jameson, who had reviewed Leavis and Thompson's *Culture and Environment* so enthusiastically for the *Highway*. Jameson had also been close to Orage at the *New Age* and was for a while a communist. Chapman was also an influential agent in

securing Edward Thompson's appointment at Leeds in 1948 cf. chapter 7.

28 Guy Chapman, 'The Common People', *Highway*, January 1939, p97.

29 *Ibid*.

30 Ifor Evans 'A New Line in Literature', *Highway*, Nov. 1938, p11.

31 *Ibid*.

32 See especially G. H. Thompson, *The Field of Study for WEA Classes*, Workers' Educational Association, London 1938.

33 Karl Polanyi, 'What Kind of Adult Education?' *Leeds Weekly Citizen*, 21 September, 1945, p5.

34 Karl Polanyi, 'Adult Education and the Working Class Outlook', *Tutors' Bulletin*, November 1946, p10.

35 *Ibid*, p9.

36 *Ibid*, p10.

37 *Ibid*, p11, emphasis in the original.

38 *Ibid*.

5.

Karl Mannheim:
the émigré intellectual and the
'sociological turn'

The rise of authoritarian and fascist regimes in central Europe after the First World War impelled many radical intellectuals to uproot from their own cultures and seek exile. A steady stream of mostly Jewish intellectuals, many with affiliations to Marxist and Weberian sociology, trekked westward across Europe, and by the mid-1930s many of them had taken refuge in Britain. Although they were highly qualified academically, many were unable to find permanent posts in British universities; Arnold Hauser, the art historian, for example, was forced to take a menial position as a clerk in a film company office while engaged in writing his massive *Social History of Art*. Hauser had taught art history for many years in the Vienna *Volkshochschule* and for him and others like him, adult education was not simply the only pedagogical space open to them, but also the most desirable.

Karl Mannheim, Hauser's distinguished colleague from the Budapest *Sonntagkreis* days, was also attracted to adult education although through the generosity of Morris Ginsburg and his colleagues, Mannheim secured a post at the LSE. He was invited to take a lectureship in London in the early 1930s and, through his involvement with progressive Christian and Socialist networks, came to exercise a considerable influence over educational debates in Britain. He initiated a radical challenge to traditional British empiricist approaches to sociology by suggesting a holistic 'Study of Society' curriculum which could totalise all sociological phenomena. Mannheim saw adult education as a potential vanguard of the new sociology and actively encouraged members of the Tutors' Association, the professional organisation of tutors in adult education founded by R.H. Tawney, to lead the way. Mannheim's theorising of the role of émigré intellectuals was also very influential. He argued for a critical engagement with the host culture in the belief that the intellectual culture of the émigré could revitalise that of the host by introducing new perspectives rather than passively accepting old orthodoxies.

An important element in this process of cross-cultural exchange was the cultural and intellectual networks centred on Christian Socialism and adult education. These circles included the political philosopher A.D. Lindsay, Master of Balliol College and chair of the Oxford Delegacy; the poet and publisher T.S. Eliot; the historian and political writer G.D.H. Cole; Harold Laski; and a range of centre-left and left but non-communist figures. This chapter centres on the trajectory of Karl Mannheim, his acceptance and influence within these circles. It argues that Mannheim and his colleagues from the 'other Frankfurt', such as Paul Tillich and Adolph Löwe, introduced a tradition of Marxist and Weberian inspired sociology into the largely positivistic British ethos. It also seems likely that the 'socialist humanism' of this émigré intervention had a critical effect on the small British Marxist intellectual culture, which was until then dominated by Soviet-style dialectical materialism. Mannheim may well have paved the way for the reception of the Marxism of George Lukács which was so important to the formation of the nascent British New Left after the break with communism in 1956. Adult education tutors were central to this new formation and the creative dialogue initiated by Mannheim and his colleagues was a key precursor.

The reception of the English edition of *Ideology and Utopia*

There is no doubting the excitement, and frustration, with which the publication of Mannheim's English translation of his *Ideology and Utopia* was greeted in British adult educational circles in 1936. It was 'an important and exasperating book' but one which, according to the reviewer in the *Tutors' Bulletin*, was almost unreadable. [1] The style was so tortuous and repetitious to British ears, he continued, that it was a painful business to drag oneself through the first hundred pages. But, for those with the stamina to do so, the effort was richly rewarded. The subject matter was not unfamiliar since, 'The Marxists, in their vigorous way, have deafened us with the doctrine that many of our opinions are determined by social forces'; but Mannheim had progressed beyond this to an analysis of the forms of knowledge themselves. After briefly discussing the main points of Mannheim's argument, the reviewer, Sprott, raised the question much beloved of British epistemologists: what is the status of the proposition that 'knowledge is socially determined?' since the proposition itself must also be socially determined. Problem of infinite regress.

Sprott wisely left the question unanswered and turned to what was perhaps the more urgent question: what was the role of 'intellectuals'? Here what Mannheim had to say was undoubtedly of seminal interest to English adult educationists, who were not generally speaking comfortable with the term 'intellectuals'. Although the term 'intelligentsia' had been coined in Orage's *New Age* before the First World War, the educated British layman still regarded it as suspiciously foreign. People preferred the term 'scholar' to intellectual and by and large took that to mean a crusty type of elderly don resident in Oxford or Cambridge. At a stretch, the related term 'academic' could be applied to lecturers in redbrick universities, but even the relationship of this group of people to 'society' was regarded as tenuous. However, possibly because the typical tutor in adult education was, by contrast, intensely engaged with society and social movements, they were not thought of as 'scholars' or academics and in the eyes of much of academia, regarded as little better than subversive propagandists. Probably the only groups which systematically used the term 'intellectual' were working-class militants, where it was more often than not a term of abuse, usually applied to fellow-travelling academics.

It came as a welcome surprise to adult educators, therefore, to see the term 'intellectual' being used in a positive and systematic way by Mannheim, who moreover, appeared to be offering a way out of the interminable wrangling over 'commitment' and 'objectivity', which, it was felt, were mutually exclusive. Mannheim suggested it was possible to be both an intellectual and at the same time committed to the cause of social progress. For those on the left who were reluctant to surrender themselves to the authority of the Communist Party, Mannheim seemed to suggest a role somewhere between partisanship and detachment. Sprott commented:

> He believes that the intellectuals, a group not attached to any class interest, can achieve a comprehensive view by identifying themselves with every conflicting attitude, realising the value and disvalue of each form of one-sidedness, and attaining thereby a synthetic point of view which incorporates all the good in each separate position, and in which the distortions are neutralised. [2]

But did this not produce too detached and 'scientific' an attitude? That would be to confuse 'objectivity' with 'neutrality'. Mannheim, like Polanyi, believed that since pure detachment was not human, politically committed positions towards social problems were inevitable. Choice and decision would never be eliminated, therefore, but the great change would be that irrational motivation could now be brought under rational control. In the process of discovering the forces of historical necessity, intellectuals could legitimately unite with those social forces deemed most likely to work for the desired and rational changes.

Sprott commented that Mannheim appeared to believe in two kinds of related forces: those associated with divergent social and class interests on the one hand, and those inherent in mankind in a general sense on the other. The duty of the intellectuals was to discover the 'objective' nature of the latter and wilfully to choose their course. In order to do this Mannheim believed in the need for an imperative, or utopia, to drive humanity on. Intellectuals had to discern whether the ideals implicit in imperatives were in accord with 'true' human interests and not merely distortions derived from partial class points of view. Here, then, was a role which the intellectual working in adult education could perhaps grasp quicker than most, for it appealed both to their professional need for objectivity and to the commitment most felt for progressive movements. But it had the further distinction of releasing those who felt that the Labour Party was irreparably compromised by Ramsay MacDonald's Nationalist government from the obligation to submit to the authority of the Communist Party as the self-declared agent of progressive change.

Contrary to the opinion of his reviewer, Mannheim had taken great pains with the English translation of *Ideology and Utopia* and had also substantially revised it to take account of the British context. Wherever possible he had found an appropriate English idiom, even if it meant that the literal meaning of the German had to be revised. He believed that the specific role of émigré intellectuals like himself was to bring, in as constructive a way as possible, their 'estranged' insights to bear on an engagement with the host culture in order to avoid being either ghettoised or simply absorbed. As a result he threw himself into work with a variety of progressive causes almost as soon as he arrived in Britain, the most important of which was adult education. The same issue of the *Tutors' Bulletin* that carried the review of *Ideology and Utopia* also carried a shortened version of a paper he had given to the Tutors' Association Annual Conference in April 1937. This was called 'Adult Education and the Social Sciences', and, in short, it suggested a vanguard role for adult educationists in revolutionising the teaching of sociology.[3] Instead of the positivistic studies of discrete problems in the Webbite and London School of Economics tradition, the opportunity offered by adult education, he argued, was for an overall study of human society in its original setting. Mannheim suggested that sociology should now be taught as a *holistic science* which connected, rather than compartmentalised all areas of human experience. This must also have been an exhilarating moment for adult educationalists, who usually entered what they saw as a vocation with a commitment bordering on missionary purpose but found themselves frustrated by conventional academic divisions of knowledge and specialisations.

Mannheim confirmed this sense of mission by the almost messianic way he addressed the grand themes of society. He argued that the central purpose of education was the rebuilding of man and society but educationalists today were faced with problems unknown in earlier, more stable societies. Since the future could not be predicted with any certainty it was impossible to anticipate the situations society would face. Everyone, not just children, therefore needed continuous re-education, not just because of the current state of dissolution and chaos, but because every phase in the breakdown also brought about a corresponding attempt at a general reorganisation. Society could not hope to recover unless the millions striving to find new responses to their own situation could be brought to realise that they were not working simply for themselves but contributing to a general reorganisation. The epochal transformation society was undergoing only appeared to be chaos so long as people failed to see the common theme running through all these experiences, namely, the gradual rebuilding of man and society.

The situation in Britain, Mannheim felt, differed from a Europe rapidly succumbing to authoritarian regimes. In Britain, the process of transformation appeared to be taking a much more gradual course, leaving time for more careful preparation of the ground. But, equally, the new situation was producing new kinds of students 'who do not come to us simply because they wish to spend their leisure in a more sensible way than the rest of their comrades, but adults who are beginning to realise the problems of a new era'.[4] These students were beginning to connect their own personal struggles with a growing realisation of the existence of a wider 'society' and as their outlooks widened they were beginning to touch on issues which formerly appeared to be the concern of diplomats, economic experts and politicians. This new kind of student, Mannheim, insisted, 'no longer sees the economic order of the political system of a country as simply the traditional hereditary outcome of some special historical development but as working machines which may be judged by their effects'.[5] In this way, the personal and the political assumed a common identity, the authority of experts was questioned and knowledge itself could be separated from power.

In Europe, Mannheim continued, democracy was being challenged by rising dictatorships and extreme expressions of nationalism, while new forms of group hatred were destroying traditional solidarities. What was peculiarly *modern* about these was that they were not the product of spontaneous outbursts of emotion but were a kind of trained hatred manipulated by 'professionals' in mass control. As a result, propaganda symbols, education, habits of thought and attitudes appeared in a new light and, Mannheim suggested, it was becoming increasingly clear that they were part of a social system; as the system changed so its symbols changed. Society now had a more clearly distinct form which could be perceived as a set of interrelations. Even personal character itself, he argued, was to a great extent the creation of society at a particular historical epoch.

Sociology, however, had not really caught up with the understanding of this new kind of student. It was still operating at the level of the zoologist who describes different animals and their organs without knowing anything about general biological processes. Thus, while many specialist studies of basic social processes existed, there was no overall study of society which could show the systematic relationships within it. The urgent task for sociology now was to reconstruct the total social setting in which specialist studies could occur. In this short but powerfully condensed article Mannheim insisted that now was the time for properly constituted, inter-disciplinary studies of culture and society to be carried out.

> In a few years it will seem strange that there was an age in which it was possible to accumulate an immense knowledge in sciences such as biology, psychology, anthropology, history, history of literature, economics, economic history, political science, sociology, criminology and the social services, without relating them one to another. It will be strange to an age to come that one studied all these disciplines concerned with human affairs without realising that they were parts of the one coherent whole we call society.[6]

Although this foresight is remarkable in itself, it is the range of related disciplines that is interesting. This really should be seen as an important moment in the genealogy of British cultural studies, which bore fruit only in the post-war years. Mannheim considered the interrelation of many more elements than actually came together in post-war cultural studies, which were initially based in literary studies, history and sociology.

But the key absence was a *totalising* framework of society within which all the related disciplines could be assembled: without this there was no ultimate frame of reference. Constructing this frame of reference, Mannheim believed, was even more important in adult education than in the conventional academic institutions, since adult education had to deal with what Stuart Hall later called 'the dirty outside world'. [7] Adult educationalists could not bury their heads in the sand of some specialism but had to face problems which presented themselves in their original settings 'as organic parts of a social interaction where nothing stands by itself'. [8] The tasks facing those in adult education were therefore of two kinds. In the first instance, to widen the scope of existing sociological studies by relating them concretely to their original setting. Secondly, a very specific task, to develop a new three-year curriculum called the 'Study of Society'. The objectives of the new curriculum would be to re-interpret the results of special subjects in the context of social interaction, starting with the deliberate description and analysis of the social forces and social structures which underlie any transformation of society. Mannheim generously acknowledged to his audience of adult education tutors that attempts at this approach had already been made with some success (indeed, as Raymond Williams suggested, Tawney's own tutorial methods could be seen as pioneering them), but it now needed to be made a priority. He suggested an experimental programme be set up, the effect of which would be to 'revolutionise' established teaching practice.

It has not yet been possible to establish how concretely Mannheim's prescriptions were acted on or whether they simply dissolved into the general structure of feeling in adult education circles. The almost immediate onset of the war may well have had the effect of postponing any attempt at a general strategy. Many post-war tutors, however, acknowledged Mannheim's influence, for example John Rex, who as a member of the Leeds Extra-Mural Department in the late 1940s regularly taught 'Study of Society' courses on the Mannheim model. The interdisciplinary approach that Mannheim encouraged did have enormous effect but, as he acknowledged, such interdisciplinary teaching was already well established in adult education. Perhaps Mannheim's role was to give these informal practices academic legitimacy and to focus on the need for a totalising sociology, a priority which was also subsequently to exercise the British 'new' New Left. [9]

We now need to look more closely at the processes whereby Mannheim came to exert an influence on British adult education, and the specific intersection of cross-cultural influences at that time. Mannheim left Frankfurt in 1933 and remained for a while in Holland where he stayed with his friend Révèsz, then professor of Psychology at Amsterdam. He also lectured at Leiden, Groningen, Antwerp and Utrecht. It may have been here that he met Harold Laski for the first time, as Laski was one of the main speakers at a conference on 'Philosophy, World and Life', together with Martin Buber, Helmuth Plessner, George Gurvitch and Carl Mennicke. He was invited to undertake post-graduate teaching at London School of Economics (LSE) by William Beveridge, the Director, on the initiative of Morris Ginsburg, Professor of Sociology at LSE. Mannheim, also considered moving on to the USA to a temporary post at the University of Wisconsin. Had he done so, like his contemporaries at the Frankfurt Institute, Adorno, Marcuse and Horkheimer, it would have been another story. However, not the least because of the open-hearted reception the Mannheims received from both Ginsburg and Harold Laski on their arrival in May 1933, they decided to stay in London.

Another incentive was the generosity of his colleagues at LSE. Beveridge and Laski's proposal that the faculty members should deduct 2 per cent of their income to provide for displaced German teachers was unanimously agreed, and in October Mannheim was appointed temporary lecturer in sociology. Despite the insecurity of his position, Mannheim seems to have worked tirelessly at LSE, and subsequently at London University's Institute of Education, for a 'third way' between the communism of the Soviet Union and the free-market capitalism of the USA – at least half of his salary came from the Rockefeller

Foundation. [10] Britain appeared to him best placed to realise such a strategic development because it was neither so saturated as Europe by totalitarian ideologies, nor so hooked on the anarchy of the 'free-market'. On the contrary, it had a liberal democratic polity founded on a strong civil society and bolstered by the wealth of the world's largest empire. The serious fissures in the British political fabric, however, exemplified in its lack of industrial modernity, high unemployment, marked class divisions and archaic political system, meant that it offered the opportunity for the kind of planned reconstruction and spiritual revival that Mannheim favoured.

A.D. Lindsay and the Christian Socialist Moot

Mannheim was accustomed to working within collaborative intellectual formations. He had, for example, as a young man been a member of Lukács's Sunday circle in Budapest around 1919, at the time when Lukács was attempting to adapt his Weberian-inspired sociology to Marxism, a period which produced his seminal work *History and Class Consciousness*. Subsequently, when he became Professor of Sociology in 1930, Mannheim led the group of intellectuals characterised by Dick Pels as 'the other Frankfurt' – other, that is, to the more well-documented Institute for Social Research of Max Horkheimer, Walter Benjamin, Theodore Adorno, Herbert Marcuse and co. [11] As distinct from the radical cultural Marxism of the Institute's members, this other Frankfurt group was associated with a more social-democratic revisionism and ethical socialism. Its members included Paul Tillich, Adolf Löwe, Carl Mennicke, Kurt Reizler, Norbert Elias and Hendrick de Man, most of whom were now in exile, Löwe, Tillich and Elias also emigrating to England. This group was, according to Pels, sensitive to issues of social psychology, the sociology of culture and 'socialist humanism', being 'less constricted by the framework of Marxist materialism'. [12] Pels suggests that with Mannheim's involvement with this group some of the moderate left and religious-socialist atmosphere of Frankfurt was transported to Britain [13] but it would perhaps be more accurate to say that, having been forced to leave the group in Frankfurt, Mannheim identified with a homologous group in Britain to which he brought some elements of a more European totalising theory.

One of the most important relationships Mannheim formed was with the Master of Balliol and Vice Chancellor of Oxford University, A.D. Lindsay. Lindsay was part of that Balliol group of Guild Socialists and Fabians which included R.H. Tawney, G.D.H. Cole, Alfred Zimmern, Arnold Toynbee, Archbishop Temple and, at one time, the philosopher T.H. Green. It was deeply committed to the ideals of the adult education movement, which they regarded as a kind of vocation. This circle also intersected with Anglican religious formations of which the most significant in intellectual terms was the Christian Socialist 'Moot' organised by J.H. Oldham. This also included a number of leading intellectual conservatives such as the poet T.S. Eliot and philosopher Michael Oakshott. Thus participation in this group led Mannheim to the heart of a circle of people who, through their writing, their command of educational and publication complexes, and their religious activities, exerted a considerable influence on both conservative-progressive and progressive-conservative public opinion. It was a group which, although individual members were strongly committed to differing allegiances (cf. Eliot who was an Anglo-Catholic in religion, a classicist in literature and a royalist in politics), was peculiarly able to transcend these differences in the name of the 'national' culture.

In Lindsay's case (as in that of fellow adult educationalist Michael Sadler, who had moved from Leeds in 1925 to become the Master of University College, Oxford) there was also a strong identification with Germany, which came in part from their admiration of the German university system, but also from their youthful engagement with the neo-Hegelianism of T.H. Green, Bernard Bosanquet and F.H. Bradley at Oxford. This had imparted a powerful respect for the German philosophical tradition and for the achievements of German high culture, which they never entirely lost, but which under Green's influence was mediated by British liberalism. This attachment was sharpened by the threat posed to the German university system by Nazism, which in particular pre-occupied Lindsay, for whom it meant an end to the tradition of dispassionate enquiry and a perversion of university standards. Many of the stream of German academic refugees that flowed into Oxford during the

1930s were indebted to Lindsay's energies in trying to find academic places for them.

The German connection was also fostered by Lindsay's Christian commitment. He believed passionately in keeping open international links with churches as a way of frustrating national rivalries and, with Bishop Bell of Chichester, made links with the anti-Nazi theologian Dietrich Bonhoeffer. Lindsay later contrasted the heroic stand taken against the Nazis by Bonhoeffer's 'Confessing Church' with the less impressive record of the German universities. [14] He also drew prophetic parallels between the German youth who, through the apathy and despair of unemployment, welcomed Hitler's rise to power, and the case of young unemployed adults in Wales displaying increasingly anti-social behaviour. Lindsay felt that 'the non-bookish majority who were bored stiff by full-time schooling' could have their capacities developed better in other ways and suggested full-time camps where they could learn a trade and receive an 'education in citizenship'.

Oldham's Moot was formed in 1938 to preserve the momentum of the international conference of 'Church, Community and State' organised in July 1937 at Oxford. [15] Lindsay invited Mannheim and a number of other exiles, including Löwe and Tillich from Frankfurt and, later, Michael Polanyi, to join what was in fact an informal think-tank. Woldring suggests that Mannheim was invited to join because of his energy in propagating his views at conferences and in sending members his publications. He appears to have been the most active member of the Moot, one of the few to attend all the meetings and one of its most vigorous publicists. The group met four times a year for a weekend and concentrated their discussions on the crisis in western culture, the nature of social change and the meaning of Christianity in society. Some of the papers prepared by Mannheim for group discussion were later published under the title of *Diagnosis of Our Time* (1943) and also as an expanded part of *Man and Society*.

Perhaps what appealed to Mannheim most was Oldham's idea of a self-constituted active 'order' which could initiate a revolution from above. Although there are clear authoritarian overtones in this idea, it was an attempt to revive something of Coleridge's idea of a 'clerisy', or body of learned men, which could give moral and spiritual leadership to the community. T.S. Eliot had already proposed such a thing in his *Idea of a Christian Society* and was to elaborate it further in *Notes Towards a Definition of Culture* (1948), a book which was probably stimulated by the Moot meetings and had seminal effect on post-war conservative thinking. Mannheim was criticised by some of his radical émigré friends for membership of this group because of its religious tendencies but he appears to have believed that the Christian tradition was one of the great supporting pillars of Western civilisation. The group, moreover, appealed to that non-democratic element of his thought which celebrated the élite role of intellectuals. For him the group represented the opportunity for socially committed intellectuals to intervene in the reconstruction of society. In a section in *Diagnosis of Our Time* which had been intensely discussed by the Moot, he argued for a planned society which was spiritually integrated, a new party system characterised by a developed right to criticise, a new form of education and a new sociologically-informed morality which had to inculcate a 'consciousness of the whole'. Pels comments that, 'If Mannheim's missionary élitism never left him, neither did he escape the lure of the concept of totality; both remained present as conduits towards intellectual authoritarianism'. [16]

In his discussions with Lindsay, education occupied a primary place in the process of reconstruction. The two men developed a warm personal relationship which Lindsay was to characterise as the meeting between his own Anglo-Saxon pragmatism and Mannheim's German organicism. While both shared a dreadful awareness of the crisis facing democracy from Germany, Lindsay's pragmatic approach was to deal with the most urgent issue and assume the rest would take care of itself, while Mannheim insisted that everything affected everything else and that the part could not be modified without altering the totality of social relations.

Nevertheless, there was substantial mutual respect. Lindsay believed that Mannheim's influence in promoting the need for the sociological approach was enormous. [17] For his part, Mannheim much admired Lindsay's books *The Modern Democratic State* and *Churches and Democracy*, which he saw as prophetic. 'Here I am', he once exclaimed, 'a German theorist, actually learning from an English empiricist'. [18] Lindsay, however, was not sure how much he learned and felt that Mannheim nursed an over-theoretical approach; despite his best intentions, he could never quite get across to English audiences the distinction between dictatorial and democratic planning. Lindsay's interpretation of what Mannheim meant by 'planning', however, was not simply impositions from the top down but planning at all levels of social life by everyone affected. The crucial intervening step was the development of awareness of the whole by the many through education. Thus each group in society had to think out its own jobs, but only by overcoming its own partial consciousness through an awareness of the interrelatedness of everything.

From the Moot meetings and personal discussions, Lindsay's and Mannheim's relationship developed into joint publishing ventures. Mannheim began work with the publishers Kegan Paul, (later Routledge, Kegan Paul) on what became the International Library of Sociology and Social Reconstruction, with Lindsay on the editorial board. This was a remarkably ambitious intervention, and the first to launch the serious sociological study of culture into British intellectual life. Amongst other publications in the series was, for example, Arnold Hauser's tremendously influential *Social History of Art*, which was the first attempt in English to apply Marxist political economy to art. Complementing this, in 1941 Lindsay began working for Chatham House on a series of books on the workings of democracy with Tawney, Ensor and others. Although Mannheim was asked to draw up a preliminary plan for the series, it was so vast it had to be seriously reduced and in the end Mannheim's own volume for the series was never finished. Lindsay's own contribution was *The Modern Democratic State*, which was to become a standard undergraduate textbook in political philosophy, especially in the USA.

By 1943 Mannheim was established at the London Institute of Education, a position he may well have acquired through his contact with the Director of the Institute, Fred Clarke, also a member of Oldham's Moot. [19] Meanwhile Lindsay was preparing for the new post-war era in education by taking what he called 'the WEA idea' into higher education, formulating plans for a new university to be established in North Staffordshire, a project in which he involved both G.D.H. Cole and Mannheim. Lindsay was impressed by the way in which university extension in the late nineteenth century had promoted the foundation of a number of provincial university colleges. They were a product of the New Universities Movement, which was critical of Oxbridge's ivory tower remoteness from modern industrial life and called for greater social relevance in higher education. Lindsay was convinced that it was time to renew this missionary spirit and, because of his long association with North Staffordshire and its historic importance to the WEA (through Tawney's tutorial classes), he felt that this was an opportune moment to launch the new idea of a university.

Adolph Löwe's recently published *The Universities in Transformation* had also greatly impressed him and it became one of the inspirations for the new University of Keele. Löwe, then working in Manchester, was also interested by what the nineteenth-century English universities had offered students and had attempted to draw lessons from them. The three elements he thought most important were, firstly, a specialist professional training, secondly, training in the art of living together through the college system and, thirdly, a *Weltanshauung* or general understanding of society as a whole. [20] However, the forces of modernity in the twentieth century had increased the drive towards specialisation and departmentalism to such an extent that the *Weltanshauung* element had disappeared, leaving students with no more than a fragmentary grasp of the society they lived in. In a striking parallel with today, Löwe commented that when the universities started to enrol a much larger share of the population the previous consensus on ideas and values gave way to 'spiritual bewilderment, fears as to economic prospects, and scepticism or radicalism. The universities more and more retreat from their positions as the interpreters of moral culture'. [21] As a result, Lindsay was convinced that the new breed of university educated specialists was becoming, in the worst sense of the term, 'an intelligentsia' cut off from any broader understanding of how their specialism fitted in to contemporary society. Lindsay was also impressed by Löwe's proposals for turning modern language schools into 'Greats' schools, in which history, literature and politics could be studied along with language. But to develop this idea further he wrote to Mannheim asking him to 'turn your great mind' on to the subject of a new school of sociology, anthropology and psychology. The results of Mannheim's intervention produced a stress on 'social awareness' which became a key element of Keele's degree courses.

A second influential text for Lindsay was Ortega y Gasset's *The Mission of the Universities*, published in English in 1946. Even more than Löwe's book, this focused on the question of culture and, in contrast, offered a somewhat medievalist and Christian approach. It was concerned with what it called the 'New Barbarians' who were learned in one thing and ignorant in everything else: the products of a system of specialisation in which a broad cultural education had been replaced by narrow training and research. Ortega argued that what the system had lost was the question of proportion and a genius for integration and seeing things whole, which was essential to the idea of culture. Clearly this chimed in with both Löwe's and Mannheim's holistic concerns but added what Lindsay perceived as a spiritual dimension. He believed that cultural unity was essentially Christian and must hinge on a 'vital' faith but that this should not be imposed nor become an orthodoxy. The phrase the 'New Barbarians' achieved a notorious currency in right-wing circles and indeed this whole side of Lindsay's approach was later used by conservative critics of more open and democratic access to higher education, quite against his own instincts.

Mannheim's diagnosis

The tolerance and friendship extended to German intellectual refugees by Lindsay and the Christian Socialist circles was plainly influential in the reception of Mannheim and other members of the Frankfurt group in England. Without the Moot and its sense of missionary purpose, particularly in the field of education, the émigré perspective might simply have foundered. I have tried to argue that Mannheim sought and found a homologous social/ideological formation to that which he had experienced in Frankfurt, the 'other Frankfurt', which was reformist, broadly religious without being orthodox, and orientated towards practical problems of culture rather than the more culturally élitist positions of intellectuals like Adorno. While these were all in a sense contingent factors, there seems to be at least one other material element in this cross-cultural transaction and that is the nature of the ideas themselves. As we have seen, Mannheim's intervention in the discussion of the Tutors' Association generated great interest because of his speculations on the role of intellectuals and the function of sociology. These ideas seemed to offer adult education tutors legitimation for their committed stance on social questions on the one hand, and a certain professional distance on the other. They also upheld the traditional interdisciplinary approach taken in adult education, with the validation of experience, but offered a totalising theory of society in which to contextualise those subjects.

These positions were further elaborated in a number of texts published in English by Mannheim. As we have seen, the English edition of *Ideology and Utopia* (1936) was tailored specifically to the British context. At least two other publications also addressed the specific situation, *Man and Society in an Age of Reconstruction* (1940) and *Diagnosis of Our Time* (1943) as well as the many lectures and broadcasts Mannheim gave throughout the war years. He was markedly a 'public intellectual' in the tradition of Ruskin, Morris, Tawney and Cole, whose orientation, although serious, was as much towards the intelligent layperson as to the academy, if not more so. The notion of a continuing system of adult education was a persistent theme and a model for future civilisation, foreshadowing contemporary debates on the need for a 'learning society'. Mannheim's whole project in Britain seemed to hinge on the importance of developing a fully educated, socially aware adult population through a totalising sociological education. Within this, thinking reflexively about his own situation as a refugee émigré intellectual, he saw his role as negotiating between European and Anglo-Saxon modes of thought. He also set himself to intervene constructively in the conjunction of sociology and education, and between practical social reforms and the reformed university, judging correctly that the British system was in urgent need of modernisation. [22]

What is fascinating in this respect is just how swiftly sociology rose to challenge the traditional domains of philosophy and literature in Britain, and how the 'Science of Society' approach became the model for radical interdisciplinary studies. It could be argued that Mannheim's sociology of knowledge approach radically undermined the validity of traditional epistemology as a basis for the study of knowledge, until it was itself eclipsed by other continental approaches in the 1980s. The sceptical relativism of this position gave eloquent justification to the 'conscious partisanship' of intellectuals which was influential in the formation of the New Left in the late 1950s as was, more worryingly, his belief in the élite role of intellectuals on its cadre mentality. His belief in sociology as the master science took root among marginal and left intellectuals, especially during the 1960s when there was a rapid expansion of departments of sociology, particularly in what was then the polytechnic sector.

A significant result of this approach and Mannheim's own involvement in it, was the translation and introduction of Lukácsian ideas into the New Left in the early 1960s, although, ironically, it had the effect of sidelining Mannheim's own approach. Mannheim retained a lingering fidelity to the Marxist notion of class-consciousness, which he also flexibly adapted to questions of gender and age, long before it became academically accepted. He was also marked by his early contact with Lukács's analysis of the reification of the proletariat as the self-conscious subject of history, but had argued for the need for reflexive self-awareness on the part of intellectuals. This was confirmed in the judgement of a contemporary analyst, Morris Watnick, who remarked, 'For it was Lukács's highly instrumental Marxism, more than anything else, which suggested to Mannheim than all social and political doctrines which pass for knowledge might better be regarded as 'existentially determined' doctrines, i.e. as elaborate rationalizations of group interests – mainly the interests of classes – which must distort the actualities of social life if they are to serve those interests effectively'. [23] Because of its more uncompromisingly Marxist approach, the Lukácsian analysis of culture, however, appealed more to the coming radical generation of intellectuals than Mannheim's, whose *Essays on the Sociology of Culture* (1956) was relatively ignored. By contrast, it has been argued, the interest taken in Lukács by the New Left and the translation of his *The Historical Novel*, prepared the way for the reception of Edward Thompson's *The Making of the English Working Class* in 1963, the first major work of British history to represent the working class as a conscious agent in its own history. [24]

Mannheim's career, then, is both an illustration of the impact a gifted and energetic émigré intellectual can have on the host culture, and also an instance of a general movement of cross-cultural influence. The effects of this exchange are still being played out in British intellectual life, where the reception and integration of European radical ideas threatened to supersede domestically generated ones. However, the main difference is that, as French post-structuralism has swept all before it, the British radical intellectual ear has become more attuned to Parisian playfulness, rather than to Frankfurt's high seriousness. Although the totalising sociology that Mannheim advocated became a totemic cause of the New Left in the early 1960s, the 'linguistic turn' and the neo-conservative backlash against sociology in the 1980s has made it unfashionable. What cannot be denied, however, is that it transformed the existing practice of academic sociology by making it confront the issue of culture and, by harnessing it to the interdisciplinary practices of adult education, paved the way for the post-war generation of cultural studies.

Notes

1 W.J.H. Sprott, Review of Karl Mannheim's, *Ideology and Utopia*, in *Tutors' Bulletin*, no. 20 Feb. 1938, p23.

2 *Ibid*, p25.

3 Karl Mannheim, 'Adult Education and the Social Sciences', *Tutors' Bulletin*, no. 20, Feb. 1938, pp27-37.

4 *Ibid*, p28.

5 *Ibid*, p29.

6 *Ibid*, p30.

7 Stuart Hall, 'The Emergence of Cultural Studies and the Crisis of the Humanities', *October*, 53, 1990, pp11-23.

8 Mannheim, 'Adult Education and the Social Sciences', *op cit*, p31.

9 See the seminal text: Perry Anderson, 'Components of the National Culture', *English Questions*, Verso, London 1991.

10 Henk E. S. Woldring, *Karl Mannheim, The Development of his Thought*, Van Gorcum, Assen/Maastricht 1986, p40.

11 Dick Pels, 'Missionary Sociology between Left and Right: A Critical Introduction to Mannheim', *Theory Culture and Society*, vol. 10, no. 3, August 1993, pp45-68

12 *Ibid*, p46.

13 *Ibid*, p51.

14 He was, however, disturbingly impressed by Kurt Hahn, the German founder of the public school at Gordonstoun, to which the current heir to the throne was sent, and felt that if Hahn's system was more widely adopted 'it might save the universities from producing an intelligentsia', quoted in Drusilla Scott, *A.D. Lindsay*, Blackwell, Oxford 1971, p265.

15 Pels, 'Missionary Sociology between Left and Right', *op cit*, p50; Woldring, Karl Mannheim, *op cit*, p59.

16 Pels, 'Missionary Sociology between Left and Right', *op cit*, p52.

17 Scott, *A.D. Lindsay, op cit*, p266.

18 *Ibid*, p267.

19 David Kettler *et al.* (eds), *Karl Mannheim*, Chichester 1984, p151.

20 Scott, *A.D. Lindsay, op cit*, p338.

21 Quoted *Ibid*, p339.

22 Kettler *et al.* (eds), *Karl Mannheim*, op cit, p150.

23 Morris Watnick, 'Relativism and Class Consciousness: Georg Lukács' in Leopold Labedz (ed), *Revisionism: Essays on the History of Marxist Ideas*, George Allen and Unwin, London 1962, pp142-165, p156.

24 John Goode, 'Thompson and the Significance of Literature', in Harvey J. Kaye and Keith McClelland (eds), *E.P. Thompson, Critical Perspectives*, Polity, London 1990, pp183-203.

6.

Between Cultures:
Richard Hoggart and popular culture

Richard Hoggart was born in Leeds in 1918 and was educated at Cockburn Grammar School and Leeds University. After service in the Second World War he joined the Department of Extra-Mural Studies at the University College of Hull where he stayed until 1959. He founded the Birmingham Centre for Contemporary Cultural Studies (BCCCS) in 1962 and was its Director until 1973, when he became Director of UNESCO. His life has been fundamentally engaged with the education of adults and the study of cultural change. His approach is marked by investigations in to the margins of 'high' and 'popular' culture, and by his use of the methods of the one to explore the other. Perhaps more than anyone, he was responsible for the siting of cultural studies as an academic pursuit, and for initiating the remarkable series of studies of popular culture which have distinguished the discipline of cultural studies in Britain.

The establishment of the BCCCS was the most important institutional development to have taken place in the evolution of the new subject. The fact that it was born within a department of English studies has strengthened, perhaps, the assumption that cultural studies was simply an outgrowth of that discipline, whereas it is clear from Hoggart's own accounts that it was much more in the way of caesarean rupture from the host than an easy

118

birth. Indeed, the funding for the Centre had to be raised from external sources and a few of Hoggart's erstwhile colleagues regarded the MA in Cultural Studies with scorn – his 'nice line in cheap hats'. [1] Hoggart's own debts to Leavis are clear but highly mediated. While Q.D. Leavis's *Fiction and the Reading Public* and F.R. Leavis's and Denys Thompson's *Culture and Environment* were both important inspirations in dealing with the question of forms of writing and society, Hoggart brought to the work his own experience as a working-class child and a wealth of reading and contact drawn from elsewhere.

Most significant, of course, was his work in adult education between 1946 and 1959. In one sense his output in this period appears more Leavisite in tone than anything he produced later but even at this point he registers a sharp dissent from the Leavisites and their methods. Hoggart's intellectual formation is far too varied to place him simply in one camp or another, and this is due, at least in part, to his engagement with adult working-class students – his own people, he would say – mediated by his own struggles between fascination with and repulsion by the style of the liberal academy.

When he was a staff tutor at Hull, Hoggart wrote extensively on adult educational matters in the adult education journals, especially *Adult Education*, the *Highway*, the *Tutors' Bulletin* and in a journal founded by his mentor at Leeds, Bonamy Dobrée, the *Universities' Quarterly*. Most of his articles were serious and valuable discussions on how to teach literature to adults, which still repay reading today, but others are about the 'movement' itself. It is perhaps hard for those who did not experience teaching within adult education in the post-war period to appreciate how vocational this work was. It was not merely a profession, although the debate about standards and quality raged throughout the period, but a mission with its own teleology. As we have seen, the adult education 'movement' was the site of fierce ideological contestation, especially over the definition and value of the term 'culture', which, in the context of the Cold War as it developed post-1947, led to heated exchanges between its workerist and culturalist wings. It was in the context of one of these exchanges that Hoggart wrote what could be interpreted as one of his more Leavisite pieces.

'Prolegomena to the Second Session' was printed in the *Tutors' Bulletin* in November 1947. Its title already stamped with the sign of 'erudition' and its text liberally sprinkled with classical and biblical literary constructions, it was a polemic against the over-democratisation of teaching within adult education and a demand for an 'aristocratic' aesthetic education. Hoggart's central argument was that the humanities had for too long taken second place to the social sciences in adult education, with the result that those who came for enlightenment were given only 'bread'. In effect, the minority who came to adult education were being starved of an aesthetic education because of a narrowly political outlook which argued that workers needed to know how the economy, politics and society actually worked before they could become cultured. Historically, feelings were just as strong on the other side of the debate. As one of the founders of the French *Universités Populaires*, Georges Deherme, remarked in the 1890s, outraged that the university extension teachers were offering only literature classes, the workers came for bread and they were given only cake. As we saw in chapter four, the debate had raged in the late 1930s over concerted attempts at modernisation led from the centre by men like W.E. Williams, editor of the *Highway*, and fiercely resisted by those like G.H. Thompson in the provinces. The battle was cut short by the Second World War, but with the onset of the Cold War the tensions were revived. In his article, Hoggart asked, ingenuously, whether 'all this [current argument] was, on the historical side, caused by the proletcult versus Universities/W.E.A. battle of some years ago'. [2]

In this 1947 article, Hoggart shifted the terms of reference in an interesting way, claiming that the catchment group for adult education could no longer be classified by social class. They now came from all ranks of society but they were what he called 'the dispossessed' or, borrowing Arnold Toynbee's phrase, the 'internal proletariat'. For this group, according to Toynbee, 'proletarianism is a state of feeling rather than a matter of outward circumstance'. [3] For Hoggart, this class - defined by its cultural loss or scarcity, rather than sociological position - could now be identified as all those 'who are reacting deep down against the vile mass culture of our day', who were to be found at all levels of society – '*homo vulgaris Northcliffii*'.

Hoggart quotes a large chunk of Toynbee, reviving the familiar, anti-materialist argument of the turn of the century aesthetic movements, that the materialist aims of modern society can only produce spiritually impoverished citizens. What he adds, however, is a contemporary gloss: those who protest against the shallow pseudo-values of this society in the name of 'life's depths', he says, turn to 'us' (adult education) for nourishment but are only offered in return 'functional action for democracy'. [4] Adult education's orientation towards social studies can only produce social functionaries. There may be those who have an admirable social conscience, which he applauds, but, just as likely, products of this system are 'the well-meaning, twisted souls compulsively manipulating their particular piece of social machinery ... the obsessive ritual of a stunted heart'. [5]

The antidote to this functionalist approach to adult education, Hoggart suggests, is 'the development of the aesthetic sense, the training of taste'. [6] But, of course, not everyone wants this and, ultimately, the true subjects of this education he suggests are 'the few': 'I think in short, that we havn't (sic) sufficiently catered for the few in any generation who care seriously ... and who, unless they can make some sort of communication with one another, are liable to be crushed by the dead weight of the "inert uncreative mass".' [7] This, without the tone, was the theme of some of E.M. Forster's wartime broadcasts. Hoggart is aware he risks accusations of snobbery and undemocratic practices. He also does not want to be seen to cavalierly dismiss the puritan virtues of those who pioneered the movement and he speaks with irony of those who call for more cultural subjects to be taught because the main battle by organised labour for political power has been won. But, he says, 'Is there a sadder sight than a class of introverts, cut off from all positive joy, turned furiously onto "social purpose" and having that incapacity for joy strengthened and their lack rationalised?' [8] There is a need, he says, for 'a more generous enthusiasm'.

The remainder of the argument seems to borrow substantially from Herbert Read, whose *Education through Art* had been published by Faber in 1943. Hoggart argues that any sense of values not informed by a developed aesthetic sense is bound to be crude, and that poetry, in particular, is 'a liberating sensitising force' which contains a vital part of the answer to our present problems. [9] He illuminates his point with a quotation from *The Memoirs of a Revolutionist* by the anarchist philosopher, Peter Kropotkin, which is extremely interesting in that it points to the necessary inter-disciplinarity of aesthetic education:

> as he (the teacher of the literature) speaks of the development of the language, of the content ... and the diverse aesthetical, political, and philosophical currents it has reflected, he is bound to introduce that generalized conception of the human mind which lies beyond the scope of each of the subjects that are taught separately. [10]

In fact, this goes beyond inter-disciplinarity because it posits the study of literature as the meta-discipline, which is of course truly Leavisite, but it at least holds tight to a notion of relevance. This moves Hoggart, in ways reminiscent of the nineteenth-century university extension pioneers, to assert the need for 'a bigger conception of our work' but he also notes that this 'smells suspiciously of an attempt to create a body of samurai' which should be guarded against. [11] Drawing back a little from the implications of this, he restates his argument by saying that you can't cure a disease which has its roots in imaginative starvation by overdoses of material mechanical panaceas, because the awful phenomena of present social life are only the outward signs of inner spiritual breakdown. Significantly, his concluding remark is to call for a 'charismatic education' 'which comes ex Weber via Mannheim'. [12]

So, while Leavisite in tone, what Hoggart's 'Prolegomena' reveals is a considerably wider net of references, extending from Wells and Lawrence's pre-First World War ideologies to Herbert Read and Karl Mannheim. It's probably not a piece Hoggart would want to be remembered by, and it contrasts sharply with later, more tempered writings, but it speaks of a young tutor early in his career, at the onset of the Cold War, grappling with the relevance of his discipline to expressed social needs, which is more than just Leavisism.

Over the next few years the opposition between culturalists and workerists in adult education grew sharper, as is well-documented by Roger Fieldhouse. [13] It was strongly coloured by the political climate of the Cold War but cannot in the end be reduced to that. Although the subtext of much of this argument was in fact a political witch hunt against communists within adult education, there was still a real argument about pedagogy which focused on the nature of class education. With J.F.C. Harrison and Roy Shaw, who had both recently been recruited into Raybould's Leeds Department of Extra-Mural Studies, Hoggart wrote a position paper in the *Tutors' Bulletin* of Autumn 1948, entitled 'What are we doing? The burden of their argument was that the WEA was being held back from addressing a wider audience by its narrow adherence to a notion of working-class education. This was hotly contested by the communist, John Vickers, who was then in charge of the residential Wedgwood College in Staffordshire. In reply, Hoggart *et al.* argued that workers' education in the class sense was incompatible with the larger or 'true' ends of adult education and the direction suggested by Vickers would be to hand the WEA over to the trade-unions. Thus 'cultural' education was identified with the modernisation of adult education, opening it out to a wider public and freeing it from its working-class base. This class base was to be one of the spectral elements haunting the pedagogical discussions of WEA in the post-war decades.

The first issue of *The Critic*, set up by Raymond Williams and Wolf Mankowitz as a left engagement with Leavisism, received a prickly review from Hoggart. An article on art he found 'stiff with the thorny jargon of the clan Leavis' and continued: 'Have we lost the mandarins only to deliver ourselves to the bilious proctors?'[14] He did not much like Raymond Williams either: 'To begin with there is too much jingling of critical loose change, notably by Raymond Williams, who tricks out the sound stem of a dialogue on actors with rosettes of brightly turned platitudes'.[15]

Not the most generous of welcomes to a new colleague's efforts and significant, perhaps, of his own isolation from the intellectual new left.

His dilemma in regard to literature teaching is most disarmingly revealed in a letter to his mentor Bonamy Dobrée in 1946, written from Redcar. It shows him trying to construct a middle way between the extremes of 'social-responsibility' teaching and the 'corrosive' Leavis boys:

> The literature picture in adult education a horrid one though simply defined. On one hand we have the 'literature-for-social-responsibility' school (who have been assassinated time & time again by all the best tutors on every possible platform & periodical – but who still go on, (so little *communication* is there even in a field as narrow as this)); on your far side are the 'debunking' 'pruning' (mainly Leavis trained) boys (the young ones mainly) who insist, rather too completely for me, that all we can do is to attack debased language & sentiment by a series of set exercises designed to debunk the mass of suggestive material which conditions *all* adult students (and from which only the Leavis boys are free? – that's a cheap crack but these Leavis students are so utterly corrosive one suspects them all of being conditioned themselves by Leavis's own antipathetic attitude [take it to pieces and put each bit under the microscope] to any enthusiasm.) Somewhere in the middle are, I fancy, most tutors who enjoy reading, try to communicate their joy, meet with many disappointments and don't quite know *what method to employ*. As a result a lot of them gradually seem to have worked out a bright cheerful 'hours with the great masters' technique which does *not* get at their students' real problems. [16]

Leavis, then, or at least his boys, were as much the enemy in adult education as its own brand of 'social-responsibility' literature tutors, by which Hoggart probably means those who taught literature strictly from the standpoint of how it illuminated the struggle of the working-class for justice and equality, also known as 'the sociological approach'. Perhaps the real weakness of this tendency implied by Hoggart's criticism is that the actual literariness or formal qualities of literature was utterly subordinated to its moral or social critical element, such that 'second-rate' literature was preferred if it was politically sound to 'literary' plenitude. The problem for the literature tutor was how to deal with, and presumably move on from, texts which adult students, particularly labour movement activists, found valuable and stimulating, such as Tressell's *Ragged Trouser'd Philanthropists*, Gissing or Dickens. The art was in finding a way of reading these texts which valued but transcended their sociological content and critically examined the language used.

The relationship of Richard Hoggart to Q.D. Leavis was shrewdly summed up by Raymond Williams in 1957. Although there seems to have been little contact between Hoggart and Williams, until the publication of the *Uses of Literacy* in 1957, they were aware of each other's activities. This shows some of the consequences of adult teaching, which leaves the tutor relatively isolated from collegiality, but it might also indicate the withdrawal from political activism of both in the 1950s. Hoggart did, however, teach a summer school with Edward Thompson on Conrad. [17] Williams's estimation was that the *Uses* was a comprehensive and intelligent account of contemporary commercial writing and welcomed it as a natural successor and complement to Q.D. Leavis's *Fiction and the Reading Public*. But, Williams added, Hoggart had steered away from Mrs Leavis's abstraction of 'the reading public' and, by shifting perspective, had instead approached readers as individuals competent to bring their own appetites, experience and critical capacity to their reading 'and to judge the documents with this reference'. [18] He also noted perceptively Hoggart's debt to George Orwell from whom 'Hoggart, in terms of literary method, seems to have learned a great deal'. [19]

Although worried by what he saw as an unsatisfactory jumbling of literary forms in *The Uses*, Williams nevertheless acknowledged that even here Hoggart had achieved something new, namely the quality of 'personal and social observation of a feeling kind' and that 'Hoggart is much more reliable on all this than Orwell: he writes not as a visitor, but as a native'. [20] What Williams indicated, therefore, which offered a valuable but apparently ignored departure from the usual narrative of Leavisite fundamentalism in cultural studies, is Hoggart's alternative location in the non-academic tradition of popular journalism represented by Orwell. The fact of his working-class experience was, for Williams, a telling one that distanced him both from the public-school boy Orwell and, by implication, the rarefied (Cambridge) world of the Leavises.

Class and Culture

Certainly this memory of his own childhood working-class experience was mediated by his later literary education, an experience and an education which Hoggart himself has painstakingly and honestly documented on a number of occasions, most famously in *The Uses*, but also in *Speaking to Each Other*, where he writes fondly of Bonamy Dobrée and latterly in his autobiographies. More than anyone else connected with the formation of British cultural studies, Hoggart's reflections on his own life have been an enduring pre-occupation (Williams, arguably, does it in his novels, especially in *Border Country*, but the formal distancing of a fictional form preserves his impersonality) and a documentary source for the sociological record. Edward Thompson was almost completely silent on his own autobiographical formation,[21] and Stuart Hall has only more recently begun the process of recovering his own background. In Hoggart, as Williams noted, personal and social observation are interwoven, such that his own experience is often presented as the evidence for the social observation he is making.

Unlike Williams, who grew up in a strongly political climate and with a remarkable tradition of educational self-help in the Welsh labour movement, Hoggart experienced class as an *exclusion* from culture and intellect. In a conversation with Raymond Williams in 1959 which was published in the first edition of *New Left Review*, Hoggart confessed,

> I felt from your book [*Culture and Society*] that you were surer, sooner than I was, of your relationship to your working-class background. With me, I remember, it was a long and troublesome effort. It was difficult to escape a kind of patronage, even when one felt one was understanding the virtues of the working-class life one had been brought up in – one seemed to be insisting on these strengths *in spite of* all sorts of doubts in one's attitudes.[22]

126

For him, Williams's life in rural Wales was a moment of an 'organic' relationship among working people, something that still existed in the townships of the West Riding but was no longer to found in an industrial town like Leeds. That way of life already seemed to belong to the past, whereas Leeds signified modernity. Instead of the organic, Leeds represented itself to him as great 'blocks' of people where relations were defined spatially or geographically rather than by trade or labour. In true modernist fashion, the divisions of space in a town like Leeds predominated for Hoggart over the solidarities of time and occupation.

His long march out of this alienating environment took him via Cockburn Grammar School to the University of Leeds, which, although only a couple of miles across town to the north, was light years away in every other sense. The patronage Hoggart mentioned in his talk with Williams was perhaps of a familiar pattern inscribed into the history of the University of Leeds from the time of Michael Sadler and Frederic Moorman. Sadler was the Vice Chancellor most responsible for transforming what, according to the historian Maurice Beresford, had been little more than a jumped up technical college into a true university between 1911 and 1925. As secretary for the Oxford Delegacy in the 1890s he had been a leading light in the university extension movement which had seen as its prime object the conversion of the northern working-classes. He was a Ruskinian whose message, he told a WEA audience in 1913, was to leave 'no Giotto among the sheepfolds' and he was personally responsible for nurturing the career of the remarkable Jewish painter Jacob Kramer. [23] Similarly, Frederic Moorman, Professor of English Language at Leeds until his untimely death in 1919, had turned Herbert Read's career into the path of literature and art in 1912. The patronage of gifted working-class and disadvantaged students by liberal intellectuals is well enough known as, perhaps, the balm of an otherwise savagely discriminatory educational system.

Dobrée and style

For Richard Hoggart, the man who assumed that role was Bonamy Dobrée, Professor of English while Hoggart was an undergraduate. Dobrée seemed through his urbanity, wit, connections and ultimately his 'style' to embody the best of English high culture, which for Hoggart was also a matter of 'class' as expressed in physicality and gesture. He remembered him as 'a man of great intellectual sparkle, and great physical charm. But that charm had to express itself in the precise restrained codes for physical gesture used by the English upper class. It belonged to a separate compartment from his lively intellect – the style of that had been picked up on his slightly eccentric road through parts of academic life and the literary-artistic circle he moved in (Eliot, Lawrence, Read, Moore)'. [24] Hoggart was particularly struck by his teaching in which the manner and the matter seemed to fuse carrying erudition lightly and imparting it in an almost offhand way. He encouraged the chosen few of which Hoggart was one: 'Each year Bonamy Dobrée seemed to pick one or perhaps two students to keep an eye on. We were probably the brightest in both the good and bad senses of that word. We were intelligent but also likely to be quirky and offbeat ...' [25]

Although he was perceived as mingling in Bohemian circles, Dobrée himself bore the marks of the military gentleman, for example roundly discouraging Hoggart from taking up the study of psychology as an option because he felt he needed all his time to develop his literary studies, a rebuff Hoggart carried with him for many years. It was as if 'the culture' had spoken to remind him of its absence in him, his own hollowness. Dobrée represented the upper class, the southern gentleman who had become genuinely affianced to the north because of its different quality of life, its otherness. He represented also 'France' and cosmopolitanism as against English provinciality – a peculiarity of the English intellectual upper class seems to be that the more 'upper', the less 'English' they are – a point of reference for Hoggart's intellectual journeying in the years to follow and, perhaps most crucially, he was 'not-Leavis'.

Dobrée's style of teaching was to communicate the sheer pleasure in the *excess* of reading:

> [His lectures] were exciting and stimulating rather than comprehensive or exhaustive. He deliberately moved across the formal boundaries of specialisms. He laced his lectures with side-comments, odd *aperçus* from other disciplines, sudden changes of level, irruption into contemporary affairs. I can trace the origins of some of my own less formal literary-and-social interests to incidental comments he threw out – on Faulkner and violence in literature, for instance. [26]

Remarkably post-modern, in fact. This clearly is part of the non-Leavisite genealogy of cultural studies: the anti-Puritanism of the cavalier, in its best sense, style – replete with disregard for disciplinary boundaries, formal niceties, appropriate tone, relishing the social reference which the modern defenders of the faith so dislike and call dilettantism.

Despite his fascination with Dobrée's style, little of it rubbed off. There is no sense in which Hoggart seemed to want to emulate his mentor *socially*, although as a teacher he was always committed to nurturing his students' pleasure in the text. Rather, Dobrée acts as a key reference point for Hoggart's dogged determination to interrogate his own class difference and, increasingly, the margins between the Hunslet childhood and the post-educational maturity. Dobrée is a kind of fascinating and exotic other to his own psycho-social formation.

The People's Army

Like Thompson and Williams, Hoggart's wartime experience in the army focused his attention on adult education. The close comradeship, the hours of talk and the classroom-like nature of the unit which he commanded, an anti-aircraft position, gave him opportunities to 'teach' in what became almost a standing seminar. It seemed only natural that towards the end of the war he should become an education officer. Perhaps one of the biggest single institutional developments was ABCA, the Army Bureau of Current Affairs, which operated as a kind of distance learning organisation, producing readable and informative pamphlets on current affairs, which could form the resources for educational work. Hoggart threw himself into this work, which he later regarded as having done 'a terrific amount to waken political consciousness in the army'. [27] By 1945 he reckoned that the soldiers were much more politically conscious than they had been three years before, and that 75 per cent would vote left in the coming general election. [28] He recounted how a soldier in OCTU had written to him saying that 'our companionship wasn't a bad substitute for a university in wartime'. [29]

It was during these sessions that Hoggart found he could give rein to the peculiar mix of textual practice with social commentary that was his literary education. Significantly, one object of his educational work was the 'large nucleus of very poor bolshies to whom I try to show the error of their ways', men with 'melodramatic minds' because they were 'not trained otherwise'. [30] He was also impressed by the autodidacts that he met, including the red-headed charcoal burner from the New Forest who read Carlyle rather than the *Daily Mirror*. [31] The self-improvement tradition of the nineteenth century was still active among the archaic crafts in rural areas and but for the army it might have gone almost unnoticed.

During this period in his letters to Dobrée, Hoggart noted a range of intellectual influences. He kept up with Cyril Connolly's eclectic literary journal, *Horizon* (which was forwarded to him regularly by Dobrée), and he expected great things after the war from Storm Jameson (an earlier Leeds graduate and protégé of Alfred Orage). In his letters to Dobrée he comments on Coleridge's theory of the imagination; the building of an aesthetics in Jacob Epstein's autobiography; G.D.H. Cole, 'who says what a lot of us are thinking', Rilke's poetry, which helped him to understand the 1930s; and the communist literary journal, *Our Time*, whose 'literary criticism smells'. [32] He very much admired Louis MacNiece's 'Epitaph to Liberal Poets', which so finely drew the consequences of the managerial revolution and the poet's subjection to 'tight lipped technocratic conquistadors'. He found Orwell, Pritchett, Betjeman and Pudney, 'a few of those spare, critical, well-informed writers … who are well suited to our times' and who had done great things for English didactic prose; Orwell in particular he greatly admired. [33]

Signs of the future direction of his own work could perhaps be seen in his admiration for Edmund Gosse's autobiographical *Father and Son*, which he thought was impressively literary, and also in his contact with an Italian Professor at Naples called Binni. Binni was something new, a kind of 'Italian Empson' whose recent work was regarded as a 'hotchpotch of psychology, anthropology and economics'.[34] He also met the Italian philosopher, Benedetto Croce, who despite his opposition to Mussolini had been left more or less alone and who was doing a 'superhuman job around here'.[35] Croce's approach to cultural questions had had enormous influence on Antonio Gramsci a few decades earlier and may also have had an impact on Hoggart. It was at this time that he told Dobrée that he would like to lecture in a training college or university after the war, but definitely not school teaching. But he also wanted to do 'something social' and to that end was interested in the plans for a post-war ABCA in which W.E. Williams was said to be involved.

A remarkable sign of his activity was the Three Arts Club he organised in Naples, which for a while became a significant cultural centre. Resembling the Arts Club that Orage founded in Leeds in 1903, which became the radical centre of Leeds cultural life, the Three Arts Club was a bold attempt to provide a focus for members of the armed forces in Naples with an interest in the arts. It encouraged painters and held exhibitions of their work, organised musical recitals, concerts, poetry readings and dramatic productions. It was also a place where social and military hierarchies were levelled by art: 'There was a democracy of artistic interest and of degrees of artistic talent which obliterated class and rank once they came through the door. In that sense the chemistry of the place was immediate and extraordinary'.[36] Its most consistent work was in producing publications, for which material flooded in from around the Mediterranean, the most notable being *Verses from Italy*, which appeared in September 1944 and *Comment from Italy* in 1945, which also included stories and essays. *Voice from Italy* and *Four in Hand* appeared in the same year. An editorial decision was taken not to use anything from poets published before the war and to concentrate on those who drew on the experience of war itself, which resulted in the discovery of much new talent, including many who were working men. Although he asked T.S. Eliot to write a preface for a pamphlet, Hoggart received a dusty reply.[37]

As the war drew to a close, Hoggart's interest in adult education sharpened; and he was increasingly convinced of the importance it would have in the post-war period of reconstruction. During the war he had been extremely gloomy about the prospects for cultural renewal and had at times come close to advocating a messianic movement. Feelings such as this were not uncommon among young intellectuals at the time, nor was Hoggart alone in seeing adult education teaching as a vocation for those seeking a social, moral and political renaissance in Britain. The Beveridge Report of 1942 and Butler's Education Act of 1944 encouraged the sense that there could be no return to the 1930s, that people had not gone through all the sufferings of the war simply to return to the old social injustices and inequalities.

Extra-mural teaching

Teaching classes in Middlesbrough for the University College of Hull's Extra-Mural Department had not been Hoggart's first choice of a job, but once there he found the patronage of Percy Mayfield, his head of department, a literature man, most congenial. Adult education was expanding rapidly in the post-war climate, thanks to the election of the Labour government in 1945, many of whose members had strong ties to the WEA.

The benefits of adult teaching also included a long summer break in which to get on with writing and research. Initially, Hoggart had wanted to write a brief guide to the 1930s poets, much as Dobrée had done for the Cresset Press on the 'Victorian Age' and the 'Present Age'. Indeed, the WEA's popular pamphlet as an introduction to a variety of social and cultural problems was a major resource for adult students between the wars and had been emulated by ABCA. The 1930s guide, however, turned into Hoggart's first book, which was the first major study of W.H. Auden, in the preparation of which Dobrée had been very helpful. With Mayfield, Hoggart lobbied Cresset for a reprint of the Dobrée guides as essential to his work in adult education. Hoggart had clearly found his vocation and wrote to Dobrée that he enjoyed the work enormously and was quickly establishing a reputation. As a result of an article in an adult education journal he was asked by Adult Education to write a piece restating the aims and standards of tutorial class work to open up the debate.

More than any other educational area, perhaps, adult education was a site at this stage for ideological contestation over cultural meanings. Its already politicised nature, a result of its historical constituencies, experimental pedagogies and marginal status, bred strong factional feeling. Cultural interpretation, therefore was often formulated against or in reaction to other well-formed ideological positions. The passions raised here came into play at the onset of the Cold War. In a letter to Dobrée Hoggart notes:

> I should have added, à propos of our work, that there's a small group of neo-Thomist tutors – whom I like, but who I suspect are as a result of recent events, in danger of helping the anti-Communist witch-hunt – one of them, inspired, it seems, by Middleton Murry's new book – was talking yesterday about 'fighting the last fight'. I havent (sic) read the book and of course I care as much about what's happening in Central Europe as they do – but it seems to me that for people of any responsibility to start talking like that at this point is disastrous. I wonder how undergraduates are taking it; it's the thirties with a new twist. I feel like a little sober (but by no means flippant) stoicism – but it's very fashionable just now. [38]

As the 1950s progressed, the urgency and political passions of the immediate post-war years faded. *Horizon* closed in 1950 and the Penguin New Writing series was wound up. Hoggart discovered new 'intellectual pabulum' in the work of Lionel Trilling, whose *Middle of the Journey* in 1947 and *The Liberal Imagination* in 1950 marked for him the arrival of major new critical influence. Apart from listening a lot to the Third Programme and going to the films, he also read Koestler and Orwell anew and the novels of Graham Greene began to appear on his syllabuses. But most of all Eliot's *Four Quartets* and Toynbee's *A Study of History* became essential reading and re-reading. What is quite significant is Hoggart's almost complete estrangement from any department of English Studies, especially that at Hull. Brett, the head of department, later invited him to meetings, but the internal members of staff, in a rather memorable image, circled the wagons against the incursive Indian. To be in adult education was to experience one quite dramatic sort of intellectual isolation, at least from mainstream academic life. But this was also the space that allowed experimental work, forced in part by the demands of adult students but also by its distance from the constraints of internal academic discipline.

Hoggart quickly took a leading role in the intense nation-wide discussions about the nature and purpose of adult education.

Contact with other extra-mural tutors was relatively infrequent, however, apart from members of the Leeds department, Roy Shaw, James Cameron and J.F.C. Harrison, as we have noted. Shaw was especially close and formed a life long friendship with Hoggart that continued through Shaw's directorship of the Arts Council. Raybould, whom Mayfield regarded as little more than an 'academic businessman',[39] attempted to poach Hoggart for the Leeds department but, following his wife's instincts, Hoggart opted to stay with Mayfield, who moved him from Middlesbrough down to Hull where he could be more centrally involved.[40]

Later he observed of this milieu: 'A considerable number of men and women, some of whom became well-known afterwards, chose to enter university extra-mural work in 1946 and 1947, and a fair amount of their time was taken up explaining, to themselves as well as to others, just why; why what they were doing seemed to them more interesting, more worthwhile, than internal teaching and for that matter than intellectual journalism'.[41] They knew that the larger academic and literary world regarded their work as old-fashioned and quaint, which as we have noted had the effect of saving them from some distractions, but despite some defensiveness, all believed in what they were doing.

Raybould was the leading apologist and reformer of the post-war period. His determination to establish university standards in extra-mural work won him many enemies but raised both the status and productivity of extra-mural tutors. He was proud of the work of his tutors, especially Edward Thompson (despite his active membership of the Communist Party), whose *William Morris* and *The Making of the English Working Class* became landmark texts in the new social history. Hoggart thought Raybould 'exemplary' and in the best sense, like Mayfield and the Principal at Hull, Nicholson, 'provincials'.[42] Like Edward Thompson who also thought of himself as a 'provincial intellectual', Hoggart and other extra-mural tutors creatively explored this non-metropolitan space in ways neglected by mainstream academia, and they populated it with such a rich complexity of cultural life that the mainstream was in the end forced to take notice.

As a consequence, the practice of literature teaching was always threatening to spill over its allotted space eclipsing the broader aims of adult education. It was in one of these highly wrought exchanges in the adult education journals that Hoggart first came into contact with Raymond Williams, then teaching on the south coast for the Oxford Delegacy. The two men argued about the distinction between social justification and possible political direction, and Hoggart notes that they were somewhat puritanical in their judgements. But unlike members of internal university departments, they could not dismiss the 'popular' with an easy shrug, because adult students lived in that world and did not care for it. They came to the study of literature, he believed, in the hope that it would speak to their condition in profound ways. Confronted with these high expectations, he argued, the adult tutor had to use a strategy of indirection. Literature was not a manual for solving existential problems, but if read with openness and understanding the pleasure it gave would reveal itself as relevant to life in unexpected ways. The tutor also had to shed the 'armour of specialist language' and talk to the adult student as an equal. [43]

The redefinition of the subject began to take place therefore, partly under pressure from the institutional setting of limits and partly in response to the continual need to answer the demand for 'relevance', which Hoggart took to mean more than simply what 'could be fitted into the Co-op shopping bag of "social realism"'. [44] But his most important insight was that the methods of literary criticism and analysis were relevant to 'the better understanding of all levels of writing and much else in popular culture and the way people responded to them'. [45]

From literary to cultural studies

In one sense this was a move into the territory of the anthropologist and the argument for this kind of project had already been made in the work of Karl Mannheim before the war. The boundaries of sociology and literary studies were beginning to blur under the pressure of demands for a more holistic study of society. [46] However, Hoggart was less interested in these theoretical questions and insisted that it was the experience of adult teaching itself which made the crucial difference. Raymond Williams's *Culture and Society*, he believed, would have been a different book if it had been written while teaching internal undergraduates in a traditional university setting. Similarly,

Edward Thompson's *The Making of the English Working Class* is rooted in his direct experience of taking tutorial classes with working-class adults in the rugged but friendly industrial townships of the West Riding of Yorkshire. [47] Adult tutors, Hoggart believed, had a very special sense of the of the direct social importance of their day to day work, a sense of the major injustices in the lives of working people, and were deeply suspicious of the class-based nature of British society. Moreover, the sheer marginality of extra-mural work, which did not compete for grants with internal departments because of its separate 'Responsible Body' status, meant that any potential hostility to its work from internal departments became, instead, sheer indifference.

Hoggart spent little time theorising the move from literary to cultural studies since they appeared to him such a natural extension of his adult educational work. The boundaries of English studies were constructed within internal departments only after the pioneers of university extension had done their initial work and it was clear that part of that process had been the paring away of the formal aspects of literary study from the social context. The extension pioneers such as Churton Collins and Frederic Moorman, on the other hand, had always seen English studies as part of a social project which, as we have seen, was the construction of a modern English identity. [48] In some ways the emergence of cultural studies as a distinct pedagogy in the late 1950s was a re-construction of that original project in new circumstances.

Notoriously distrustful of literary theory, Hoggart has been content to say no more than that he was led almost inexorably to move from the study of literature, academically defined, to work on many other aspects of contemporary culture, 'chiefly but not only in words'. [49] His debt to Q.D. Leavis's *Fiction and the Reading Public* and to similar material in *Scrutiny* is recorded in *The Uses of Literature*, but her wholesale rejection of popular culture was not in itself an adequate response. Hoggart wanted to see to how people brought good instincts to poor writing within 'a social setting that provided its own forms and filters for judgements and resistances'. [50] Influences which took him in that direction came from Orwell and C.S. Lewis, as we have noted, and Ezra Pound, who argued that 'when language goes rotten' thought and feeling decay with it. [51] Pound's book *Guide to Kulchur* (1938) was described by his biographer as a recklessly libellous attack on 'the gang of punks, pimps and cheap dudes' now ruling in England, which Faber had thought it politic to tone down. [52] Its title already indicated the transformation of the Arnoldian subject in the context of the oncoming 'mass' society.

Notes towards a definition

The book, which began its incubation as *The Abuses of Literacy*, owed its origins to this process. Some early sketches for elements later worked into the book had been published by George Orwell, then literary editor of *Tribune*, the newspaper of the Labour left, as early as 1946. Hoggart himself described it as a sort of guide or textbook to aspects of popular culture, which was an attempt to adjust Mrs Leavis's work by setting that culture in the context of readers' lives. [53] In effect it was written back-to-front because he initially began with writing what became the second and theoretical half of the book. The pressure of having to provide a context, however, led him to write the sketches of working class life which drew heavily on his own childhood. Some have called this an example of a 'narrative of exile' written by one who no longer lived that life, exiled by education and status, but this is to misunderstand the process. Hoggart was constantly revisiting the scenes of his youth, still physically close to him at Middlesbrough, in his dialogue with his adult students, who would confirm, modify or deny his own accounts with reference to their own lives. This accounts for the relative lack of nostalgia (except, perhaps, around the absent mother) in Hoggart's writing. There is a complete absence of the heroic, militant working class familiar from more left-wing accounts which worried Klingender. [54]

Nevertheless, some of the pieces were written for the sophisticated middle-class audience of the BBC's Third Programme. One of the most controversial chapters, 'Scholarship Boy', brought him more correspondence than anything else he had written, mostly from those who also had emigrated from the working class via a Grammar School education, concurring emotionally with his account. So these were not by any means desert island accounts of a lost childhood but an engaged working over of the issues with his own students. [55]

Another neglected element in the discussion of the origins of cultural studies is the importance of the adult educational three year 'tutorial class' itself. This was one of the key innovations brought about by the formation of the WEA in 1903 and was in essence a contract between students and tutor to focus in depth, for one evening a week over three winters, on a specific line of study. This almost puritanical seriousness of study was demanded by the pioneers of the WEA, who forced the rupture with what, by the turn of the century, they experienced as the decadence of the university extension movement. They were no longer content with what had often become the leisured ramblings of university dons giving 'popular' lectures to the deserving poor. Probably looking to the example of the French syndicalist-inspired *Universités Populaires* movement, they sought both relevance and commitment from their tutors. One of the earliest practitioners of the tutorial method was the historian, R.H. Tawney, whose own social history has to be counted among the intellectual foundations of historical cultural studies. His debt to the sociologist Max Weber is well-known, but few have asked what moved him in that direction. The answer is suggested by Hoggart:

> He and other early tutors also said that their tutorial classes helped them redefine their subjects, that social history or industrial relations began to look different if you discussed them for three years, week after week, with adults who had had much living evidence of social history and daily experiences of industrial relations. For me much later, similar implicit but powerful challenges to the definition of my subject – English literature – led me to move out to an area I called contemporary cultural studies. [56]

Hoggart believes the potential is still there for this intense tutorial work. The argument that, once greater access for working-class students into university had been created, adult education was no longer necessary, is patently false. Adult education did (and perhaps still does) something different, namely it works with students, collectively as well as individually, for socially relevant ends without unnecessary regard to formal academic boundaries. As such it is ideologically and as a practice quite distinct from full-time undergraduate education and from the whole paraphernalia of awards and assessment which have been forced on it. The era of 'mass' higher education – the adjective is ironic – will not for the foreseeable future include the majority of working-class children for whom in later years adult education could provide for their first tentative steps.

Critical hindsight

Richard Hoggart's trajectory eventually took him right out of adult education and into mainstream departments of English, first at Leicester and then at Birmingham universities. His interest in communications and cultural matters had already led to his involvement in external work in the arts with the BBC, the Arts Council, and a number of national committees. At Birmingham, because it soon became apparent that a centre for the study of contemporary culture could not be set up within the School of English, Hoggart quickly began work on an alternative institutional base. The Birmingham Centre for Contemporary Cultural Studies was the first of its kind. In forming the Centre he believed that the work could be divided into roughly three areas, namely: the historical and philosophical; the sociological; and thirdly, for him the most important, the literary critical.

In his work as an adult tutor, Hoggart and many others had roamed through all these disciplines as a matter of course in their day to day work, but both *The Uses* and Raymond Williams's *Culture and Society* had received hostile criticism from specialists for this and it was clear that the interdisciplinary approach was going to have to be much better informed methodologically. Edward Thompson, too, knew he would have to tighten up his scholarship after the critical mauling of *The Making*. But, as Hoggart commented, the specialists were remarkably backward in putting forward their own more general interpretations. [57] Although initially he took his methodology from literary criticism, his recruitment of Stuart Hall from the editorship of *New Left Review* began a turn towards sociological and theoretical areas that Hoggart himself did not feel equipped to engage with, and which ultimately frustrated him.

Without the commitment of university intellectuals to organised social movements, especially the 'working-class movement', the context for such work would not have evolved. Hoggart's work on his own personal development and his dogged commitment to ploughing a furrow between academic specialist 'detachment' and an overly constraining political commitment has been central to the whole enterprise. This has attracted political criticism from both left and right. Edward Thompson, noting his 'explicit hostility' to Marxism, generously acknowledged that Hoggart along with Williams and Hall had thrown a lifeline to those 'old Marxists' around the *Reasoner* group who were trying to work out of the 'theoretical disaster' Marxism had created for itself and 'helped tow us out'. [58] Less charitably, Perry Anderson condemned Hoggart's work to the theoretical stone age of the 1950s, 'which blurred the specificity of the superstructural complex which is society's original thought and art'. [59]

Of all 'the founding fathers', Hoggart's work has focused most closely on contemporary popular culture and in particular on that 'women-centred' environment of the working-class home. This has attracted the hostile attention of feminists, who, not incorrectly, see the mother portrayed simply as conduit for male cultural ambitions. Bea Campbell notes how his autobiographical account already lacks that mother-centred family and suggests he is drawing on received cultural versions. She feels it is recognisably related to Orwell's nostalgic drawing on the memory of an 'older order'. [60] But it may be possible to say, as Sheila Rowbotham has said of Thompson's *Making*, that a space was opened for the further investigation of the specific ways that working-class women have functioned in the creation of contemporary culture.

Swindells and Jardine suggest that it is possible to see Hoggart's work as moving the left on from a negative critique of contemporary culture into active involvement with it, especially in school reform. [61] In this sense he follows Leavis's concern for education which was, of course, reinforced by his own experience. This strand fed directly into the debates about comprehensive schooling and echoes of Hoggart are evident in Brian Jackson and Denis Marsden's *Education and the Working Class*, which subsequently became the *bête noir* of Thatcherism. But there is a distinct sense of Leavis's yearning for a lost organic 'community' in Hoggart's work and Swindells and Jardine argue that by collapsing his 'lived experience' into a personal memory of a domestic past Hoggart is in the end unable to produce a politicised account of the relation between culture and working-class life. This is undoubtedly true, especially since any notion of a working-class movement is largely missing from his work, but it is not the whole story. It draws attention to the uses of autobiography in showing connectedness between the personal and the political at many levels and it enlarges our understanding of that area so neglected by Marxist analysis: civil life. In many cases the adult education class was, and perhaps still is, a microcosm of civil life, as Hoggart himself argues, and the complex negotiation of difference and agreement that takes place in the best classes could provide a model for its renewal. [62]

Notes

1 John Corner, 'Studying culture: reflections and assessments. An interview with Richard Hoggart', *Media Culture and Society*, Vol. 13, 1991, pp137-51, p146.

2 Richard Hoggart, 'Prolegomena to the Second Session', *Tutors' Bulletin*, November 1947, pp7-10, p7.

3 Quoted *Ibid*.

4 *Ibid*, p8.

5 *Ibid*.

6 *Ibid*.

7 *Ibid*.

8 *Ibid*.

9 A formulation with which Edward Thompson would not have disagreed, cf. his essay on Christopher Caudwell, E.P. Thompson, 'Caudwell' in J. Saville and R. Miliband, (eds), *The Socialist Register 1977*, Merlin, London 1977, pp228-276.

10 Hoggart, 'Prolegomena' *op cit*, p9.

11 *Ibid*, p10. This was the project outlined by H.G. Wells in his eugenicist text *A Modern Utopia* (1910).

12 *Ibid*.

13 Roger Fieldhouse, *Adult Education and the Cold War*, Leeds Studies in the Education of Adults, Leeds 1985.

14 Richard Hoggart, 'One Kind of Critic', *Tutors' Bulletin*, July 1947, p15.

15 *Ibid*.

16 Richard Hoggart to Bonamy Dobrée, letter 27, 22 Dec. 1946, Bonamy Dobrée Collection, Brotherton Library, University of Leeds.

17 Richard Hoggart, *A Sort of Clowning, Life and Times 1940-1959*, Oxford University Press, Oxford 1991, p132.

18 Raymond Williams, *The Politics of Modernism*, Verso, London 1990, p25.

19 *Ibid*.

20 *Ibid*, p27.

21 Except for an intriguing comparison with Raymond Williams in his review of *The Long Revolution* in *NLR* 9.

22 Richard Hoggart and Raymond Williams, 'Working-Class Attitudes', *New Left Review*, No. 1, Jan./Feb. 1960, pp. 26-30, p26

23 Tom Steele, *Alfred Orage and the Leeds Arts Club 1893-1923*, Scolar, Aldershot 1990, p200.

24 Hoggart, *A Sort of Clowning, op cit*, p50.

25 Richard Hoggart, 'Teaching with Style on Bonamy Dobrée' in *Speaking to Each Other*, Pelican, London 1973, p191.

26 *Ibid*, p199.

27 Richard Hoggart, letter to Bonamy Dobrée, No.16, 26 Oct. 1944, Dobrée Collection, University of Leeds.

28 Richard Hoggart, letter to Bonamy Dobrée, No.19, 11 June 1945, Dobrée Collection, University of Leeds.

29 Richard Hoggart, letter to Bonamy Dobrée, No. 3, n.d., Dobrée Collection, University of Leeds.

30 *Ibid*.

31 Richard Hoggart, letter to Bonamy Dobrée, No.1, n.d., Dobrée Collection, University of Leeds.

32 Hoggart, letter to Dobrée, No.19, *op cit*.

33 Richard Hoggart, letter to Bonamy Dobrée, No. 26, n.d., Dobrée Collection, University of Leeds.

34 Hoggart, letter to Dobrée, No.16, *op cit*.

35 Richard Hoggart, letter to Bonamy Dobrée, No.12, 18 December 1943, Dobrée Collection, University of Leeds.

36 Hoggart, *A Sort of Clowning, op cit*, p54.

37 Hoggart, letter to Dobrée, No.19, *op cit*.

38 Richard Hoggart, letter to Bonamy Dobrée, No.128, Tues. 10 Feb., no year but before 1951, Dobrée Collection, University of Leeds. Who this group were is unclear. It may have been associated with the journal *Humanitas*, which Hoggart occasionally wrote for, or inspired by the teaching of Father Herbert Rickabee at Manchester University – some other adult tutors who converted to Roman Catholicism, possibly under his influence, included Walter Stein and Roy Shaw at Leeds. Jacques Maritain's *Art Scholastique*, which had recently been translated, may have been a touchstone for the group.

39 Hoggart, *A Sort of Clowning, op cit*, p114.

40 An arrangement was made with Raybould where Hoggart's old patch and even his house were taken over by a new Leeds staff tutor, the sociologist John Rex.

41 Hoggart, *A Sort of Clowning, op cit*, p92.

42 *Ibid*, p121.

43 *Ibid*, p126.

44 *Ibid*, p129.

45 *Ibid*.

46 Not only in Britain, of course, but in the work of, for example, Levi-Strauss in France whose 'The Structural Study of Myth' and *Tristes Tropiques* appeared in 1955. Although there is no evidence that Hoggart was aware of Levi-Strauss at this time or arguments within current French thought, the correspondence of interest was to prove crucial for later developments and may have inspired the

programme of translations into English undertaken by the New Left.

47 Hoggart, *A Sort of Clowning, op cit*, p96. This stress on experience rather than theory, although ultimately problematical, is an important rejoinder to those over-theoreticised accounts of the formation of British cultural studies which tend to neglect the context of its own formation.

48 Brian Doyle, *English and Englishness*, Methuen, London 1989.

49 Hoggart, *A Sort of Clowning, op cit*, p134.

50 *Ibid*, p135.

51 *Ibid*.

52 Noel Stock, *The Life of Ezra Pound*, Penguin, London 1974, p452.

53 Hoggart, *A Sort of Clowning, op cit*, p141.

54 *Ibid*, p142.

55 One of my copies of the *Uses* belonged to Jim Roche who was until 1956 a Communist Party organiser in Yorkshire, born and brought up in Leeds, and who with Edward Thompson and John Saville, was involved in setting up the *Reasoner*. This is covered with his own notes and comments which both take issue with and enthusiastically concur with Hoggart's observations.

56 Hoggart, *A Sort of Clowning, op cit*, p94.

57 Hoggart, *Speaking to Each Other, op cit*, p239.

58 E.P. Thompson, 'The Politics of Theory', in R. Samuel (ed.) *People's History and Socialist Theory*, Routledge & Kegan Paul, London 1981, p397.

59 Quoted in Julia Swindells and Lisa Jardine, *What's Left, Women in Culture and the Labour Movement*, Routledge, London 1990, p124.

60 Beatrix Campbell, *The Road to Wigan Pier Revisited*, London p222.

61 Swindells and Jardine, *What's Left, op cit*, p125.

62 See Michael Collins, *Adult Education as Vocation*, Routledge, London 1991.

7.

Edward Thompson and the West Riding: Cold War and cultural struggle

A Cold War appointment

At the age of 24 Thompson had completed his degree at Cambridge with a first in the History tripos part one, had served three years in the war, worked in the railway brigade in Yugoslavia and Bulgaria, and had spent some time in the USA. He had taken a war degree in 1946 but stayed on for another year undertaking 'research of a largely undirected nature in English literature and social history'. [1] He really wanted to be a poet but he had long had an interest in adult education and, as it was unlikely he could live by his writing, he decided to try teaching.

During the year Thompson spent on his private reading and researches and 'working on some writing on my own account' [2] he served his apprenticeship as a part-time tutor for the WEA, and in April 1948 he applied for the post of staff tutor in the newly-formed Department of Extra-Mural Studies at the University of Leeds. His mentor in this was Frank Jacques, District Secretary of the WEA's Eastern District, based in Cambridge. Jacques knew and liked his father, Edward Thompson senior, who was a distinguished specialist in Indian history and literature. Thompson junior, he told Raybould, had inherited much of his father's character and charm and was destined to become a top class tutor. [3] In his letter of reference in

144

support of Thompson's application, he wrote that Thompson had 'speedily developed an excellent technique as a teacher, and succeeded in stimulating and holding the interest of his students at a very high level in places which, in the past, had proved to be difficult terrain for tutors of some considerable experience'. [4] Thompson had proved himself an energetic and able tutor and Jacques would have 'used him much more widely had he decided to stay on'. [5]

But Thompson had already decided to move on. In his letter of application he reckoned he could offer teaching in three areas of relative expertise, history and political science, international relations and English literature. His qualifications for the first were self-evident. On the second, international relations, he said that he had taken no course of studies covering it but was very actively interested in it, having learned about Indian affairs from his father, and spent war service in Africa, Italy and Austria, followed by two months in the USA and two months in Yugoslavia and Bulgaria. He had also taken on ABCA and wall-newspaper work while in the army, as part of his regimental officer's duties. [6] By this time he had even written and published an account of those experiences. Perhaps his reasons for offering English literature were most interesting. He frankly confessed to having no qualifications whatsoever for lecturing in it, but said that it 'has long been my chief interest, both in my attempts as a practising writer and as a field of study'. [7] He confessed that his knowledge was unorthodox and patchy but that the discipline of teaching a course would force him into systematic study.

Jacques, who was his chief referee for the post, was almost unstinting in his praise. Thompson was a charmer but there were some qualifications. Dwelling on the 'objectivity' of his teaching, Jacques made plain that although it was beyond question, 'if he had an interpretation of any factor or sequence of factors which he felt it important to contribute to the discussions, he did so, being extremely careful to emphasise that this was merely an interpretation, his view, etc.' [8] What signals would this send to the Registrar, intended or otherwise?

His reservations became clearer in a private and confidential letter addressed to Raybould personally, sent three days later on

17 April 1948 where he expressed some thoughts of the kind normally exchanged on the telephone. Yes, Thompson had inherited many of his father's great abilities, but there was a great 'but' underlined for emphasis: *'But* – he is a member of the C.P., and a very sincere one, if you know what I mean by that, and do not dismiss it as an impossibility'. [9] It had obviously given Jacques great heartache to reveal this, so much so that his syntax becomes overstrained:

> I tell you this because, so far as I can contrive to prevent it, I have accord to any C.P. member the chance to use the opportunity presented by groups of students for their indoctrination. And have been thoroughly cursed and hated, and openly attacked for this ... I only weary you with what would otherwise be complete irrelevancies, to try to shew that I think there really is something potentially very fine about Thompson. And that I know his integrity to be of an unusual order. [10]

Thompson thus had great potential. He had taken a wrong turning perhaps, taken up a youthful enthusiasm, or caught an ideological infection, but, with time, he would come good.

> He's a good teacher, who will improve and reach the very top class. And the greatest means to the improvement still necessary (remember his comparative youth, inexperience) will be because he is so keen and that will bring out of him all that his students need from or demand of him. In patience, in sympathetic understanding, in unremitting labour, hard and endless. [11]

So the discipline of almost biblical labour would temper his steel and bring him to the paths of righteousness. Jacques's severe Puritanism, echoing what was at the heart of the great tradition in adult education, compelled him to speak out, but he also knew what was required to draw the deviant back to the fold. Jacques let Thompson know at once about his letter to Raybould. 'Do believe me', he implored Thompson, 'that this is not an unkindly act, nor one born of the recent decision to purge ourselves with hyssop in high quarters, but out of regard for both you and the W.E.A.'. [12] This was almost certainly a reference to the Wedgwood Memorial College affair. Ernest Green the National Secretary of the WEA, partly in response to accusations by the TUC General Council of communist bias in trade union schools conducted by some members of the Oxford Delegacy, had decided to confront John Vickers, the communist Warden of the Wedgwood Memorial College. There followed some fraternal bloodletting as a result of which the Oxford Tutorial Classes Committee held an inquiry into the Queen's College trade union school, about which there had been allegations. Despite the uproar the inquiry found only that the allegations were 'somewhat imprecise' and that communist tutors were not *per se* unfit to be tutors. John Vickers's contract was not renewed the following year. [13] However, as a result of these and other allegations which marked the onset of the Cold War it was clear that an informal blacklist of communist tutors was being drawn up. [14]

Jacques, while well-known for his uncompromising attacks on the communist and far left, was not content to tar Thompson with the same brush. Indeed, as his again near-biblical language displayed, he felt that men with his energy were essential for the health of 'the movement', but there was another big But: 'But others beside myself, I'm very glad to say, who cherish the people who are the W.E.A., are similarly determined that, so far as it can be prevented, the opportunities presented by these same good people – for good they are, and often great, – shall not be used for their indoctrination by any one, be he Pollitt or Pope'. [15] Thompson was counselled, as were a whole generation of adult tutors on the left, not to let his politics interfere with his teaching.

Raybould's response to Jacques's letter was to hold back for some weeks and to consult with Fred Sedgwick, the District Secretary of the Yorkshire (North) WEA district. ('We still feel that we would like to think a little longer about it as there are so many tricky issues involved.' [16]) It is likely that Sedgwick's wisdom prevailed for, although more than a little suspicious of communist activities, he would not discriminate against individual party members. Much later, in a memorial speech for Sedgwick,Thompson spoke of his 'active toleration', rather than mere tolerance, of political positions he disagreed with. [17]

As so often when he found his beliefs challenged, Jacques's letter drew a long and eloquent reply from Thompson, which provides a memorable statement of his youthful relationship to

Marxism – Marxism, interestingly, rather than communism. He began almost by thanking Jacques for letting Raybould know he was a communist because he did not want a job where he would have to keep it dark, as he had had to in the army, even when the colonel talked of 'the next war with Russia'. [18] He thought anyway that Raybould already knew because he had informed Guy Chapman so that there should be no misunderstanding. Although courteous, his letter was not going to let Jacques entirely off the hook:

> On the question of principle, of course, I would ask if you would take the same precautions with a member of the Conservative Party, – who in my opinion might be a real danger to the movement? There is still a myth in some circles that anything on the left is 'political', whereas a dyed-in-the-wool Tory interpretation of international affairs, the British Constitution, or the Glorious Revolution is 'non-political'. [19]

Thompson recounted an incident in which his father was refused permission to do some voluntary educational work with troops on Salisbury Plain because he had invited such dangerous leftists as the classicist Gilbert Murray to address them. He also, he confessed, had had his own fears about indoctrination from 'immature partisans of all creeds and parties' especially in Cambridge, but he felt that there was misunderstanding of what a 'Marxist interpretation' of a subject may be, which was not to be confused with 'Communist indoctrination'.

> Any Marxist worth the name is only interested in finding out the truth. In history for example he will make use of the Marxist guide lines, and according to the Marxist method he will examine social relations, the ownership of the means of production, the changing relations of production, at a very early stage in any enquiry. But if he is worth anything he will know that he can't 'interpret' any period or problem until he knows the facts inside out. What you, I suspect, quite rightly, fear is the Marxist, who spends his time giving a shoddy general interpretation, ramming class-war down the throats of his class, without really knowing his stuff. I don't think you would object to Christopher Hill, for instance, or Maurice Dobb giving their interpretation of the facts and the causations of a period on which they were admitted experts ? [20]

His defence of history teaching was in fact impeccably liberal, but with the important reservation that it was not possible ever to be impartial about the facts deployed:

> No-one can suppress his attitude in teaching history, whether he's a Fabian, a Tory or a Marxist. If he could then history would only have entertainment value for people today, and would have nothing to do with citizenship in the present. The important thing is that the class should always be given a fair cross section of the facts on which to make up their own minds, and that the lecturer insofar as it's in his power be intent on giving them this raw material for their own minds to work on, and not on converting them to his attitude without going through the whole process of making up their minds for themselves. But an attitude he *must* have (even unconsciously) if he's going to select or reason facts at all, and to ask him to suppress it totally can only be to ask him to give some other presentation with which he is not in agreement. [21]

Thompson thus felt it was impossible to divorce presenting historical facts from an attitude towards those facts. But he also felt he was insufficiently familiar with any period to give a full Marxist interpretation of it. He was, however, opposed to methods of teaching history, such as he had encountered at Cambridge, which attempted to separate out particular factors, such as Constitutional, political theory or economics, for exclusive study. 'I think it just makes nonsense of history, and that the first fascinating thing to show is the intricate pattern of reactions, interrelations and causations at every level'. [22] He said that he would, moreover, jib at the approaches of Bryant and Rowse and warn his classes against the 'misleading and shoddy' social history of Trevelyan who 'has forgotten all the clouds and scrupulously painted all the silver linings, looked at the Industrial Revolution through a glass of mellow port, dismissed the Scottish evictions in about six lines, etc. etc'. [23] He was also not convinced that Cole's view of Chartism and the Webbs' of trade unionism were the only ones. His concern was to express these relations as a totality:

149

On the positive side I should always try to show an organic development in the historical period. That is, emphatically not an inevitable development or a development necessarily for the better, but a casual [causal?] relationship between one great event and the other; showing that, while we can never predict the course of history, we may by the study of past history gain the insight to win a measure of control over the present. [24]

Thompson could not see how this could possibly be conceived of as indoctrination by Jacques. Significantly, he told Jacques that he was keen to teach courses in English literature because this was a field far less open to accusations. He concluded the letter by asking Jacques to indulge his desire to lay out his stall, because Marxists were so often accused of having axes to grind when in practice many of them were 'far more tentative and less prejudiced in their approach than the average Whig'. [25]

This letter concluded the correspondence and Thompson was subsequently appointed to the post. Raybould was later proud to have appointed a communist, but may have been careful not to appoint any more and for all the communists who were appointed because of their father's good name, how many others were the victims of the private note or phone call? Thompson just squeezed in before the door closed. As John Saville recalled in a recent History Workshop Conference devoted to Edward Thompson, by 1948 there were virtually no longer any jobs given to communists in higher education and even Christopher Hill was worried about the renewal of his fellowship. It was clearly a close call for Thompson and we can only speculate whether, without his appointment, what he called his 'West Riding book' *The Making of the English Working Class*, would ever have been written.

Raybould's department had been formed only two years earlier under the benevolent eye of Charles Morris, the Vice Chancellor, and in the teeth of opposition from the WEA under George Thompson. But Thompson had retired and his place as District Secretary was taken by Fred Sedgwick, who although utterly committed to working-class education, had nothing like George Thompson's suspicion of the university. The generation of class warriors which had made the WEA such a force in Yorkshire in the inter-war years was also melting away, many thinking that with the election of the Labour government and the foundation of the welfare state, their job was done. The district, once proud of having probably the highest proportion of manual workers in its classes, was like the rest of the country seeing a rapid decline. In the ten years from the end of the war, nationally, the proportion of manual workers in classes fell to only 16 per cent (although in Yorkshire the figure was probably significantly higher). Edward Thompson's colleague, the historian J.F.C. Harrison, noted also the decline in membership and income, and that, in order to fulfil the demand for Extra-mural provision not met by the WEA, universities were forced to expand non-WEA provision. [26]

Thompson undoubtedly believed he was coming to the heartland of the English working class movement. In fact, he found in many places moribund branch organisations dominated by an old guard which, although still full of rhetorical fire, often lacked the necessary energy for the educational class struggle. Thus, where he expected to find hot-beds of militancy he was greeted with some suspicion and not a little ennui. As he wrote to Raybould some years later, 'when I came I had an over rosy picture of the organisational strength and initiative of WEA branches, went through a period of disillusion and as a result felt inclined to point out shortcomings where they contradicted the somewhat optimistic generalisations about the WEA sometimes put forward.' [27]

He refused to despair and the evidence of his personal commitment and organisational energy is widespread. He settled in Halifax, rather than Leeds, where he systematically worked with the local West Riding branches to establish classes, making himself available for single lectures, fixing up preparatory meetings in the summer and autumn before the courses began, personally visiting branch members, and recruiting new and often young members himself. In his reply to Raybould's questionnaire about branch organisation, he gave the example of Todmorden and Middlesbrough where his classes were made difficult in the early stages by the extremely weak state of branch organisation and he noticeably fails to conceal his impatience:

Press advertising and a public lecture at Todmorden brought one or two recruits: but all other work was done by the Branch Chairman ... who found the work beyond him, while the Secretary ... proved to have been a mistaken election, since he did nothing (as Mr. Sedgwick and Mrs. Race will confirm). I did some door to door canvassing of old members myself, but found most of them too old to be much interested. [28]

At Middlesbrough the situation was rescued but at a high cost:

The Secretary was taken ill at a critical time. Even before this, my suggestion that instead of a preliminary meeting a well advertised public lecture should be held was not taken as seriously as it should have been. Only 7 or 8 attended the 'lecture'. It should be said that the first class members took upon themselves the job of recruiting, did it well, and the class is established. However, one result of this is that the majority of class members are teachers & clerical workers, among whom the first class members were found: i.e. no fresh ground has been broken. [29]

In his early years Thompson therefore found himself in the anomalous but not unusual position, as a staff tutor, of having to stimulate the voluntary movement. He concludes his letter to Raybould in true missionary style: 'I think we should ask for more support from old class members, who retain an interest in the WEA, and in large centres, retain their membership, in interesting their own friends or members of their trade union, party, or other organisation. How far, and in what way, it is possible to get this sense of responsibility re-established is another matter'. [30]

Despite his impatience with the movement which so clearly failed to live up to his expectations, he proved an able and a popular tutor. For the first three years he taught only courses in English literature. His syllabi, although quite eclectic, were quite conventional for the period with no obvious Marxist pitch to them. The most featured critic on his book lists is F.R. Leavis. This no doubt reflects the bias of the departmental library which supplied the books, but also the virtual lack of an English Marxist critical tradition. For his 1949-50 Bingley literature class his 'further reading' list did include Christopher Caudwell's *Illusion and Reality* and Ralph Fox's *The Novel and the People*, but as Andy Croft notes, buried in amongst the massed tomes of Richards, Leavis, Forster and Cecil, they must have looked like 'rare and rapidly obsolete products of a stunted tradition'. [31] But Croft asks, what other Marxist critical texts could he have included? 'The critical writings of Gramsci, Benjamin and Bakhtin were then unknown in Britain, Brecht was known only as a dramatist and Lukács's *Studies in European Realism* was not published in English until that year'. [32] He was happiest teaching poetry rather than fiction, which he found rather arduous and intractable and frequently invited specialists such as colleagues at Leeds, Arnold Kettle and Kenneth Muir, to take classes. On one occasion, Croft notes, the Bradford novelist John Braine was invited to a class. In the manner then pioneered by the Leavises, Thompson also analysed advertisements and newspapers.

A curious feature of the period from 1951-1955, when he was writing *William Morris,* is just how infrequently Morris turns up in Thompson's syllabi (although this might be due to the lack of a popular edition: the Pelican edition of Morris's selected writings and design edited by Asa Briggs, then at Leeds, did not appear until 1962 and Lawrence and Wishart's *Three Works,* edited by A.L. Morton, not until 1968). Croft points out that during this period Thompson was increasingly teaching social history courses and his literature teaching declined, but then *William Morris* is as much a work of history as it is of criticism. In fact, as we shall see later, John Goode points out that in this respect the book was peculiarly ahead of its time. [33]

As with all new tutors Thompson's classes were inspected periodically by a senior tutor. Bill Baker visited his literature class in Cleckheaton on a cold night in January 1949 and wrote to Raybould that he did not expect to find Thompson at ease with a class because of some views he had aired in the Tutors' group, which betrayed, Baker thought, 'lack of knowledge of the character of W.E.A. classes'. [34] His heart sank even lower when Thompson unexpectedly sprang a play reading on the group. But the class joined in 'with abandon' at times and Thompson gave 'just the right kind of judicious introduction on "background" and comments on the text' of Jonson's *The Alchemist.* Baker also found that the class were getting a lot out of young Thompson and that even the branch chairman, whose passion was for politics and economics, found himself surprised to be enjoying it so much. The chairman, said Baker, 'was impressed by the way in which Thompson wove a pattern through his talks' and enjoyed especially the section on the Romantic poets. Baker was quite impressed but withheld judgement for the time being. By the end of the year however he had no such reservations. Thompson's literature class at Bingley was, he told Raybould, one of the most satisfactory classes that he had ever visited, 'quite first-class' in fact. [35] But there were qualifications of another kind:

> The class clearly appreciated Thompson; one keen member told me in conversation how much he was getting out of the course. He regretted that they had no manual workers in the class (though they were all branch members of the W.E.A.), and he asked me whether the W.E.A. provided more elementary or popular courses, for he doubted whether the course they were enjoying would be suitable for a group of manual workers. Quite clearly Thompson's material and method would need modification with a group of lower attainments or capacity, and I am inclined to think that he is happier with the kind of group which Bingley has provided. [36]

To be sure Thompson enjoyed the stimulation offered by an intelligent and well-read group as Baker opines but he was not content with only that kind of group. He went deeper into the working-class heartlands of the West Riding, offering classes where, in conventional terms, there was little joy to be had. One such class was in the village of Shepley near Huddersfield. It was a struggle, no doubt a class struggle, with a class of older workers, small in numbers, and finding the textual analysis Thompson required of them more than taxing after a hard day's work. It demanded much of the tutor to find a cultural coding for literary criticism outside the academy in a working-class community. Thompson made it clear in his report that such classes were for him much more vital than the more culturally congenial classes of the larger towns. But he had to justify them against Raybould's demands for 'university standards'. Thompson argued that such classes, may be performing a more worthwhile function than a class of far higher standards, confining its membership to the professional section of a large centre of population. In the latter case the result may be only to encourage an intellectual elite. At Shepley, a small industrial valley, it is necessary to grapple more realistically with the problems of standards and popular culture. It is unlikely that the active trade-unionist will find in himself a specialist interest in problems of literary criticism or 'intellectual climate'. Must he therefore be denied an opportunity to gain acquaintance with major works of literature under qualified guidance? Even if the going is hard and the results unspectacular, this sort of class must be kept alive. [37]

Such an argument was generally in tune with George Thompson's *Field of Studies for WEA Classes* (1938), that the importance of extra-mural work lay less in meeting the demands of the academy than in nurturing a working-class community. But Edward Thompson differed in maintaining a belief in the absolute value of *literary* studies, which he was confident could be disentangled from the 'bourgeois' values of which George Thompson was profoundly suspicious.

The question of university standards, encouraged by Raybould, dominated debate in the department in its early years and it is astonishing to find that within two years of being appointed, Thompson takes a fundamentally oppositional stance. In one of a remarkable series of discussion papers published within the department during 1950, Thompson took issue not only with Raybould but with a number of his colleagues, including Roy Shaw. He was particularly unhappy with Raybould's coveted 'Olympian detachment' of the extra-mural tutor who moved somewhat like a god among the lower orders dispensing enlightenment. This was not how he saw it nor, he argued, how the authors of the WEA tutorial class movement had seen it in 1903. The mythical notion of the detached 'objectivity' of the tutor, he believed, could not be sustained and only made matters worse because the aim of the movement was precisely to heal 'the divorce between the institutions of higher education and the centres of social experience'. [38] The obsession with university standards unbalanced the implied dialectic, by failing to value the experience and understanding of the class members. The aim of his paper was, therefore, to suggest that the use of the term 'university standards' only sanctified a theory of adult education which was actually hostile to the healthy development of working-class adult education. It was necessary on the contrary, 'to suggest that the dynamic of the tutorial class movement has been derived not from any one educational theory or practised inculcation of "attitudes", but from a fruitful conflict or interplay between the scholarship of the universities on the one hand and the experience and social dynamic of the students on the other'. [39]

This was much closer to George Thompson's view of the matter. He had not wanted control of the tutorial class movement to slip into the hands of the universities, and accordingly had opposed the formation of a department of extra-mural studies at Leeds. However, for Edward Thompson the dialectic should not be unbalanced the other way with the assumption that 'experience' or 'social purpose' was all, because study and the desire to master a discipline were also vital elements in the formation of true understanding. The tutor, while being prepared to have hitherto accepted academic judgements corrected in the light of the student's experience, must not on the other hand 'abandon his teaching' to the necessary distortions and limitations of this experience: 'Thus in a healthy tutorial class, a struggle constantly took place between the scholarship of the tutor and the social dynamic of the movement'. [40] It was precisely this dialectic which had made the tutorial class movement so full of possibilities, 'the interplay and conflict of abstract, passive, contemplative experience and concrete active, productive experience'. [41]

But just how healthy was the movement now? Against those who, with the weary fatalism of worldly academia, were preparing to accuse him of romanticising the movement whose cause he embraced, Thompson produced a passionate defence, which foreshadowed the enormous project he was embarking on. He accepted that much of the life had drained out of the movement but,

It is easy to deplore the loss of social dynamic and the changing social character of classes, and lay the blame on the workers themselves or upon a particular social situation over which we have no control. But we cannot sit around waiting for some social cataclysm to arouse the same kind of dynamic as has been evident before. We must use every means to ensure the maximum efficiency in the changed social context. [42]

One strategy the WEA might therefore take up was,

that there should be more provision of classes in social history, and especially history of the working-class movement, taught through the extensive use of local illustrations and documents, on the pattern of many successful classes in the Eastern District ... Such classes might help to effect a loosening up of the situation, by placing the gains of the present in the perspective of the struggles of the past, and by prompting a desire to extend and defend them. [43]

So by seamlessly joining education to political consciousness and the desire for change, Thompson made it clear that he thought it impossible for tutors to remain detached in the approved academic manner. Tutors, moreover, occupied a privileged position within the movement.

We should be constantly aware that weaknesses in the movement may reflect failures in our teaching, or an incorrect attitude on our part. Why for instance, do we find trades councils, trades unions, and local Labour party branches in the West Riding today rejecting the approaches of the WEA in favour of a loyalty to the N.C.L.C., even when the N.C.L.C. has ceased to provide classes? Can it be that the atmosphere of our classes is too 'pure and clear'? Can it be as tutors that we have given the impression that we welcome them into our classes only on our terms, asking them to leave their suspicion outside the class-room door: instead of welcoming them in, suspicion and all, yes, even welcoming the suspicion as a rich ingredient of the class? Can it be that we are (without deliberate intent) allowing the University to stifle the WEA? [44]

Here clearly outlined was his own project which led to *The Making of the English Working Class*: the reconstruction of working-class histories as struggles rather than as the process of an inevitable evolution towards progress and enlightenment. Some years later he was to criticise Raymond

Williams's *Long Revolution* precisely for its failure to mark the element of struggle in the creation of culture. As Fred Inglis remarked in his study of British socialism, Edward Thompson's *The Making of the English Working Class* provides 'a new past to live from; it changes the social memory so that differently understanding how the present came about, the agent thinks forward to a new set of possibilities'. [45]

Nevertheless, although Raybould was the ultimate target of this polemic, he was not unsympathetic to Thompson's point of view, as long as the outcome could be seen as scholarly. Thompson's next step was to begin the process of rescuing the documents and records of what he readily recognised were the terminal stages of the old West Riding Labour movement. He convinced Raybould that the department should systematically set about collecting them and establish an archive. Raybould's response was to send out a circular to co-operative, trade-union and ILP branches asking for their help in achieving this aim. His letter was couched very much in the terms set by Thompson. The interest of his tutors, he said, was not just in teaching but in researching various aspects of the history of the movement 'work which the department strongly supports and wishes to extend'. [46] He continued,

> We believe that in preserving the memory of the past of the Labour movement and in analysing its development, particularly in our own West Riding – probably the most important part of the country as far as Labour history is concerned – they are performing a vital function for the movement, since failure to understand the past leads inevitably to confusion in present thinking. [47]

There was no mistaking Thompson's excitement over the project, when he wrote a month later to a colleague:

> p.s. Did I tell you I have now established contact with the Bradford ILP and paid a visit to inspect their records just before Xmas. I have given them a copy of Raybould's letter, and they have promised to consider it at their next meeting, Jan 10th, I think. There is every chance that we may get the whole lot, since there are only a few old people hanging on. The whole lot includes valuable

minutes from the 1890s, many of Jowett's paper (sic) and cuttings, bound volumes of the old Bradford Pioneer, etc etc. If they reply officially to the Department please let me know at once. We shall need a van and also some tact to get the lot away! [48]

A glimpse of the kind of history Thompson was *not* interested in comes in a letter from Thompson to Stanley. Joe Thornton, a retired Leeds Labour alderman, for whom Thompson had great respect, wanted help in publishing his reminiscences, but Thompson was of the opinion that they were likely to be 'excessively anecdotal and rambling and of little historical or scientific value'. [49]

As well as devoting time to building this archive, Thompson listened intently to the experiences narrated by his students, well aware that these might be the last of that heroic generation which founded the modern labour movement. As late as 1964 he still heard reminiscences of conditions of work which he felt really belonged to the period of Engels's *Condition of the Working Class in England*:

> Within living memory in Morley, it seems, miners have worked lying down in eighteen inch seams, children have been in the mills at the age of nine, urine has been collected from pub urinals for scouring ... It is difficult to believe that the Industrial Revolution has yet occurred in Morley, and next year's syllabus (in the later nineteenth century) will seem like a tour through the space age. [50]

In these classes his method of getting students to work on original documents stimulated recollection, discussion and argument, the latter being essential to what he regarded as a successful class. Thus textuality, the stylistic study of documents and hermeneutics, disciplines which passed over from literary study, became essential tools in the study and writing of history. This corresponded to Thompson's idea of interdisciplinary work and his notion that to subject memory and experience to the test of academic discipline lifted it out of the realm of mere antiquarianism. What distinguished Thompson's work and that of a number of his colleagues was the belief that his students' own experience could be successfully interrogated for historical material if it was treated in the proper context of disciplined study.

This approach can properly be called a cultural study: one which combines elements of academic literary and historical practice, interacting with popular culture. But what did Thompson understand by the term 'popular culture' which he had used in his report on the Shepley class?

Popular Culture and Cultural Struggle

Given that Thompson's approaches to culture are usually a response to a particular context rather than the product of structured theorising, a number of elements can be identified: hostility to American commercialised popular culture, an active critique of the orthodox Marxist reduction of cultural phenomena to some economic 'base', and a belief in the historical strength of the English subaltern classes to resist hegemonic culture through their own rituals and institutions. He also believed in the value of the nineteenth-century Romantic critique of capitalism, which, although it emanated from middle-class and lower middle-class intellectual and artistic dissidents, was capable of integration into the socialist project.

In this sense, Thompson shared Karl Mannheim's and C. Wright Mills's views on the relative freedom and historical duty of the intellectual. Like Ruskin, Carlyle, Morris, Tawney and Cole, who saw their primary duty to the 'people' rather than the academy, Thompson, with Raymond Williams, has to be seen as the last in the line of great public intellectuals. He was first and foremost an 'educator' but one who changed its nineteenth-century assumptions. Although Dorothy Thompson recently characterised his approach to teaching as a 'master/apprentice relationship',[51] Thompson saw his responsibilities as not simply to lay before his adult classes his trained intellect and understanding, but also to encourage his students to value their own understanding and experience – often in face of what 'education' was telling them. The conservative nineteenth-century view of working people – that they were empty vessels into which, if anything decent was to be made of them, learning had to be poured, or alternatively, that they were cesspools of superstition and irrationality, which had to be scoured clean by the academic sanitation department – was abhorrent to him.

160

On the other hand Thompson was sceptical of that Rousseauesque populism which assumed common people were *instinctively* in possession of the truth. Culture was the product of creative work and intellectual understanding, although it might well be embodied in popular *collective* forms whose origins were lost. In 'Homage to Tom Maguire' he wrote, 'Nothing in history happens spontaneously, nothing worthwhile is achieved without the expense of intellect and spirit'.[52] Like Raymond Williams, he believed in a continuous popular culture which was persistently anti-hegemonic even if at times it seemed to use the language and symbolism of the dominant culture. He argued vigorously against Williams's view, however, that this had evolved a common way of life. Instead, he insisted, it should viewed as a way of *struggle*, because in so far as a consensus had emerged, it was only the temporary resolution of class conflict, in which the dominant order was forced to concede something of value to the subordinate classes in order to extract their agreement to be ruled. In this view he clearly paralleled Gramsci's notion of 'hegemony', when Gramsci himself was relatively unknown, even inside British Communist circles. While Williams appeared to suggest that the evolution of consensus was an organic process, Thompson insisted that only further struggle and resolute defence of the gains made were essential. As a result of these arguments in the early New Left it was clear that Williams modified his own approach towards the Marxist approach Thompson was suggesting.

He also set a high value on the Romantic critique of capitalism which Williams had charted in his book *Culture and Society*. William Blake in particular, as Thompson demonstrates so powerfully in his final book, epitomised the strength of the poetic refusal of the 'cash nexus' of market values. While Williams tends to stay within the 'literary' moment of the critique, Thompson shows the embeddedness of Blake's ideas in real historical movements. Blake is seen luminously in the context of Muggletonian dissent and is thus rescued from the academy and returned to the 'people'.

161

Literature and Poetry

For both Williams and Thompson literature and literary criticism have had a special place in the cultural struggle. Thompson's historical work is replete with literary references and, perhaps not unproblematically, he is happy to use literary works as original source documents. What he does here, however, is not merely to show how literature reflects society, as Marxist orthodoxy of the time would have it, but how it creatively works back on that society and revises it: Marxist heresy perhaps, but one of which Marx himself was guilty as when he said in the *Communist Manifesto*, that 'All things solid melt into air'. As John Goode has argued, 'Thompson's concept of consciousness as historical agent teaches us more about the actual behaviour of literary texts in history than most of the analyses of the behaviour of signifiers'.[53] Poets occupy a special political place:

> What a remarkable contribution to our nation's political discourse they've made – think of Langland, Chaucer, Marlowe, Milton, Marvell, Pope, Wordsworth, Blake, Shelley, Byron ... Their voices weren't some extra condiment like H.P. Sauce, shaken on the British plate. They weren't interior decorators who made the place more pretty. They were part of what life was about, they asked where society was going.[54]

Following Christopher Caudwell, whom he greatly admired, Thompson asserted that through its power of transforming and estranging conventional modes of thought, the 'poetic' has been an essential cultural tool. Thompson understood Caudwell as saying something deeply at odds with the orthodox Marxist approach to culture at that time, which was that the concrete modes of poetry can reach deeply into language's normal affective modes in such a way as to convey an experience which can totally transform the subject's attitude to life. 'It was', he said, 'this direct concrete operative power of poetry which continues to afford a challenge, the possibility of revolutionising inherited modes of consciousness'.[55] This is, of course, a recognisably Romantic stance, but Caudwell's contribution to it had been to attempt a materialist understanding of the process. Thus the 'literary', for Thompson, occupies a special place in anti-hegemonic popular struggle and can't be dismissed as either part of the hegemonic cannon, or merely high-brow decoration. Poetry belongs properly to popular culture.

Thompson's historical work, John Goode reminds us, actually begins with a literary biography, that of William Morris, in 1955. In his first years at Leeds, as we have seen, he taught only literature classes and this massive work was begun as a way of discussing with his working-class students, 'the significance of literature to their lives'.[56] He continued: 'I was seized by Morris. I thought, why is this man thought to be an old fuddy-duddy? He is right in with us still ... Morris took the decision that I would have to present him. In the course of doing this I became much more serious about being a historian'.[57] *William Morris* was written because Thompson wanted to illuminate a cathartic moment in British history when a great poet had thrown in his lot with socialism, something which the academic historical record had erased. 'Morris' exists as sign in more ways than one and opened up another front in Thompson's cultural struggle. Morris's 'moral realism' was, for Thompson in 1955, a critique of the Stalinist Marxism of the British Communist Party's leadership.[58]

The term 'popular culture', however, was not one to which he was unequivocally committed, and he uses it in ways with which some contemporary theorists would not be comfortable. It does not appear at all in the index of *The Making*. The notion of a popular culture as a spontaneous effusion was quite foreign to him and he had no sympathy for the elision of popular with 'mass' or 'commercial' culture. From the beginning, Thompson took a high tone. The popular culture he was concerned with was, as we have seen, a product of work and intellect on popular experience. Nothing for him could be worse than subversion of this activity by the flood of Hollywood films, comic books, and easy consumerism of the post-war period. As a young communist in the early 1950s he believed that, because of the betrayal of the ideals of socialism by the failing Labour government, the British working class was about to be swamped by American popular culture: 'In place of the great proletarian values revealed in class-solidarity and militancy, we now have, even among sections of our working-class movement, the values of private living growing up – the private fears and neuroses, the self-interest and timid individualism fostered by pulp magazines and Hollywood films'.[59]

Thompson characterised this as the 'slaughter house culture' of an imperialist power already deeply implicated in a hot war in the far east, where it was napalming Korean civilians, while simultaneously generating a cold war against the Soviet Union. This view was in line with the new cultural policy of the British Communist Party, at last waking up to the need for the 'cultural struggle'. But this was not unique to the world view of communism, and American popular culture was also demonised by F.R. Leavis and the *Scrutiny* group. Richard Hoggart, too, was alarmed about the effect of mass culture, especially its newest element, television, on the sturdy independence of the working class:

> Most mass entertainments are in the end what D.H. Lawrence described as 'anti-life'. They are full of corrupt brightness, of improper appeals and moral evasions. To recall instances: they tend towards a view of the world in which progress is conceived as a seeking of material possessions, equality as moral levelling, and freedom as the ground for endless irresponsible pleasure.[60]

Most tutors in adult education shared a common repugnance of 'mass' culture, which they wanted to distinguish from something that was authentically 'working class' or 'popular' culture, which they linked with historically broad-based but also moral movements. In *Customs in Common* (1993), Thompson cautions against sweeping generalisations on 'popular culture', and he stresses the element of plurality:

> a culture is also a pool of diverse resources, in which traffic passes between the literate and the oral, the superordinate and the subordinate, the village and the metropolis; it is an arena of conflictual elements, which requires some compelling pressure – as, for example nationalism or prevalent religious orthodoxy or class-consciousness – to take form as a 'system'. And indeed the very term 'culture', with its cosy invocation of consensus, may serve to distract attention from social and cultural contradictions, from the fractures and oppositions within the whole.[61]

The consequence of this was that unless any instance of 'popular culture' was placed firmly within a specific historical context little could be generalised from it. Indeed Thompson himself in that book is much more interested in what he calls 'the plebeian culture which clothed itself in the rhetoric of "custom".' [62] Even here he is doubtful that it could be completely severed from hegemonic culture as a whole, and he moves to a position of considerable cultural relativity when he suggests that, in different historical contexts the same set of beliefs can have different meanings. In some circumstances he makes clear that so-called 'conservative' customs and traditions, such as, for example, the 'patriotic' agitations on behalf of Queen Caroline may be rebellious. [63] It could be said that popular culture is only of interest for Thompson insofar as it sustains resistance or rebellion. Nevertheless, he did believe in something like a continuous popular culture which was counter-hegemonic: 'a very vigorous self-activating culture of the people, derived from their own experiences and resources. This culture, which may be resistant at many points to any form of exterior domination, constitutes an ever-present threat to official descriptions of reality'. [64]

His specifically Marxist purchase on this populism was, in the words of Ellen Meiksins Wood, to see 'the magnetic force of class in the transformation of a continuous popular culture'. [65] But there is still some ambiguity here, or at least something unresolved it seems, because Thompson wants on the one hand to project a popular culture which is somehow spontaneously self-renewing but, on the other hand, one which had continually to be remade. The question is: remade by whom? What seems to be lacking here, symptomatically perhaps, is some theory of 'the intellectuals'.

As Kate Soper has pointed out, Thompson rejected his friend C. Wright Mills's reliance on intellectuals as the *sole* agent of change (in the face of an 'apathetic' working class) [66], but he was obviously profoundly conscious of his own role in the class struggle as a communist, educator and intellectual. His reluctance to theorise the role of intellectuals may well have been because he was dubious of the category as such – there were, for him, only specific people thinking and acting in specific ways. But Thompson did recognise the existence of special groups within cultures. In his essay 'Outside the Whale' he makes the strong assertion, later picked up by Kate Soper, that 'the shape of cultural history is decided by minorities'. [67] If this is so what has happened to his notion of continuous popular culture? 'Outside the Whale', which first appeared in 1960, was Thompson's critical commentary on George Orwell's apology for intellectual quietism, 'Inside the Whale' – the essay in which Orwell, nearly forty years before Francois Lyotard, announced the death of the grand narratives 'progress' and 'reaction'.

Thompson, by contrast, insisted that intellectuals should play a leading if not to say galvanic role in cultural struggle, and he abhorred the climate of quietism emanating from T.S. Eliot, Orwell, and the unworthier brand of contemporary cynic like Kingsley Amis, which he plainly saw as *trahison des clercs*. What is not so clear, however, is his conception of the relation of intellectuals to the working-class movement. On the one hand he satirised those media commentators who believed that 'Revolutionary ideas were middle-class "constructs"; they never could be engendered of their own accord within the soil of working-class culture, where all ideas and relations are dense, local, particular and inarticulate'. [68] He also had little sympathy for those middle-class intellectuals, fearing their own deracination, 'pressing their noses against the windows of the Working-Men's Institutes and rotting housing estates, seeking to gain vicarious participation in the rituals of the dense and the concrete'. But there was also the fact of 'Marxism', which did not automatically spring from the soil of working-class culture but from the labour of middle-class intellectuals. The problem was in part that the main intermediary between the realm of Marxist ideas and the working class had been, precisely, the Communist Party, and it was here that the role of intellectuals was anything but clear. As the long series of bitter disputes leading up to the break with the party in 1956 and the formation of the *New Reasoner* showed, the party's intellectuals were no longer content to embrace the officially sanctioned version of Marxism.

The British Road to Socialism

For a long time, as Andy Croft makes clear, one of the British Communist Party's most vibrant aspects was its cultural activity. [69] During the 1930s the party was a source of patronage and education for young writers to whom it could offer publication in literary journals and an introduction to left publishing houses like Lawrence and Wishart. At the same time, its active historians' group, under Dona Torr and Christopher Hill, was setting a new agenda for British social history. It was also a profoundly cosmopolitan group; in particular, refugees from Nazism brought non-Soviet European Marxist perspectives like that of the Lukács group and the first translations of Antonio Gramsci. The party acted both as a club providing mutual support and education and as a mentor group. Dissident intellectuals and writers were attracted to it in part because it provided alternative arenas for serious cultural debate to those commanded by Bloomsbury and the aesthetic elite so hated by Leavis, but also because it offered a partisanship with working people.

During the 1930s, the party adopted a relatively laissez-faire approach to its cultural groups and allowed them considerable rein, but later disputes between the groups and the party leadership grew bitter. Initially, the central committee was relatively uninterested in culture or intellectuals, which were regarded as desirable as long as they made no attempt to interfere with party policy but remained largely ornamental. With the onset of the Cold War, however, the party leadership realised the growing political significance of culture and in 1947 established a National Cultural Committee to 'co-ordinate' the work of the ten specialist cultural groups, including the Writers Group, under the chairmanship of Emile Burns. As Andy Croft again notes, the Cold War was shaping up on the literary high ground, as exemplified by Crossman's *The God that Failed*, and increasingly the party's view was that culture was too important to be left to intellectuals.

As the orthodox Marxist models of economic determinism became less defensible, the party was sensitised to the power of ideologies and forms of representation in shaping class consciousness. The Twenty-Second Party Congress, inspired in part by the writing of Mao Tse Tung and the Chinese Revolution, called for a cultural struggle alongside the political struggle. Thus, 'The British Road to Socialism', the party's new political programme, had to be supported by some more developed understanding of what Britishness, or Englishness, actually was. Under the auspices of *Arena*, the most prestigious of the party's cultural journals, a series of important conferences on aspects of culture were held, to which many of the party's intellectuals contributed, including the young Edward Thompson.

These conferences were important in establishing the ground on which the cultural struggle should be fought. In one important sense it was to construct an alternative sense of national identity to that associated with imperialism and oppression. This was the Britain of patriotism without jingoism, of 'dear old England', and the *British* Road to Socialism. It was clear that in these conferences the idea of a militant 'class' culture was strategically giving ground to that of a national 'common' culture. For example, in a conference given over to an examination of Britain's cultural heritage, George Thomson, the classicist and one of the party's most respected intellectuals, argued that it was wrong to think of 'culture' as exclusively bourgeois, since in Britain this so-called bourgeois culture was also the heritage of socialism. It was, as the proletarian philosopher Tommy Jackson had argued, in some senses a revolutionary culture and English literary realism, as Gorky had said, was pioneering. [70] Thomson saw the cultural struggle as having two main thrusts. The first was to encourage 'worker-writers', so that writing was seen not simply as a class-bound activity and would have the effect further of uniting intellectuals with the workers and, most importantly, being *tempered* by them. The second was to interpret the existing cultural heritage in the light of Marxism-Leninism. He gave the fairly uncontroversial example of Gay's *Beggar's Opera* and also he quoted Caudwell's dictum that the struggle should 'drag the past into the present and force the realisation of the future'.

However, since Caudwell's unorthodox approach was regarded by the leadership as heretical if not schismatic, this was more contentious. A fierce debate over Caudwell raged in the pages of the party's journal *The Modern Quarterly* during the period 1950-51 when most of the party's big guns were lined up to demolish him and other dissident intellectuals within the party. But the staunch defence of Caudwell by

George Thomson, in particular, inspired Edward Thompson into re-thinking the role of culture in the class struggle. He was persuaded by Caudwell's refusal of the reduction of consciousness, in orthodox Marxist theory, to passive reflection and mechanical materialism. [71] This broke with the base and superstructure model and allowed a much more flexible interpretation of cultural determinants to be developed. In some ways the use here of Caudwell's cultural theory appears to parallel Gramsci and perhaps to foreshadow Althusser's conception of the 'relative autonomy' of the spheres of ideology.

In his own contribution to the conference called 'The American Threat to British Culture', Thompson made perhaps his first major intervention into the party's cultural debate with a talk on 'William Morris and the Moral Issues Today'. Here he took a militantly vanguardist position, which was that 'we' had to win people for life and not wait for a new kind of person to appear until after the revolution: 'We must change people now, for that is the essence of all our cultural work'. [72] The implication was that cultural activity was relatively independent of economic determinants. Morris's 'moral realism' was clearly in his sights at this time and the significance of the talk is that he interpreted the *political* project of the party as in major part to be achieved through *educational* objectives. This correlates strongly with his professional role as an adult educator.

As we have seen, an equally heated debate over culture was exercising the adult education movement. In the pages of the *Tutors' Bulletin*, in the previous year, Thompson had already urged the WEA to adopt a cultural policy which would give the same amount of energy to campaigning for the extension of cultural facilities to the people as they had given for educational facilities. [73] He urged that the WEA should change its attitude on cultural matters from high-minded and distanced study to actual engagement with living cultural activities. The Shakespeare class, for example, should not turn up its nose at the local amateur dramatic production but get stuck in and dirty its hands with *popular* culture.

Thompson's intervention demonstrated the serious change in direction that younger militants were taking, away from 'pure' politics classes and into the arena of culture. In what appeared to be a serious rapprochement between the traditional class purism of the now retired G.H. Thompson and the culturalism of W.E. Williams, Thompson argued that workers' education had to take into account the 'cultivation of the individual' which was necessary for the education of the 'citizen'. The point of cultural education was to ensure more active participation of 'the movement's' students in the social activity represented by the art under study.

> There is no case for attacking a class in music or literature because it does not produce a crop of Labour councillors, but there may well be a case against a class in which no member became actively engaged in local dramatic or musical societies, gave service on a library committee, promoted the activities of the Arts Council, entered controversies in the local press upon municipal theatre or music, or kept abreast in an alert and communicative way with contemporary developments in the arts. [74]

Here then was a definite shift of focus, the opening up within education of a cultural struggle alongside the political struggle. Thompson implicitly challenged both the limitations of his namesake and the centralism of W.E. Williams, a strong advocate of the newly created Arts Council. Essentially the debate at the time was about resources to foster the emergent regional and local cultures, rather than the mainstream Arts Council approach of imposing a 'national' culture upon a supine provinciality. But, Thompson recognised: 'the scales today are weighted so heavily by commercial forces interested in the degeneration of standards, by forces of mass suggestion, by the environment and routine of industrial life against any healthy cultural activity that every sign of health must be carefully fostered'. [75] This marks continuity with the language of Leavisism in anathematising the commercial trivialisation of mass culture but, unlike Leavis, Thompson asserts local self-determination and democratic vitality. In effect, this particular view of cultural struggle was the one most influential in the formation of cultural studies. It was not intended, however, to produce a new academic discipline, but to serve as an active political strategy, conducted on the margins of the academy: rough, moralistic, unrefined but responsive to popular movements and, for the tutors concerned, utterly vocational.

Somewhere between party and class and between the educational institution and 'the people' there had to be space for the relative autonomy of intellectuals in what those intellectuals had defined as 'the cultural struggle'. To return to his polemic against Orwell, Thompson insisted that what the leadership, the intellectuals and educators should now be offering was as much moral as political. It was enabling rather than directive: to give 'the valley to the waterers, that it bring forth fruit' and not to attempt to impose some new 'utopia' from above.

> The post-war generation grew to consciousness amidst the stench of the dead, the stench of the politics of power. They opted instead for the politics of personal integrity ... The old Left, because it refused to look evil in the face, because it fudged the truth about Communism or suggested that human nature could be set right by some stroke of administration, appeared mechanical, 'bullying', dehumanised: it could only speak the language of power, not of socialised humanity.[76]

All this is of course richly suggestive of the relationship of intellectuals, as a group, to common or popular culture, but Thompson never theorised it fully. It is perhaps significant that Antonio Gramsci's name rarely appears in his work and that Gramsci's work on the role of intellectuals was not taken up. However, in his concerns with agency and moral choice, it has been suggested by Robert Gray that 'Thompson's emphasis on culture seems to conceive it as a privileged space for the formation of moral agents.'[77] So to return to the idea of popular culture and its capacity to resist the dominant culture, it could be suggested that Thompson sees, as it were, passing between and through cultural spheres, individual moral agents, thoughtful, concerned and actively working on the material of culture itself in a spirit of critical renewal.

In this view there seems to be no need to conceive these people as a professional class as Mannheim does, as they can be drawn from any stratum of society. Thompson's own love of the craftsman intellectual, shared with William Morris, is plain throughout his work; his antagonism towards the academic bacon-slicer is equally well known. His own inability to tolerate the intra-mural university (as opposed to the extra-mural one) for more than a few turbulent years, led him to temporarily sideline his own specialist trade as historian and become a full-time peace campaigner in the early 1980s, speaking eloquently of his own moral choices. Popular culture is not, then, simply the organic secretion of the people but the active engaged work of moral agents from whatever quarter, in pursuit of a 'humanised' society. What is equally clear is that, although these agents may only be in a minority at any one time, they require a common culture to sustain them. This is not a 'populist' solution to the question of popular culture and seems to suggest an elite upon whom the burden falls. But it is an elite without élitism, it is renewable and replaceable from a common ground, it has no privileges or exceptional rights of birth or wealth, it is responsible for the common good and it is profoundly moral.

Adult education was, therefore, crucially involved in the production of those 'organic' intellectuals who might renew the common culture. Instinctively, it seems, Edward Thompson was drawn to this mode of work, where he remained for seventeen years, helping to form a generation of worker intellectuals. If this formulation now seems quaintly outmoded it is not necessarily because Thompson was just a provincial intellectual who did not understand the finer points of theory, but because his active concerns lay beyond the academy's repelling walls. Without the work of education, the distinction between a culture of the people and a commercial 'mass' culture servicing hegemonic needs, may disappear for good.

Notes

1. E.P. Thompson, letter to the Registrar, 18 March 1948, University of Leeds, Central Filing.
2. *Ibid.*
3. Frank Jacques, letter to the Registrar, 14 April, 1948, University of Leeds, Central Filing.
4. *Ibid.*
5. *Ibid.*
6. E.P. Thompson, letter to the Registrar, 18 March 48, *op cit.*
7. *Ibid.*
8. Frank Jacques, letter to the Registrar, 14 April, 1948, *op cit.*
9. Frank Jacques, letter to S.G. Raybould, 17 April 1948, University of Leeds, Central Filing.
10. *Ibid.*
11. *Ibid.*
12. Frank Jacques, letter to Thompson, 23 April 1948, University of Leeds, Central Filing.
13. Roger Fieldhouse, *Adult Education and the Cold War*, Leeds Studies in the Education of Adults, Leeds 1985, p42.
14. Personal witness of this was given to me by Ron Bellamy, formerly of the Oxford Delegacy and University of Leeds.
15. Frank Jacques, letter to Thompson, 23 April 1948, *op cit.*
16. S.G. Raybould, letter to Jacques, 24 April 1948, University of Leeds, Central Filing.
17. E.P. Thompson, Memorial Lecture for Fred Sedgwick, tape transcription.
18. E.P. Thompson, letter to Jacques, 28 April 1948, University of Leeds, Central Filing.
19. *Ibid.*
20. *Ibid.*
21. *Ibid.*
22. *Ibid.*
23. *Ibid.*
24. *Ibid.*
25. *Ibid.*
26. J.F.C. Harrison, 'The WEA in the Welfare State' in S.G. Raybould, (ed), *Trends in Adult Education*, 1959, p1-29; Peter Searby & the Editors, 'Edward Thompson as a teacher: Yorkshire and Warwick' in *Protest and Survival, the historical experience, Essays for E. P. Thompson*, John Rule and Robert Malcolmson, (eds), 1994, p6.
27. E.P. Thompson, letter to Raybould, 3 February 1954, Department of Adult Continuing Education Archives, University of Leeds.
28. *Ibid.*
29. *Ibid.*
30. *Ibid.*
31. Andy Croft, 'Walthamstow, Little Gidding and Middlesbrough: Edward Thompson, Adult Education and Literature', *Socialist History*, No. 8, 1995, p39.
32. *Ibid.*
33. John Goode, 'Thompson and the Significance of Literature', Harvey J. Kaye and Keith McClelland, (eds), *E.P. Thompson, Critical Perspectives*, Polity, London 1990, pp183-203, p190.
34. W. Baker to Raybould, 19 January 1949, Department of Adult Continuing Education Archives, University of Leeds.
35. W. Baker, class visit report, 26 November 1949, Department of Adult Continuing Education Archives, University of Leeds.
36. *Ibid.*

37. E.P. Thompson, Joint Committee class report for first year literature class at Shepley 1948-9, Department of Adult Continuing Education Archives, University of Leeds.

38. E.P. Thompson, 1950, 'Against "University" Standards', University of Leeds, Department of Extra-Mural Studies, Adult Education Papers, Vol. 1, No. 4, p31.

39. *Ibid*, p18.

40. *Ibid*, p35.

41. *Ibid*, p36.

42. *Ibid*.

43. *Ibid*.

44. *Ibid*.

45. Fred Inglis, *Radical Earnestness*, Oxford University Press, Oxford 1984, p199.

46. Circular from S. G. Raybould dated November, 1954, Department of Adult Continuing Education Archives, University of Leeds.

47. *Ibid*.

48. E.P. Thompson, letter to Crowley, 28 Dec. 1954, Department of Adult Continuing Education Archives, University of Leeds.

49. E.P. Thompson to Stanley, 1 July (no year), Department of Adult Continuing Education Archives, University of Leeds. In the same letter Thompson writes 'I did wonder to what use that room in which we started to build a labour movement archive is now put?' What happened to this archive?

50. E. P. Thompson, Joint Committee report of a social history class in Morley 1963-4, Department of Adult Continuing Education Archives, University of Leeds.

51. Dorothy Thompson, Lecture at Ruskin College, 'A Day for Edward Thompson', 23 April 1994.

52. E.P. Thompson, 'Homage to Tom Maguire' in *Essays in Labour History*, Asa Briggs and John Saville, (eds), Macmillan, London 1960, p314.

53. Goode, 'Thompson and the Significance of Literature', *op cit*, p189.

54. E.P. Thompson, *The Heavy Dancers*, Pantheon, New York 1985, p6.

55. E.P. Thompson, 'Caudwell' in J. Saville and R. Miliband, (eds), *The Socialist Register 1977*, Merlin, London 1977, pp228-276, p271.

56. Henry Abelove *et al.* (eds), Visions of History, Manchester University Press, Manchester 1983, p13.

57. *Ibid*.

58. The second edition of *William Morris*, published in 1977, had the same effect on the neo-Stalinism, as he saw it, of Althusserianism.

59. E.P. Thompson, 'William Morris and the Moral Issues Today' in *The American Threat to British Culture*, Arena Publications, London 1951, pp25-30, p29.

60. Richard Hoggart, *The Uses of Literacy*, Pelican, London 1957, p340.

61. E.P. Thompson, *Customs in Common*, Penguin, London 1993, p6.

62. *Ibid*.

63. E.P. Thompson, *Customs in Common*, op cit, p93.

64. *Ibid*. p87.

65. Ellen Meiksins Wood, 'The Debate on Base and Superstructure' in Harvey J. Kaye and Keith McClelland, (eds), *E.P. Thompson, Critical Perspectives*, Polity, London 1990, p146.

66. Kate Soper, 'Socialist Humanism' in Kaye and McClelland, *E.P. Thompson, Critical Perspectives, op cit*, pp204-232, p218.

67. E.P. Thompson, 'Outside the Whale' in *The Poverty of Theory and Other Essays*,

Merlin, London 1978, p21.

68. *Ibid*. p24.

69. Andy Croft, 'Authors Take Sides: Writers in the Communist Party, 1920-1956' in *Opening the Books: New Perspectives in the History of British Communism*, Kevin Morgan, Nina Fishman, Geoff Andrews, (eds), Pluto, London 1995.

70. George Thomson, 'Our National Cultural Heritage' in *Britain's Cultural Heritage*, Arena Publications, London 1952, pp3-19, p13.

71. E.P. Thompson, 'Caudwell' in *Socialist Register 1977*, J. Saville and R. Miliband (eds), Merlin, London 1977, pp228-276, p244.

72. E.P. Thompson, 'William Morris and the Moral Issues Today' in *The American Threat to British Culture*, London Arena Publications, 1951, pp25-30, p30.

73. E.P. Thompson, 'A Cultural Policy', *Tutors' Bulletin*, Summer 1950, 7-12, p11.

74. *Ibid*, p8.

75. *Ibid*, p9.

76. E.P. Thompson, 'Outside the Whale' *op cit*, p31.

77. Robert Gray, 'History, Marxism and Theory' in Kaye and McClelland, *E.P. Thompson, Critical Perspectives, op cit*, pp153-182, p174.

8.

Raymond Williams
and the invention of cultural politics

> But its (adult education's) whole spirit, most admirably expressed by
> the WEA at its best, is of growth towards a genuinely common culture,
> an educated and participating democracy. [1]
>
> Yet what is now happening, in the existing institutions, is a steady
> pressure from a late-capitalist economy and its governments to reduce
> education both absolutely and in kind, steadily excluding learning
> which offers more than a preparation for employment and an already
> regulated civic life. [2]

John McIlroy's exemplary labour of sifting out and analysing
Williams's work on adult education, for the moment at least,
would seem to make any further inquiry superfluous, and we are
all deeply indebted to him. [3] But there still may be conclusions to
be drawn about the relation of this practice to the emergence of
cultural studies which complement McIlroy's overall
understanding.

Any talk of British cultural studies and the New Left finds it
hard to avoid the pairing Thompson and Williams. They function
almost as a complementary pair in contemporary intellectual left
culture and their interaction has been a feature of the
convergence of two of the most formative intellectual streams in
British cultural studies: Leavisism and Marxism. Not that
Williams can simply be identified with the one and Thompson

176

with the other. Thompson's critique of Williams's *Long Revolution* in 1960 may have provoked one of the most substantial changes in direction for Williams – from the emphasis on culture as a common way of life to culture as the product of *struggle* between the classes; while for Thompson, Williams had 'a more constructive insight into the possibilities of socialism in this country than anyone living'.[4]

The curious thing is that, despite more than fifteen years shadowing each other, they did not in fact collaborate on a joint project until after Thompson had left the Communist Party in 1956, yet their paths might have crossed so many times before. Both were members of the Communist Party before the war, both began their degrees at Cambridge, then served in tank regiments during the war and took part in the army's adult education service ABCA. Both returned after the war to complete their degrees. Each, separately, worked for Frank Jacques as part-time tutors in the WEA's Eastern District before getting full-time appointment as staff tutors in university departments of extra-mural studies. Although now members of the same vocation – both would have hesitated to call it a 'profession' – such was the isolation of adult education tutors that these two men saw nothing of each other for a decade and apparently worked in almost complete isolation, though they were aware of each other's contributions to adult education journals and conferences and eventually each other's major publications.

Thompson's critique of *The Long Revolution* produced an illuminating graph of their two ideological trajectories in which, obliquely, Thompson reflected on their different class backgrounds: the public school boy comparing his relationship to *the culture* with that of the 'scholarship boy':

> It may be that the 'scholarship boy' who comes to Christminster undergoes quite different intellectual experiences from the middle-class intellectual who enters the socialist movement. In the first there is a sense of growth into the institutions of learning, with less of a crisis of allegiance than is sometimes suggested: the sense is that of Jude entering into his inheritance on the behalf of his own people. The dangers besetting the middle-class socialist intellectual are well enough known. But he may nevertheless, in joining the socialist

movement experience more sense of intellectual crisis, of breaking with a pattern of values: there is still a rivulet of fire to be crossed. For this reason his tendency is towards intellectual sectarianism, or – as Hardy noted in Sue – the sudden relapse into former patterns of response. But the working-class scholar may tend to persist in the illusion of Jude: the function of bourgeois culture is not questioned in its entirety, and the surreptitious lines of class interest and power have never been crossed. [5]

They were, of course, at different ends of the country. While Thompson embedded himself in the industrial West Riding, rich in the working-class institutions which characterised Williams's view of the co-operative culture of labour, Williams himself took up post on the south coast – which was just rich. Nevertheless it was a location landmarked in the folklore of working-class culture, the Hastings where Robert Tressell wrote *The Ragged Trouser'd Philanthropists*. Although for many working-class activists this was the one great novel of working-class life, except for a generous half page commentary in his *The English Novel from Dickens to Lawrence* [6], Williams appears almost to have ignored it. While Thompson as we have seen was the only Communist to be employed by Raybould at Leeds (though it was a broadly socialist department), Williams was employed at Oxford University's department of extra-mural studies, the Oxford Delegacy, 'where by 1947 nine out of the thirty full-time teaching staff, plus the Secretary of the Delegacy, were either members of the Communist party or "fellow-travellers"'. [7]

The department at Leeds under the stern directorship of Sidney Raybould was newly formed in 1946 and rapidly increased its teaching staff into the 1950s. Oxford, one of the oldest departments and under Michael Sadler a pioneer of university extension teaching in the late nineteenth century, was also undergoing substantial expansion. As Fieldhouse makes clear, this expansion was not sanctioned by the Ministry of Education who hurriedly despatched an HMI to warn them off. Moreover, their plans seriously aggravated the National Secretary of the WEA, Ernest Green, who saw imperial pretensions at work: Oxford's activities, particularly in areas of working-class education in North Staffordshire, were to spark off a serious confrontation between the WEA and the Delegacy. To make matters worse, the project by Thomas Hodgkin, the Delegacy Secretary, to establish extra-mural classes in British West Africa as part of the movement towards decolonisation, was also denounced by Lords Vansittart and Milverton in the House of Lords in 1950 as a sinister extension of the Soviet propaganda machine. [8] Both Williams's close colleague, Tony McClean and Henry Collins, who were party members, were chosen for this mission, but as in the case of North Staffordshire, no evidence of propagandist activities were found. If anything a scrupulous attention to the protocols of traditional liberal adult education were especially carefully observed, but to the Colonial Service administrators and expatriate military men, this *liberal* education looked suspiciously like subversion.

The conjuncture at Oxford was therefore more radically politicised than at Leeds, and the social class background of many of the tutors was substantially different. The communists, for example, tended to come from privileged and public school backgrounds while the labourists tended to be more working-class. Thomas Hodgkin himself was from an established intellectual Oxford Quaker family, and his communism owed as much to this dissenting tradition as it did to Marxism, and little or nothing to Soviet Communism. Hodgkin found his opponents' objections that he might be required to submit to King Street party discipline and thus compromise his objectivity little short of hilarious. Williams occasionally found himself having to mediate in internal departmental disputes because he was seen as politically independent of both the communist and labourist camps but trusted by both. It was not an especially comfortable position for, as he said, he found that intellectually he tended to think along the same lines as the communists but culturally he was much more at home with the working-class labourists. The effect of Cold War ideology after the heady years of the late 1940s was to stifle the more overt signs of communism and to establish an informal black-list of party members and known sympathisers. It was, as Williams later said, a politically dangerous time. Both Hodgkin and McLean had left the party by 1950 and after Hodgkin's resignation as Secretary of the

Delegacy a year or so later, a more conventionally labourist leadership under Frank Jessup and Pickstock was put in place. During this period Williams, who got on well with Pickstock, nevertheless used the distance between Oxford and the south coast to bury himself in his teaching and research and only emerged in the summer for occasional forays up to Oxford with Tony McLean to 'do' adult education. [9]

When it came to 'doing adult education' at Leeds, Raybould had set himself the task of designating precisely what was denotative about university adult education in an attempt to differentiate the work of his department from that of the WEA generally. For Raybould it boiled down to 'university standards', a concept he had adapted from George Thompson, but which, as we have seen, was strongly opposed by Edward Thompson. Raybould also strategically revived the older university extension classes to allow him a sphere of influence separate from the WEA where he could attend to a non-working-class clientele (as required by the university) that was already well-educated, especially those who required further professional education. Raybould proselytised for university standards throughout the adult education structure and in his frequent publications. Hodgkin took issue with Raybould in the *Highway* on not dissimilar terms to those of Edward Thompson, and he criticised the drift to intellectual conformity that Raybould's notion of standards implied. He argued that Raybould's desire for increased vocational and professional education would draw adult education progressively away from the working-class educational movement. [10] Williams sympathised wholeheartedly with this position and argued further that the notion of standards was a subtle form of gatekeeping which would tend to exclude the 'non academic' student without secondary education and would force adult education into an increasingly institutional straitjacket. [11]

Williams agreed with Edward Thompson and William Cobbett that education was not always an unalloyed good since it frequently doubled as a source of social control. Thus merely to extend an already categorised university education to working people might well be to ignore their own experience and needs.

The educational deficit, he believed, did not simply affect the working class, it was often at the heart of the university, the problem being that university did not always realise and was prone arrogantly to deny this. Adult education, Williams proposed, should be conducted as a dialogue between academics and their working-class students, in which academics were prepared to learn from their students and amend their ideas appropriately, much as G.D.H. Cole and R.H. Tawney had approached their work. A short pamphlet written by Williams in the early 1960s had a salutary effect on the new generation of WEA Organising Tutors:

> There is another main reason why tutors should join and work with the WEA. This a matter of the health of their own academic subject. There are some important examples here. There was the profound stimulus, to all the social studies, from the contact of men like Tawney and Cole with the realities of working-class life and history, through the WEA. There has been, more recently, the profound stimulus to literary and cultural studies, by the fact of contact between tutors trained in academic disciplines, affected sometimes by fashions, and students who live in less specialised cultural worlds and who force the tutors to follow the questions of value right through. [12]

This, as we have seen, was a line of argument which threaded the working-class educational movement from the turn of the century down through George Thompson and Karl Polanyi to the current generation. The implications were that the university itself must be prepared to review its own educational provision reflexively. A further consequence was that adult education imperatives themselves offered a distinctly alternative perspective, as Stuart Laing makes clear:

> The adult education experience was crucial in inflecting concern with educational standards towards a position which was neither university nor school orientated but rather addressed itself directly towards general cultural standards within the whole adult population. [In the case of Richard Hoggart's *The Uses of Literacy*] If the book's content is explicitly comparative between working-class lived culture and mass art products then it is the adult education position which provides the perspective from which the comparison is made. [13]

181

It is important therefore to see the emergence of cultural studies as coming from a period of intense ideological and theoretical debate within adult education about the nature of university education and standards and as a response to the political climate of the Cold War. As Williams remarked elsewhere cultural studies was politics by other means.

But it is also clear that it was a response to more general social change in which the post-war restructuring of British society reflected the relative strength of the organised labour movement in conditions of full employment and increasing affluence. It was in this context that Williams described his personal sense of deficit as less economic than cultural, and that despite their own working-class culture, there was a sense in which working people themselves were systematically deprived of a more generally available culture.

The Common Good

The problem that exercised Williams through his life and produced his most fruitful work was the tension between the idea of 'culture' as a way of life, 'culture' in the anthropological sense and 'culture' as the imaginative products of a people: Art. In *Culture and Society* he is relatively dismissive of working-class culture in the second sense, in that it produced little of permanent artistic value – hence his comparative lack of interest in working-class novels. On the other hand, the working-class way of life had produced the great collective achievements of the trade unions, the co-operative movement and the democratic party of labour; all as far as Williams was then concerned, were the institutions on which a future egalitarian and socially just society must be built. Even this, he admitted in conversation with Richard Hoggart, who largely ignored this aspect of working-class culture, implied that within the working class there were high and low traditions: 'The most difficult bit of theory that I think both of us have been trying to get at, is what relation there is between kinds of community, that we call working-class, and the high working-class tradition, leading to democracy, solidarity in the unions, socialism'. [14]

So even here there was a sense in which the great achievements of working-class culture were the product of a minority, Hoggart's 'earnest minority', whereas the great change that was happening in the post-war period was that the quality of art and thought would be increasingly dependent on the taste of the majority.

Williams believed that education was central to culture and that adult education in particular had been an active element in social change. It was now essential, he believed, to expand education from a minority to a majority pursuit because, contrary to the increasingly conservative tone taken by the *Scrutiny* group, Williams viewed cultured minorities now as a threat to civilisation rather than its salvation. The massive expansion of cultural production taking place in the post-war period could not be left in the hands of self-appointed coteries but must instead become democratically accountable. In trying to come to terms with his own role as an adult educator within the current rapidly changing situation, Williams came up with the following historical analysis: educational thought in Britain since the nineteenth century could be divided into three strands. The first was that of the 'Old Humanist' (within which, no doubt, Eliot, Leavis and the right wing of the *Scrutiny* group could be fitted) which regarded education as a necessarily minority pursuit and one which was 'the repository of certain values, the true golden thread in the life of man'.[15] This perspective held that education should resist the practical claims of the world and any attempt to expand and therefore dilute it. In Williams's eyes, this view had done a great deal of damage, not the least because, in the nineteenth century, in dialectical opposition to it a second group arose: the 'Industrial Trainers'. Because the Old Humanists would have nothing to do with the hard demands of an expanding and competitive economy, the Industrial Trainers comprehensively won the debates about popular education which as a consequence became increasingly vocational and skills-orientated. The modern education system, according to Williams, was a shotgun marriage between the two strands, which produced the public and grammar schools in the old humanist mould and the secondary and further education system to suit the industrial trainers.

But adult education had developed from a third strand, which was that of the 'Public Educator'. This strand, like Carlyle, saw the point of education as enabling people to think critically, a faculty which had become even more important with the advent of mass democratic society. The negative element in the Public Educator perspective was that of 'moral rescue' as epitomised by those in the Temperance Movement who were involved in the early days of university extension. But for Williams, the post-war situation made it more necessary than ever that adult education should be able to reach out and embrace the majority. He argued for the kind of integrated vision of society that both Polanyi and Mannheim had envisaged, where society recognised itself as an educative process – 'a method of association and co-operation in which the processes we separate out as politics, as economics, as communication, as education, are directly related to the reality of living together'.[16] The adult education movement, he believed, had to recognise the value of modern communications systems, including the electronic media, and could no longer simply be content with 'earnest minorities'. This emphasis on communications as a technology to be utilised rather than feared, marks Williams out more than anyone from the attitudes associated with the Old Humanists, yet his emphasis on the holistic conception of society and the common good also separates him from the Industrial Trainers.

The issue of communications was for Williams, therefore, at the heart of cultural development. In 1960, he was asked to speak on the subject at a major conference organised by the National Union of Teachers on Popular Culture and Personal Responsibility. Although he believed in the potential of mass communication, like Hoggart, he still deplored the contemporary incarnations of mass media; in this respect both men differed quite radically from the attitude later cultural studies was to take. Penguin commissioned Williams's book *Communications*, which was published as a Penguin Special in 1962. Williams makes it plain that *Communications* is a consolidation of his adult education teaching in the area of newspapers, magazines and radio. As well as detailed analysis of these particular media, Williams offers a general argument for keeping commercial interests, especially advertising, out of communications, and for public ownership of the means of production such as presses, studios, broadcasting networks and theatres. Although it set the pace for cultural analysis at the time, Stuart Laing points out that, compared with the big budget institutions that followed in its wake, the book now seems more like the work of a gifted amateur.

The most immediate institutional outcome of this strand of thinking was the inauguration of the Open University, by Harold Wilson's Labour government, which in some ways took up the radical torch laid down by the traditional adult education movement which – in some despair – Williams had by then left. With some reservations Williams was enthusiastic about the Open University which he regarded as 'a remarkable demonstration of some of the true possibilities of television'. He felt that the OU had solved some of the problems of the medium in relation to the obvious issues of clarification and questioning and making the students' own work active, through its planned printed courses. [17] However, he differed from many later advocates of what was to be called 'distance learning' by maintaining that the medium could not eradicate the work of classroom teachers. Here, as Andrew Milner maintains, Williams was in close agreement with Jürgen Habermas about the irreducible need for dialogue in the educational process. [18] Although television and the printed syllabus could impressively stretch the reach of education, they could not ultimately eliminate the class and the teacher discussing problems in common.

How to Read?

As we saw in chapter three, the teaching of literature was the primary site of ideological contestation in adult education during the 1930s. What tends to be forgotten is that literature was by no means a secured discipline. Amongst other things what the arguments had revealed was that literature teaching was a very variable occupation, the extremes of which were the historical survey approach beloved of the 'literary appreciation' school and the practical criticism of the Leavisite stormtroopers. Although unhappy with the slackness of the former approach, Williams was, from the beginning, insistent that the relation between literature and history, or literature and life, had, at some stage, to be forcibly made. However, as much as the most ardent Leavisite, he found himself having to insist on the priority of the written word: text before context, literature as literature and not as a branch of history or sociology. Thus, in some respects, in his arguments with colleagues during the 1950s and early 1960s, Williams can appear to be quite conservative, even donnish in his attitude to teaching.

The teaching of English literature in the early decades of the twentieth century was in part a victim of the WEA's demand for social relevance. The reaction of the newly confident working-class movement against the kind of literature teaching then commonplace in university extension classes tended to reduce literature to the place of social commentary. A kind of 'Shawlsworthy' syllabus evolved, featuring the more gritty realism of Shaw, Galsworthy, Dickens and Gissing, and the function of literature classes was primarily to illustrate the iniquities of the capitalist system. Not that this approach was wholly without value – as George Thompson pointed out, it certainly saved the movement from a lot of waffle about 'spiritual values' – but it relied on a tendency to treat the texts as if they were simply a transparent medium through which 'real life' could be viewed on the other side, rather than as a complex semiological system through which that 'real' world was constructed.

The great gift of 'practical criticism', as first theorised by I.A. Richards and then extended and popularised by Leavis and the *Scrutiny* group, was that it drew attention back to the text itself. By analysing the way in which the reality effect was produced and, through the analysis of tone, the way an attitude towards that reality was subtly conveyed, this method led to nothing short of a revolution in literary studies. Many of the more radical tutors found it seductive, but perhaps so seductive that many also failed to notice some of the undemocratic cultural attitudes that often accompanied it. The idea of the necessity of a cultural élite was embraced even by 'left-Leavisites' such as L.C. Knights, who in other respects was much closer to the socialist historians such as Christopher Hill.

In the mid-1940s at the beginning of his career, Williams, with Wolf Mankowitz and Clifford Collins, both of whom also worked in adult education, tried to bridge this opposition through the creation of two cultural journals, *The Critic* and *Politics and Letters*. They believed they could unite the disciplined approach to reading, which they valued in Leavis, with a left critique of society, the kind of perspective already evident in some of Knights's work. However, as Williams later conceded, they had not appreciated the profoundly anti-socialist element in Leavis's work, which, although it was genuinely hostile to the destruction capitalism had wrought on Art and the organic society, was even more hostile to Marxism and working-class movements. The Leavisite view was that 'the only way forward was back'. This was of course absolutely not Williams's perspective since for him the organic society and the working-class movement co-existed. Neighbourliness, as he once angrily protested at a Cambridge lecture – to the derision of his more sophisticated colleagues – was something he actually experienced as a way of life in his home village in Wales.

However, it was the practice of teaching adults in the context of commitment to and occasionally, as in the case of trade union education, democratic control by working-class organisations, that really appealed to Williams. It has to be borne in mind that tutors in adult education were expected to teach subjects beyond their own academic specialism in a wide variety of contexts. In Williams's case it meant that the very first four courses he taught as a staff tutor for the Oxford Delegacy were in International Relations, though by the following year he had somehow managed to transform these into *literature* classes. The chemistry of this change is not hard to appreciate. The prime resource for the study of International Relations was newspapers. In class discussion, students were encouraged to read and compare the international coverage of a variety of newspapers, ranging from the high Tory *Telegraph* and establishment *Times*, through the populist conservatism of the *Express* and *Mail*, to the popular labourism of the *Mirror* and *Daily Herald* and the communist perspectives of the *Daily Worker*. It is not hard to imagine Williams moving the discussion from the actual politics of

International Relations to the construction of the news items from which 'the facts' were drawn. Thus the world became text and the methods of practical criticism were adapted appropriately.

The 'literary turn' became a general feature of university adult education in the post-war period and resulted in a massive increase in classes. O'Connor comments that:

> the rapid increase in literature classes after the war is in part due to the increased numbers of women students and in part to the interests of the new group of tutors. Under the influence of Empson, Leavis, Murray, and Richards, lecture courses (which had often covered an enormous amount of ground very rapidly) gave way to practical criticism and in depth class work on short passages of text. [19]

However, the break was not quite as sharp as O'Connor implies. Although the method itself was drawn from Leavis and Thompson's *Culture and Environment* and Q.D. Leavis's *Fiction and the Reading Public*, what Hoggart called 'the peg in the nose' cultural élitism was not particularly congenial to adult students. One of the problems was that these classes lacked a good contemporary text-book which could combine method with illustrations. In a sense both Hoggart's *The Uses of Literacy* and Williams's *Reading and Criticism* (1950) were conceived as text books for use with adult classes. The latter was published in a series called the Thinkers Library, designed specifically for this purpose and edited by Lady Simon and two of the most influential figures in adult education, Thomas Hodgkin and Sidney Raybould.

What is interesting about Williams's account of this period is the degree of pressure literature tutors found themselves under from their more 'political' colleagues who were teaching classes in the social sciences and politics. This pressure derived in part from that unreconstructed political approach exemplified by George Thompson, which viewed literature as a 'woman's subject'. This prejudice was reinforced by the larger numbers of women now coming into adult education, and sharpened by anxiety over the declining number of male manual workers. [20] In an early comment on a contribution by Richard Hoggart to the literature pedagogy, Williams remarks on 'the sense of guilt which most literature tutors have that theirs is not a really useful subject and that it must be made to resemble social history or philosophy or logic before it can be fully accepted in adult education'. [21] This point is repeated in Williams's own article on experiments in literature teaching, written later in the same year, where he observes that a literature tutor is often regarded by others, and indeed by himself, as 'someone for whom apology must be made'. But it was precisely this sense of irrelevance that occasioned much of the new experimentation in literary pedagogy, the pressure in fact to find a social relevance for literature in its own right, not just as an annexe of history or sociology. Williams's view of the historical development of literary studies was that it had always been fuelled by controversy and experiment, of which perhaps some of the most significant examples were to be seen in adult education. The reason was that, 'Adult education travels light, with little that is settled in the way of institutions, with a variety of material shortages, and with a wide freedom to experiment. In the last fifty years the teaching of Literature to adults has accordingly been both battlefield and laboratory'. [22]

Williams's own solution to the gulf between the 'social relevance' tutors and the textual purists was to propose that the social function of literature lay in training people how to 'read', that is to read actively and critically and be able to demystify textual material. While he maintained that making correlations between literature and its social context was both necessary and desirable, especially in adult education, this should always be a most judicious operation. While, for example, social history proceeded by drawing abstractions, the discipline of literature lay in close reading. So, while inter-disciplinarity was desirable it had to begin with the recognition that two distinct methodologies needed to be learned. Such was the interest in combined classes in literature and history that he organised a conference for tutors that same year.

Williams also reflected on the need to transcend conventional academic boundaries in order to make the work of literature tutors socially relevant:

> In a different interest, a course in reading may be applied to such
> institutions as newspapers, advertisements, popular fiction, pamphlets,
> etc., and its methods of analysis adapted to examine films, buildings,
> and broadcasting. This is one of the most directly useful forms of
> specifically social training which the literature tutor can offer and
> experiments in it seem to have been successful. [23]

Here then was the way out of literary 'purism' – to adopt the methods of the purists themselves, and to move to that fuller cultural analysis which the Leavises had begun, but which, because of their ideological commitment to a cultural élite, they were unable to complete. Only in the context of a democratic popular education practice could the analysis be given social relevance. This is acknowledged to be one of the major routes by which British cultural studies emerged as a discipline. What are usually emphasised, however, are the Leavisite origins of the method, while the determining structural context in adult education is forgotten. At this early stage, however, Williams was still to a great extent captured by the purist discourses, such that he can say, 'Literature as a coherent record of human experience, needs neither apology nor external justification. It is itself, and its study as such remains one of the permanently valuable disciplines of any education'.[24] By the late 1970s, in the light of his reassessment of Marxism, he had considerably modified these ideas.

However, the centrality that Williams gave to reading as the defining discipline of literature study helped to distance it from the synoptic or survey approach to teaching, which in effect was simply a degraded form of literary history. Indeed, in some of his early classes Williams felt that he too was guilty of that approach, as in, for example, his course 'The Novel since 1800'. Progressively he restricted the number of books he covered in his courses and devised a graduated programme of readings. The crucial justification for a literature course, he felt, was that it promoted a critical approach rather than simply focusing on appreciation. This also related to the social function strand in literature teaching, which had gained popularity among adult students by treating literature as social criticism.

Williams found, somewhat to his surprise, that courses in critical theory were popular, and that his students took great relish in ticking off an 'objective correlative' whenever they found one, or discovering a whole train-load of 'ambiguity'. He was unhappy about this, precisely because a retreat into theoretical formulae was an escape from helping his students to respond adequately to works of literature. Williams was left with the dilemma of wanting to train his students in a critical discipline but realising that the direct approach of teaching critical theory was simply inadequate. If anything it was an even greater evasion of the actual practice of *reading* than the survey approach. In order to encourage a more focused response to reading, Williams therefore devised a graduated programme of courses which began with short extracts and led on to work on full texts, which he described as progressive reading rather than progressive *exercises* in reading. Such careful attention to pedagogy was characteristic of Williams but it also reflected the atmosphere of almost laboratory-like experimentation then in train in adult education, though *not* in the universities. As a consequence, Williams met with resistance from students, university administrators and the Ministry of Education, which frequently refused to accept his course proposals.

While he was experimenting in the discipline itself, Williams's classes in public expression for trade-unionists – usually neglected in commentary on his work – pushed him to consider questions of social relevance. For the most part, these courses were held for manual workers and, as McIlroy notes, probably assuaged some of Williams's frustration at his inability to get manual workers into his regular literature classes. [25] Classes in public speaking had been regular fare since university extension days, but Williams's approach was typically innovative. He regarded these courses as fundamentally about the usage of written and spoken English, and as such it is important to see his reflections here as complementing his attention to 'reading' in his regular literature classes. The differences between written and spoken language were, he came to believe, axiomatic.

In his first classes at Hastings Trades Council, the trade-union activists most urgently wanted to know about how to prepare reports and make arguments, and how to write letters and pieces for union journals and newspapers which would properly state their case. To this agenda Williams added training in logical thinking, not in itself novel, using Susan Stebbing's *Thinking to Some Purpose* and Thouless's *Straight and Crooked Thinking*, both of which had been standard textbooks in adult education since the 1930s. But then, as McIlroy notes, Williams addressed 'the essentially different kind of analysis which derives from literary criticism and which is concerned with the valuing of tone, feeling and sensibility'.[26] The courses seemed to have been effective in channelling students into longer tutorial classes and they provided the stimulus for much of the speculation which led to his book *Communications* (1962). The success of these classes enabled Williams to argue within the Delegacy that courses in English should be a necessary component of any course for trade-unionists.

The Cultural Turn

Is the truth of English studies courses for adults that they are already, in fact if not in name, cultural studies? In adult education, the urge to break away from formalist criteria and to consider questions of social relevance seems to have informed English studies from the beginning. While the undergraduate may well be content simply to learn how to apply critical criteria to textual analysis, the attitude of the adult student tends to be: 'How does this tell me more about the world in which I make my living, bring up my family, cope with death etc.?'; or in the case of the activist in social movements: 'How does this help me to change the world I live in?'

Williams's early years in adult education were characterised by a creative negotiation of this dialectic. On the one hand he produced what amounted to handbooks on reading and communications for use in class, and on the other he was turning over the theoretical question of culture again and again. If in some sense his teaching began to seem like a series of returns to the Leavisite agenda of his 'Modern Moralists' course at Cambridge – where his first adult education course on culture in 1946-7 was entitled "Culture and Environment" – Williams was also constantly seeking to transcend this intellectual legacy,

192

drawing on the work of the new British social historians and the sociological approaches introduced in the late 1930s. This double movement, which took him close to the waves of revisionist Marxism which increasingly flowed in from the continent but never entirely engulfed him, was to last the rest of his life.

A consequence of his immersion in theoretical matters was that his method of teaching increasingly incorporated longer lectures and discussion. Williams was always famous for actively engaging his students in the work of a class, on occasion getting them to sit and study a set text in complete silence for half an hour before they began to comment. But, although as a rule he believed that lectures had a deadening effect and induced passivity in a class, the excited discussion his own lectures provoked seem to have provided a genuinely uplifting experience for class and tutor alike. The first published evidence of this work was his essay on 'The Idea of Culture' (1953) from which *Culture and Society* (1956) rapidly developed. The first course with this title had in fact been given in 1948-9.

By 1950, Williams had already laid down some of the tracks for the systematic study of culture, and had contributed what constituted a set of guidance notes for tutors of 'Culture and Environment'.[27] The key text was, of course, Leavis and Thompson's eponymous book, but Williams was not altogether happy with it. He agreed that textual analysis centred on literary criticism should be the main activity, but insisted that other disciplines should also be consulted. Moreover, it was important to stress that literary critical methods had an application beyond the literary field, in cultural forms such as newspapers and advertisements, but also broadcasting, film and even architecture and town planning. As he made clear, the purpose of this kind of class was a training in awareness and judgement, but it also involved, by means of 'an incursion into comparative sociology and social history', a judgement on society as such. The main difference between the logical analysis approach advocated by Stebbing and Thouless, and what Williams called his 'culture and environment' approach, was this analysis of quality through the study of tone, method and effect.

Williams's review of contemporary critical literature in 1950 reveals just how quickly Leavisite cultural analysis was progressing in the immediate post-war period. While he recommended books by a variety of Scrutineers it was usually with qualifications. Thus, while Leavis's *Education and the University* contained perhaps the best exegesis on literary critical analysis, Denys Thompson's *Reading and Discrimination* was useful but tended to employ a kind of inappropriate snap judgement. [28] Essays by Empson, Knights, Muir and selected essays by Leavis were also recommended for the critical approach. For discussion of the press he recommended books by Norman Angell and Janet Soames and the pre-war PEP *Report on the British Press. My Northcliffe Diary* was 'invaluable', but Kingsley Martin's *The Press the Public Wants* was disappointing. Four books on advertising including one 'would-be serious anthology' were recommended. On popular fiction, Q.D. Leavis's *Fiction and the Reading Public* was 'the standard work' and Orwell's essays were useful. Also recommended was Unwin and Stevens's *Best Sellers – Are they Born or Made?*

These categories – newspapers, advertisements, popular fiction – are recognisably the material of the nascent cultural studies, but the next category 'propaganda' seems to belong to the old Leavisite agenda. Williams recommended five books on propaganda including Smith, Lasswell and Casey's *Propaganda, Communication and Public Opinion*, adding the wry comment, 'There is, of course, no shortage at all of material for analysis'. [29] No doubt the war-time boost given to official propaganda had spawned its own body of commentary, but it is possible to see the Cold War, then reaching its peak, as in fact the creature of a body of by now skilled professional propagandists, who might otherwise have found themselves unemployed in peace time. Film and broadcasting study was another important area of study to be constructed, but here Williams found little to recommend. Rotha's *Film Till Now* and Winnington's *Drawn and Quartered* were 'reasonable' but Thorpe's *America at the Movies* and Mayer's *Sociology of Film* were disappointing. Elsewhere he recommended the work his colleague Clifford Collins was doing on film sociology and Siegfried Kracauer's *From Caligari to Hitler*.

The final and most weighty category of study considered by Williams was 'Culture and Civilization', a title whose dualism reflects his debt to the nineteenth-century German tradition of literary speculation, as exemplified by Weber and Tönnies, which pre-dated Leavis. Under this heading Williams recommended Matthew Arnold's *Essays in Criticism* and *Culture and Anarchy* (recently republished by Cambridge in the Dover Wilson edition), and T. S. Eliot's *Notes Towards a Definition of Culture*. Williams was always generously disposed towards Eliot, whom he described in *Culture and Society* as a conservative a radical could be thankful for, but it still comes as something of a surprise to read Williams's note that, although he disagreed with sections of it, *Notes Towards a Definition of Culture* was 'a far more definitive book than its title would suggest'. [30]

More significantly, though, Williams felt that *Culture and Environment* itself could not be recommended unreservedly. Almost dismissively, he referred to it as 'the orthodox view' and largely derivative of George Bourne and D. H. Lawrence. Leavis's position in *Mass Civilization and Minority Culture* was 'not the only one' and Bantock's articles in *Scrutiny* outlining the same position were found to be even more unsatisfactory. For Williams, 'the assertion of a "minority" is by now largely irrelevant and in certain terms, idle and harmful'. [31] Here Williams demonstrated not so much that he was moving on from Leavis, because he never wholly shared these positions anyway, but that he had to hand another body of work, running in parallel, which was setting a different agenda.

However, the alternatives to the left of Leavis were not self-evident either. In one of the strongest statements of his own position, Williams noted, 'As one who finds himself perhaps nearer to the Marxist than the Leavis position, I would say, however, that Caudwell's books fall well below their reputation, and that they cannot be taken seriously'. [32] In any case, he continued, one ought to read the social history of the Hammonds, especially *The Bleak Age*, 'the settled and influential views' of R.H. Tawney's *The Acquisitive Society* and Christopher Dawson's *Progress and Religion*. Also relatively valuable was Lewis Mumford's *The Culture of Cities* but especially R.S. and

H.M. Lynd's *Middletown* books. He also recommended a selection of articles from his by now defunct journal, *Politics and Letters*. Finally, a book that was in his opinion so distinguished that it could not be omitted, was Ruth Benedict's anthropological work *Patterns of Culture*, which Williams rated very highly, noting, 'Her book provides the method of comparative social evaluation which is necessary both to give the work of cultural analysis full scope and to keep it relevant'.[33]

The dismissal of Caudwell is consistent with his views in *Culture and Society* and perhaps marks his great distance from the intellectual life of the Communist Party where a major controversy over Caudwell was about to break. As we have seen, for George Thomson, Edward Thompson and those who were attempting to liberalise the party and to gain ideological independence from the Soviet Union and Soviet Marxism, 'Caudwell' like 'Morris' was shortly to become a sign of the new politics. Williams's point, however, which he reiterated time and again, was that one simply could not talk about a 'dying' culture in the way that Caudwell and the generation of 1930s communists did. On the contrary, Williams argued, if one lifted the veils of communist ideology, one could see a booming capitalist economy, an expanding welfare state, an increasingly affluent working class and an extraordinary growth in cultural institutions. His distrust of ideological generalisations which failed to engage with the actualities of life is nowhere so clear.

What Williams did value, however, is what communists would have dismissed as the liberal or social democratic body of social history which had grown up around the work of historians like Tawney, the Hammonds and Cole. Much of this writing had also been generated in the context of the adult education movement originally, and only later returned to inform the academy. Although it was theoretically inspired, in Tawney's case especially by Weber, the theory did not stand in place of an engagement with the historical material. The interesting complement to this stream of theoretically inspired social history was the relatively new discipline of anthropology, exemplified in the 'whole way of life' analyses of Ruth Benedict and the new sociology. As we have seen, this new strand was itself dependent on the proselytising of the European

Marxist-inspired sociologists like Mannheim and Polanyi. As yet, however, little of this work was in translation.

At this early stage in his career then, Williams displays an extraordinary confidence in his direction and judgement and a remarkable awareness of the value of existing cultural analysis. His debt to Leavis is acknowledged but he is clear about the limitations of that approach, a critique that one feels is informed less by theoretical study than by reflecting on his own experience. For someone who feels closer to Marxism than Leavisism, though, there is a significant absence of any Marxist references. There was little available at that time, but Ralph Fox, Jack Lindsay and Alick West, whose work one feels might at least have merited a comment, are passed over in silence.

Andrew Milner makes the point that Williams's concept of cultural materialism denotes not so much a confluence of Marxism and Leavisism as a break from both. I think we can see from his adult educational practice just how the insights of the one tradition may have worked on the other. How, for example, Leavis's idealist and élitist 'culturalism' is made subject to a materialist analysis which insists that culture is ordinary and shaped by social relations, while the economic or technological determinism of orthodox Marxism is rejected in favour of a model which sees culture itself as shaping the so-called economic base. In identifying culture as both 'Art' and a 'whole way of life', Williams is, of course, following Leavis and Eliot, especially the Eliot of *Notes*. But where he differs dramatically from them is in locating a healthy culture not in the 'organic' past, which he so brilliantly demystifies in *The Country and the City*, but in the socialist future. He demonstrates, moreover, that the 'organic' tradition of Eliot and Leavis is highly selective.

In this work, too, Williams demonstrates that while theoretical approaches are a desirable antidote to the dull hand of pragmatism, they must not be allowed to degenerate into an academic theoreticism. Again it is hard not to see this conservatism gaining stimulus from his experience with adult classes whose culture, although equally intelligent, is not as rigorously focused as that of academia. Even when Williams did move to an internal academic position at Cambridge in 1961, he maintained his distance from the flood of French theory translated in the 1970s and 1980s, only, as Terry Eagleton remarked, somehow miraculously managing to prefigure them. Milner, too, points out that positions and concepts that Williams generated through close engagement with texts often resembled those developed by continental Marxists, for instance Williams's concept of the structure of feeling could be said to correspond to Gramsci's notion of hegemony, or Lucien Goldman's homologies perhaps because they all had their origins in nineteenth-century German idealism, and the idea of *zeitgeist*. But what Williams maintained in opposition to some more fashionable theories of ideology, particularly Althusser's, was that ideology could never entirely encompass all human practice. [34]

Milner also successfully demonstrates the close relationships between Williams's work and that of Bourdieu and Habermas. Bourdieu, for example, still values the category of social class as means of analysis, is suspicious of high culture, sympathetic to popular culture, and sees culture as central to late capitalist social organisation. With Habermas, Williams shares a radical democratic anti-capitalism and post-Romantic idealism, a concern for the new social movements (although Williams is more strongly wedded to the working class as the organising principle), and in particular the centrality of what Habermas calls communicative action. This dialogue and resolution was, for Williams, essential to any common culture and contrasted markedly with what he believed was the pseudo-radicalism of the negative studies of post-modernist art. These, he thought, were a moment of novelty only and not representative of an emergent culture.

Notes

1. Raymond Williams, 'Going on Learning', *New Statesman*, 30 May 1959; John McIlroy and Sallie Westwood, (eds), *Border Country: Raymond Williams in Adult Education*, NIACE, London 1993, p221.

2. Raymond Williams, *Towards 2000*, Pelican, London 1985, p151.

3. McIlroy and Westwood, (eds), *Border Country, op cit.*

4. E.P. Thompson, 1961 'The Long Revolution – II', *New Left Review*, No. 10, 34-39, p34.

5. *Ibid*, p37.

6. Raymond Williams, *The English Novel from Dickens to Lawrence*, Chatto & Windus, London 1970, pp 155-6

7. Fieldhouse, *Adult Education and the Cold War*, *op cit* . p35.

8. *Ibid*, p55.

9. Raymond Williams, 'Adult Education and Social Change' in *What I came to Say*, Neil Belton, Francis Mulhern and Jenny Taylor, (eds), Hutchinson, London 1990, pp157-166.

10. Thomas Hodgkin, 'University Standards', *Tutors' Bulletin*, Autumn, 1948.

11. Raymond Williams, *Politics and Letters*, Verso, London 1979, p81.

12. Raymond Williams, 'An Open Letter to WEA Tutors', Workers' Educational Association, London 1961; McIlroy and Westwood. (eds), *Border Country, op cit* , p224.

13. Stuart Laing, *Representations of Working-Class Life , 1957-1964*, Macmillan, London 1986.

14. Richard Hoggart and Raymond Williams, 'Working-Class Attitudes', *New Left Review*, No. 1, Jan./Feb. 1960, pp. 26-30, p26.

15. Raymond Williams, 'The Common Good', *Adult Education* XXXIV, 4, November 1961, pp192-9; McIlroy and Westwood, (eds), *Border Country, op cit*, p226.

16. *Ibid*, p231.

17. Raymond Williams, *Television Technology and Cultural Form*, Fontana/Collins, London 1974, pp54-55.

18. Andrew Milner, 'Cultural Materialism, Culturalism and Post-Culturalism: The Legacy of Raymond Williams', *Theory, Culture & Society*, Vol. 11, 1994, pp43-73, p68.

19. Alan O'Connor, Raymond Williams, *Writing, Culture, Politics*, Basil Blackwell, Oxford 1989, p9.

20. Note Tom Steele, 'Class Consciousness to Cultural Studies: the WEA in West Yorkshire, 1914-1950' in *Studies in the Education of Adults*, vol. 19, no 2, Autumn, 1987, pp109-126 on the effect of the war on this balance.

21. Raymond Williams, 'A Note on Mr. Hoggart's Appendices', *Adult Education*, XXI, 2, 1948, pp96-8; McIlroy and Westwood, (eds), *Border Country, op cit*, p44.

22. Raymond Williams, 'Some Experiments in Literature Teaching', *Rewley House Papers*, II, X, 1949-50, pp9-15; McIlroy and Westwood, (eds), *Border Country, op cit*, p146.

23. *Ibid*, p151.

24. *Ibid*.

25. McIlroy and Westwood, (eds), *Border Country, op cit*, p296.

26. Quoted in *Ibid*, p296.

27. Raymond Williams, 'Books for Teaching "Culture and Environment"', *The Use of English*, 1,3, 1950, pp134-40.

28. Thompson had read and commented on the proofs of *Reading and Criticism* which was due for publication.

29. Williams, 'Books for Teaching "Culture and Environment"', *op cit*.

30. *Ibid*.

31 *Ibid*.; McIlroy and Westwood, (eds), *Border Country, op cit*, p177.

32. *Ibid*.

33. *Ibid*., p178.

34. Milner, 'Cultural Materialism, Culturalism and Post-Culturalism', *op cit*.

9.

Conclusion: marginal occupations, adult education and social renewal

The argument of this book has been that the old formation of adult education provided a valuable marginal space which enabled creative experimentation and innovation in educational and pedagogic practices, especially between the 1930s and the 1960s. This was a period of intense social and political change in which considerable modernisation of the British state apparatuses took place, not least where education was concerned. One of the most important cultural shifts in this period was in the move away from the confrontational, class-based politics of the earlier part of the century to new concepts of the popular and the nation which incorporated or at least tried to minimise class divisions. This is a process that still continues, although it has been more one of re-mapping of class identities than their obliteration, as is frequently maintained. The move to construct the national popular has been at the expense of the centrality of the working-class identity that was the core of the old Labour movement. The generation of mass unemployment and the systematic destruction of working-class collectivist forms, which were part of the political project of Thatcherism have, of course, grossly accelerated this process. If this is the negative aspect of the process, the positive is that with the decentering of working-class identity from the leadership of progressive politics other suppressed identities have emerged. From the working-class struggle the related but distinct struggles for the liberation of women and minority ethnic identities have emerged. The politics of anti-racism and anti-sexism must be regarded as two of the most important progressive outcomes of the decline of working-class politics. The contribution of cultural studies to these struggles has been invaluable, and in shifting the focus of inquiry from the workplace and production to the home and consumption, has opened up issues formerly regarded as closed books.

This book has suggested that cultural study has long been a significant part of liberal adult education, dating back to the nineteenth century. It has tried to show that the teaching of the arts, especially English literature, has had a special significance in constructing identity for the emergent democratic classes. It has not approached this process as simply the process of enforced hegemonic repression or surveillance, as has been the burden of older, orthodox Marxist interpretations and newer, uninflected Foucauldian ones, but as the outcome of mediated negotiations between necessarily unequal power blocs, in which the liberal educator has been a central figure. This process of negotiation may have bought off revolution and enforced bourgeois hegemony, but it also enabled substantial social reforms to be introduced and forced concessions from the hegemonic bloc which a decade and half of reactionary politics has still not wholly won back. If working-class identity has always been compromised by an infusion of nationalism, it is also true that the nation has had to incorporate many 'working-class' values and institutions in order to be legitimated.

English studies may well have been invented by the liberal educators to incorporate the colonised masses into the new national settlement of Englishness, but I have argued that this had unintended consequences in suggesting other interpretations of labile texts. In adult education one of the most significant factors in affirming these other interpretations and in casting suspicion on the intentions of the hegemonic institutions has historically been the fact of the working-class movement itself. Without this movement's sceptical, though in many ways deeply conservative, approach to liberal education – as embodied in some districts of the WEA and in the Labour Colleges – the insistence on connectedness to everyday experience would not have been possible. It was, of course, a limited connectedness and despite the presence of many women in these classes their own exploitation was largely unacknowledged until the re-emergence of the feminist movement in the late 1960s. In fact WEA classes provided one of the most significant spaces for the evolution of feminist theory in Britain. Emblematic of this process were the courses taught by Sheila Rowbotham in Hackney and elsewhere, which began as courses in political ideas but underwent a paradigm shift to emerge as women's history and then women's studies in the early 1970s. Rowbotham is the first to acknowledge her debt to Edward Thompson in creating the conceptual space where those voices hidden from history could at last be heard. Women's studies courses swiftly sprang up all over the country. For example, in Leeds courses in such subjects as single-parent families, women and technology, women and anthropology, women and literature and feminist approaches to film study were evidence of the interdisciplinary range of women's studies. Within a few years one of the first MAs in women's studies was introduced, against substantial opposition, into the department of Sociology at the University of Leeds. Women's studies must not therefore be allowed to suffer an analogous fate to cultural studies and be represented as emerging fully-armed from the side of a university academic department, but should also be seen as intimately linked to a wider social movement which was testing its newly understood educational needs in the marginal spaces outside the academy.

It has been suggested that the 'truth' of English studies was always cultural studies, in the sense that the study of English has always strayed away from the narrow focus of textual study to the wider implications of that text for life and identity. Although frequently forced back by the academicians to close textual analysis, as we have seen, the demands from outside the academy were for relevance – both from the adult student who wanted to connect it to lived experience and from the liberal establishment, which wanted to connect it to the creation of national identity. These tensions existed in the university

extension movement, were made explicit in the Newbol\
and were fought out in the struggles over Leavisism in the \   .

There it might have ended had the vitality of the adult educational movement not attracted the attention of the European Marxist émigrés, who, fleeing from Nazism, were perhaps justly sceptical of the attenuated intellectual traditions of Stalinised Marxism. A new dimension to the debates was the proposition that the élite intellectual traditions of the British establishment should give way to a democratised learning society, offering education from the cradle to the grave. In this new approach to education hidebound academic specialisms were routinely transgressed. Clearly such joyful interdisciplinary irreverence would not have been admitted within the mainstream university system, and thus the extra-mural space became for many the site of the educational avant-garde. The new totalising sociology introduced by émigrés like Mannheim was undoubtedly utopian, but it was, nevertheless, remarkably suggestive.

I have tried to argue that the real effect of this argumentation was not felt until the post-war generation of tutors took up their extra-mural positions and discovered ways of linking these insights to their work with adults. Freed from the imposition of the spurious neutrality of the intra-mural university, and committed to the general cause of workers' emancipation, this was the generation that made culture and social consciousness the centre of their investigations. If this was the 'moment of culture', as Perry Anderson has suggested, it was also politics by other means. From about 1947, the Cold War informally outlawed communist politics in Britain and signalled the long-term attack on working-class industrial organisation (although the establishment was content to maintain many of the social aims). The model of social revolution based on industrial mobilisation, the general strike and spontaneous mass upheaval was no longer a mobilising myth. Also the extraordinary proliferation of cultural forms – from those backed by the newly formed Arts Council to imported American comic magazines – meant that forms of representation and expression offered themselves for analysis and critique as never before. Culture, which unequivocally served neither the dominant order nor the emergent one, was everywhere and unavoidable. Making sense of this in adult education classes became one of the most engaging common pursuits.

But this meant that some severance of the relationship between the intellectual and the working-class movement became inevitable, and with other opportunities for further and higher education emerging from the Butler and Robbins educational reforms, a fragmentation of the public for adult education and a consequent dilution of aims began. The attempt by Williams and others effectively to create a new political formation allied to a New Left politics was in retrospect heroic but tragic, and the critique of Labourism engendered by it led not to the renewal of socialist energies but to conservative reaction, which, ironically, took much of its rhetoric from the libertarian left.

What became of the project of cultural studies in adult education? In a sense what happened to it is also the story of the social and cultural transformation which later came to be called post-modernism. While the cultural struggle re-energised the left and made possible the construction of a New Left politics, it accelerated the demise of the class formations upon which the old politics was built. The politics of the point of production gave way to those of reproduction. If, as Fred Inglis remarked, Edward Thompson's *Making of the English Working Class* provided 'a new past to live from' and changed social memory, then clearly cultural study was a potent force. That text, which Thompson called his West Riding book, the outcome of his engagement with his adult education classes and political work in Yorkshire, effectively created a new history from which a younger generation of militants could break with the established political institutions and imagine alternative futures.

However, if the past could be so fickle as to transform itself under the pen of a gifted historian, what other wonders lay in store? In a sense the trap had been sprung. The 'culturalism' which Thompson had encouraged was tempered in his case and that of the 'old' New Left by the empirical discipline of submission to historical evidence and material enquiry. But many of the young Turks it encouraged had fewer reservations. Under the newly discovered sign of 'Theory' some of the 'new' New Left of the early 1960s unlocked the gates to a more fully fledged idealism. As he famously recorded, after the palace coup which ditched him and other historians and adult educationalists who had formed the original *New Left Review*, Thompson wrote: 'we found we had appointed a veritable Dr. Beeching of the socialist intelligentsia...Old Left steam engines were swept off the tracks: wayside halts ("Commitment," "What Next for C.N.D.?", "Women in Love") were boarded up; and the lines were electrified for the speedy traffic from the marxistentialist Left Bank ... Finding ourselves redundant we submitted to dissolution.'[1]

There was much more to it than this, of course. The work of Juliet Mitchell and others in the re-emergent feminist movement was in part inspired by Althusser's use of the concept of ideology, a theoretical approach which, although it debunked Thompson's use of the term 'experience', nevertheless worked in ways he had encouraged, to recreate new subjects of knowledge. But the metaphor holds. Some might argue that, through the rediscovery of the continent and the subsequent programme of translations by *New Left Review* of European Marxism and post-Marxism, the *trans-manche* theory express dumped an extremely ripe mound of manure on the seedlings of British cultural studies, only to bury some of its more fragile shoots. On the other hand, after a long period of isolation it seemed that once again British intellectual life had been opened to the centres of European ideas and this did produce significant developments.

There was, for instance, the formation of the Birmingham Centre for Contemporary Cultural Studies by Richard Hoggart, which, under Stuart Hall, used a synthesis of Althusserian and Gramscian theory to launch some extraordinarily fruitful analyses of popular culture. For adult education, the 1960s were a time of change. Raymond Williams left the Oxford Delegacy to confront Cambridge English head on, Thompson went to Warwick 'Business' University, and John Rex went to Durham. By the mid-1960s adult education had lost many of its most energetic iconoclasts to internal university departments (though in Thompson's and Hoggart's cases, not for long). At the same time, the very expansion of the higher education system that allowed these ex-WEA tutors a route into academia, also drew in many students from lower middle-class and working-class families, who previously might have looked to the WEA in mature life. The Open University, the brainchild of Michael Young, later in the decade, offered structured part-time degree programmes to adults which made the old extra-mural provision look distinctly jaded.

The effect of this epochal change in adult education was that the yoking together of the political struggle and the cultural struggle urged in the immediate post-war period was only fitfully possible. Cultural studies moved into the academic mainstream and, despite its interest in the popular, became increasingly mandarin in its discourses. It was discussed in ways that even the intelligent lay members of adult education classes found hard to grasp, often leaving the field free for the return of a more conservative liberal studies or 'art appreciation' mode of thinking. Thus the mainstreaming of cultural studies left the initial project of a popular critical education in a New Left politics stranded in a time-warp, which eternally celebrated the moment of *The Making* but seemed not to be able to move on – the exceptions being, perhaps, in the development of local studies and creative writing.

By the late 1980s, mainstream cultural studies appeared to be in crisis. Despite the undoubted successes of its mapping of the terrain of popular culture, for Jim McGuigan, one of the more damaging features of the mainstream approach to cultural studies has been the dogmatic insistence on separating contemporary cultural studies from the political economy of culture. [2] Because mainstream cultural studies regards any attempt to map cultural phenomena onto accounts of capitalist development as economic reductionism, (ironically, exactly the demon Thompson was trying to exorcise), they have lost the possibility of political engagement with social life. Instead, they comment upon social life from a distanced and increasingly ironic standpoint. In some of their more recent manifestations, mainstream cultural studies adopt an aristocratic nihilism which utterly refuses to distinguish between social life and its simulations – with ludicrous results, such as in Baudrillard's analysis of the Gulf War.

Another effect has been a kind of uncritical populism, which in a simple inversion of Leavisite concerns, celebrates virtually every manifestation of popular culture as politically progressive. While there is an understandable wish to understand and value everyday meanings in the manner of Williams's insistence that 'culture is ordinary', McGuigan insists that such a stance 'produces inadequate explanation of the material life situations and power relations that shape the mediated experiences of ordinary people'.[3] It's also not much help, he believes, for falsely modest intellectuals merely to record how well people are doing in the face of overwhelming odds. Another effect is that intellectuals themselves have become part of a new post-modern 'class' of taste-creators, hooked on fashion.

However, there has been a growing sociological commentary on post-modernism which, stemming from the work of Habermas, Bourdieu, Giddens and others, has been sceptical of the claims of some kinds of theory. With the work of Frederic Jameson and David Harvey, McGuigan suggests that it has been possible to return to sophisticated analyses of the political economy of cultural studies without falling into the trap of crude reductionism. Through this work it is possible to see post-modernism as a cultural/ideological configuration of late capitalism, which has produced both an authoritarian populism and its antagonists in new social movements.

Is there a renewed role for adult education here for the millennium? If there is, then it could be found in what Thompson, following William Morris, has called 'the education of desire'. Although utopias are currently out of fashion as collective projects, Ruth Levitas has argued that utopian thinking is still possible as a critical tool.[4] Without being prescriptive, it can stimulate a desire for a different way of being from which standpoint it can interrogate the present. One of adult education's traditional functions has been to address that mode of thinking and to help people work with that – whether it be the construction of the Labourist commonwealth in the earlier part of the century, or enabling working-class women to access the higher education movements of the 1980s. The marginal non-mainstream position of adult education has historically enabled intellectuals to open up dialogues with working people, and in its more radical forms has enabled social movements to harness intellectuals to their needs. This marginal space has to be re-occupied and used once more by educators to leave for a moment the hermetically sealed rituals of the academy where the internal debates reach scholastic dimensions of dizziness, to join the dialogues of intelligent lay persons who seek out 'liberal adult education'.

The benefits are obvious to both sides. The mere process of trying to communicate the more extreme flights of cultural theory to adult students often renders its absurdity patent – necessary intellectual difficulty is another matter. Adult education also engages with the experience of mature students, which is so different from those fresh out of school. It should also be a space in which communities and new social movements can secure the services of academics for their own projects. The undoubted excellence of many studies of popular culture could be of even greater value if it were put at the disposal of groups and agencies such as local communities, ethnic minorities, gay rights, women's movement, disabled and aged groups and so on. On a broader scale, cultural studies can enable the project of 'citizenship' to be reconsidered with far more flexible narratives of subjectivity, identity and cultural needs, and with less aesthetic impoverishment than the old Labourist cause. If cultural studies then began reflexively, to understand itself as a formation, as Williams proposed it should, then it might renew its project of a popular education.

After two decades of 'Black Studies', multiculturalism and 'work with ethnic minorities' we seem in some respects to be little further forward; if anything, we have retreated from the militancy of the 1970s and 1980s. Short-term funding for research and outreach projects, the ending of local authority community education policies and, on the part of higher education, a barely disguised zeal for black faces only so long as they come bearing large sums of their countries' sterling currency reserves has led to an incessant reinvention of the wheel. Any achievements are subsequently lost in the filing cabinets of educational institutions forced into a perpetual pursuit of government-inspired targets and never owned by the communities themselves. Communities remain impoverished. In a recent keynote speech at a Black Studies conference in Leeds Amrit Wilson, unfashionably, bemoaned the disjunction of identity politics and class politics. In the name of ethnic cultural studies there are now courses in colleges which deny the link between racism and colonialism; the notion of culture taught in these classes is static – the 'saris and samosas' syndrome. Since dynamic conceptions of culture which include struggle are entirely absent from these courses, students could reasonably draw the inference that history has somehow 'ended', and that their everyday experience of racism is somehow nothing to do with their 'culture'. Such revisionist versions of cultural studies serve only the cultural tourism of a heritage Britain, where minorities function as colourful tokens of Empire that bedeck a nation obsessed with its past.

Notable exceptions to this are participative literacy schemes, such as those in Sheffield, which have altered the agenda by genuinely empowering local communities rather than institutions.[5] Such schemes only occur where local authorities are prepared to entrust serious long-term funding to local communities and allow members of those communities to influence the outcomes. It suggests that a modest shift of funding from institutions to communities might produce greatly enhanced returns. An educational policy that recognised difference and funded communities to negotiate their own educational needs could begin to construct supra-communal identities which no longer relied on the suppression of the Other or the fossilisation of 'Culture'. This shift would recognise the power of marginalised cultures to contribute to the positive transformation of a 'common culture' since, as we have seen, such cultures are not dens of ignorance which only an enlightened middle-class culture can illuminate but sites of resistance and communal value.

As orthodox notions of 'Englishness' lose currency and legitimacy, a new post-colonial settlement urgently needs to be agreed. Education can aid this process only if it becomes a medium of dialogue for those with circumscribed power to discover their own needs and learn how they may satisfy them. In this, students' own cultures will have to be their reservoirs of wisdom and hope and the tradition of informed and committed dialogue in adult education the means of enlightenment. Reflecting on the enduring value of Williams's *Drama in Performance* nearly forty years since its first publication, Graham Holderness wrote:

> this book actually emerged from one of the most supportive educational environments in which it is possible for a teacher to work. It is probably easier to grasp and sustain the notion of culture as a collective social activity, and as a material process of production, in the context of a continual engagement with thinking and learning adult students, than in any other space in the educational system. At a time when, amid extreme political contradictions, those values that used to be sharply differentiated as 'extra-mural' and 'adult education' are becoming major priorities within the central system of higher education, it is appropriate to reinsert into active circulation a book which testifies so eloquently to the possibility of democratic educational culture. [6]

If the centre has begun to engulf the margins, then the project now must be to ensure that those values of a 'democratic educational culture', so dear to the old extra-mural formation, also shape the new 'mass' higher education. [7]

Notes

1 E.P. Thompson, 'The Peculiarities of the English' in *The Poverty of Theory and Other Essays*, Merlin, London 1978, p35.
2 Jim McGuigan, *Cultural Populism*, Routledge, London 1992.
3 *Ibid*, p244.
4 Ruth Levitas, *The Concept of Utopia*, Philip Allen, Hemel Hempstead 1990, p181.
5 See Ahmed Gurnah, (ed), 'Literacy for a Change: a special issue on the Sheffield Black Literacy Campaign', <u>Adults Learning</u>, Vol 3, No 8, April 1992.
6 Graham Holderness, 'Introduction to this Edition', in Raymond Williams, *Drama in Performance*, Open University Press, Milton Keynes 1991.
7 For a promising start in this direction see Peter Scott, *The Meanings of Mass Higher Education*, SHRE and Open University Press, Milton Keynes 1995.

Bibliography

Archival Sources

Staff papers, Central Filing, University of Leeds.
Department of Adult Continuing Education archives, University of Leeds.
The Dobrée Papers, the Brotherton and Special Collections, University of Leeds.
The Raybould Papers, Study of Continuing Education Unit, School of Education, University of Leeds.

Unpublished Material

Janet Coles, 'S. G. Raybould and the Development of Extra-Mural Studies at the University of Leeds 1946-69', M.Ed. thesis, University of Leeds 1992.
Roger Fieldhouse, 'The Ideology of English Responsible Body Adult Education 1925-50', Ph.D. thesis, University of Leeds 1984.

Printed Sources

Henry Abelove *et al*, (eds), *Visions of History*, Manchester University Press, Manchester 1983.
Benedict Anderson, *Imagined Communities*,Verso, London 1983.
Perry Anderson, 'Components of the National Culture', English Questions, Verso, London 1991.
Perry Anderson, 'Socialism and Pseudo Empiricism', New Left Review, 35, 1966, pp2-42.
Chris Baldick, *The Social Mission of English Criticism 1848-1932*, Clarendon Press, Oxford 1987.
T. K. Barrett, 'The Adult Class and Modernist Verse', *Tutors' Bulletin*, no. 7, January 1933, pp12-17.
Logie Barrow, *Independent Spirits: Spiritualism and English Plebeians 1850-1890*, Routledge Kegan Paul, London 1986.
Zigmunt Bauman, *Intimations of Postmodernity*, Routledge, London 1991.

Bibliography

Board of Education, *The Teaching of English in England, Being the Report of the Departmental Committee Appointed by the President of the Board of Education to Enquire into the Position of English in the Educational System of England* [chair: Sir Henry Newbolt] H.M.S.O. London 1921.

R. E. Brettle, 'Reviews', *Tutors' Bulletin*, no. 4, May 1932.

Asa Briggs and John Saville, (eds), *Essays in Labour History*, Macmillan, London 1960.

Dryden Brook, 'Where are we Going ?', *Highway*, Nov. 1938, pp14-15.

James Cameron, 'Education for Freedom', University of Leeds, Department of Adult Education and Extra-Mural Studies, The Raybould Memorial Lecture 1979.

Beatrice Campbell, *Wigan Pier Revisited, Poverty and Politics in the Eighties*, Verso, London 1984.

Martin Carnoy, *Education as Cultural Imperialism*, Longmans, New York 1974.

Guy Chapman, 'The Common People', *Highway*, January 1939, pp97-8.

Partha Chatterjee, *Nationalist Thought and the Colonial World: a Derivative Discourse*, Zed Books, London 1986.

Lin Chun, *The British New Left*, Edinburgh University Press, Edinburgh 1993.

G.D.H. Cole, *The People's Front*, Gollancz, London 1937.

G.D.H. Cole, 'The Lesson for Democracy', *Highway*, March 1939, pp153-55.

G.D.H. Cole 'What Workers' Education Means', *Highway*, October 1952.

Janet Coles, '"With Fire and Faith": R. G. Moulton's university extension mission to the United States', in Stuart Marriott and Barry J. Hake, (eds), *Cultural and Intercultural Experiences in European Adult Education, Essays on Popular Education since 1890*, Leeds Studies in Adult Education, Leeds 1994, pp52-69.

Michael Collins, *Adult Education as Vocation*, Routledge, London 1991.

John Corner, 'Studying culture: reflections and assessments. An interview with Richard Hoggart', *Media Culture and Society*, vol. 13, 1991, pp137-151.

Andy Croft, 'Authors Take Sides: Writers in the Communist Party 1920-1956' in Kevin Morgan, Nina Fishman, Geoff Andrews, (eds), *Opening the Books: New Perspectives in the History of British Communism*, Pluto, London 1995.

Andy Croft, 'Walthamstow, Little Gidding and Middlesbrough: Edward Thompson, Adult Education and Literature', *Socialist History*, no. 8, 1995, pp22-48.

Ioan Davies, 'Cultural Theory in Britain: Narrative and Episteme' in *Theory, Culture & Society*, vol.10, no. 3, August 1993, pp115-154.

Ioan Davies, *Cultural Studies and Beyond*, Routledge, London 1995.

H.D. Dickinson, 'Academic Standards in Adult Education', *Tutors' Bulletin*, no. 20, Feb. 1938, pp35-7.

James Donald, *A Sentimental Education*, Verso, London 1990.

John Dover Wilson, 'Adult Education in North Yorkshire', *Journal of Adult Education*, vol. III, October, 1928.

John Dover Wilson, *Milestones on the Dover Road*, Faber, London 1969.

Brian Doyle,'The Invention of Englishness' in Robert Colls and Philip Dodds, (eds), *Englishness: Politics and Culture 1880-1920*, Croom Helm, Beckenham, 1986, pp89-115.

Brian Doyle, *English and Englishness*, Methuen, London 1989.

Constance Dyson, 'The Approach to History', *Tutors' Bulletin*, July 1946, pp6-8.

Terry Eagleton, *Literary Theory: An Introduction*, Blackwell, Oxford 1983.

Anthony Easthope, *Literary into Cultural Studies*, Routledge, London 1991.

Ifor Evans, 'A New Line in Literature', *Highway*, Nov. 1938, pp10-11.

Bibliography

Roger Fieldhouse, *Adult Education and the Cold War*, Leeds Studies in the Education of Adults, Leeds 1985.

John Goode, 'Thompson and the Significance of Literature', in Kaye and McClelland, (eds), *E.P. Thompson, Critical Perspectives*, 1990, pp183-203.

Antonio Gramsci, *Prison Notebooks*, Q. Hoare and G. Nowell Smith, (eds), Lawrence and Wishart, London 1971.

Robert Gray, 'History, Marxism and Theory' in Kaye and McClelland, (eds), *E.P. Thompson, Critical Perspectives*, 1990, pp153-182.

Michael Green, 'The Centre for Contemporary Cultural Studies' in P. Widdowson, (ed), *Re-Reading English*, Methuen, London 1982, pp77-90.

Linda Grier, *Achievement in Education*, Constable, London 1952.

Ranjit Guha and Gyatri Spivak, *Selected Subaltern Studies*, Oxford University Press, Oxford 1988.

Ahmed Gurnah, (ed), *Culture for Social Renewal*, NIACE, London (forthcoming).

Jürgen Habermas, 'Modernity – an incomplete project' in H. Foster, (ed), *Postmodern Culture*, Pluto, London 1985.

Stuart Hall, 'The Emergence of Cultural Studies and the Crisis of the Humanities', *October*, 53, 1990, pp11-23.

Malcolm Hardman, Ruskin and Bradford, Manchester University Press, Manchester 1986.

J.F.C. Harrison, 'The WEA in the Welfare State' in S.G. Raybould, (ed), *Trends in Adult Education*, London 1959.

J.F.C. Harrison, *Learning and Living 1790-1960*, Routledge Kegan Paul, London 1961.

Terence Hawkes, *That Shakespeherian Rag, essays on a critical process*, Methuen, London 1987.

Eric Hobsbawm, 'The Formation of British Working-Class Culture', in *Worlds of Labour*, Weidenfeld and Nicolson, London 1984, pp176-193.

Thomas Hodgkin, 'University Standards', *Tutors' Bulletin*, Autumn 1948.

Thomas Hodgkin, 'Objectivity, Ideologies and the Present Political Situation', *Highway*, vol. 42, January 1951, pp78-91.

Richard Hoggart, 'One Kind of Critic', *Tutors' Bulletin*, July 1947, p15.

Richard Hoggart, 'Prolegomena to the Second Session', *Tutors' Bulletin*, November 1947, pp7-10.

Richard Hoggart, *The Uses of Literacy*, Pelican, London 1957.

Richard Hoggart and Raymond Williams, 'Working-Class Attitudes', *New Left Review*, no. 1, Jan./Feb. 1960, pp. 26-30.

Richard Hoggart, 'Teaching with Style on Bonamy Dobrée', in *Speaking to Each Other*, Pelican, London 1973.

Richard Hoggart, *A Sort of Clowning, Life and Times 1940-1959*, Oxford University Press, Oxford 1991.

Richard Hoggart, 'In Conversation with Tony Harrison', in Neil Astley, (ed), *Tony Harrison*, Bloodaxe Books, Newcastle 1991.

Ian Hunter, *Culture and Government, The Emergence of Literary Education*, Macmillan, London 1988.

Fred Inglis, *Radical Earnestness*, Oxford University Press, Oxford 1984.

N. A. Jepson, *The Beginnings of English University Adult Education – Policy and Problems*, Michael Joseph, London 1973.

N. A. Jepson, 'Leeds and the Beginning of University Adult Education', *Proceedings of the Leeds Philosophical Society*, Literary and Historical Section vol. VIII, Part III

Bibliography

Harvey J. Kaye and Keith McClelland, (eds), *E.P. Thompson, Critical Perspectives*, Polity, London 1990.

Anthony Kearney, *John Churton Collins, The Louse on the Locks of Literature*, Scottish Academic Press Ltd., Edinburgh 1986.

Michael Kenny, *The First New Left British Intellectuals After Stalin*, Lawrence and Wishart, London 1995.

David Kettler *et al.*, (eds), *Karl Mannheim*, Chichester 1984.

Leopold Labedz, (ed), *Revisionism: Essays on the History of Marxist Ideas*, George Allen and Unwin, London 1962.

Stuart Laing, *Representations of Working-Class Life 1957-1964*, Macmillan, London 1986.

Ruth Levitas, *The Concept of Utopia*, Philip Allen, Hemel Hempstead 1990.

Carl Levy, (ed), *Socialism and the Intelligentsia 1880-1914*, Routledge Kegan Paul, London 1987.

Carl Levy, 'Education and self-education: staffing the early ILP' in Carl Levy, (ed), *Socialism and the Intelligentsia*, 1987, pp135-210.

B. T. McCully, *English Education and the Origins of Indian Nationalism*, Peter Smith, London 1966.

Jim McGuigan, *Cultural Populism*, Routledge, London 1992.

John McIlroy, 'Teacher, Critic, Explorer', in Morgan and Preston, *Raymond Williams*, 1993.

John McIlroy and Sallie Westwood, (eds), *Border Country Raymond Williams in Adult Education*, NIACE, London 1993.

Angela McRobbie, 'New Times in Cultural Studies', *New Formations*, 13, Spring, Routledge, London 1991, pp125-152.

Karl Mannheim, 'Adult Education and the Social Sciences', *Tutors' Bulletin*, no. 20, Feb. 1938, pp27-37.

Karl Mannheim, *Ideology and Utopia*, Kegan Paul, London 1936.

Karl Mannheim, *Diagnosis of Our Time*, Kegan Paul, London 1943.

Karl Mannheim, 'The Sociology of Intellectuals', *Theory, Culture and Society*, vol. 10, no. 3, August 1993: pp45-68.

Stuart Marriott, *Extra-Mural Empires: Service and Self-Interest in English University Adult Education, 1873-1983*, Nottingham Studies in the History of Adult Education, University of Nottingham, 1984.

Ellen Meiksins Wood, 'Falling Though the Cracks: E.P. Thompson and The Debate on Base and Superstructure' in Kaye and McClelland, (eds), *E.P. Thompson, Critical Perspectives*, 1990, pp125-52.

Ellen Meiksins Wood, *The Pristine Culture of Capitalism*, Verso, London 1991.

Andrew Milner, 'Cultural Materialism, Culturalism and Post-Culturalism: The Legacy of Raymond Williams', *Theory, Culture & Society*, vol. 11, 1994, pp43-73.

W. J. Morgan and P. Preston, (eds), *Raymond Williams, Politics, Education, Letters*, Macmillan, London 1993.

Francis Mulhern, *The Moment of Scrutiny*, Verso, London 1979.

Alan O'Connor, *Raymond Williams, Writing, Culture, Politics*, Basil Blackwell, Oxford 1989.

Dick Pels, 'Missionary Sociology between Left and Right: A Critical Introduction to Mannheim', *Theory, Culture and Society*, vol. 10, no. 3, August 1993, pp45-68.

Oliver Pickering, *Sir Michael Sadler: a Bibliography*, with biographical essay by Stuart Marriott, Leeds Studies in Adult Education, Leeds 1982.

Karl Polanyi, 'What Kind of Adult Education?', *Leeds Weekly Citizen*, 21 September 1945, p5.

Bibliography

Karl Polanyi, 'Adult Education and the Working Class Outlook', *Tutors' Bulletin*, November 1946, pp. 8-14.

Jonathan Rée, 'Socialism and the Educated Working Class', in Carl Levy, *Socialism and the Intelligentsia*, 1987, pp211-18.

Jonathan Rée, *Proletarian Philosophers*, Clarendon Press, Oxford 1984.

Kristin Ross, *The Emergence of Social Space, Rimbaud and the Paris Commune*, Minnesota University Press, Minnesota 1988.

Sheila Rowbotham, 'Travellers in a strange country: responses of working class students to the University Extension Movement, 1873-1910', *History Workshop Journal* 12, Autumn 1981.

Sheila Rowbotham, *The Past is Before Us, Feminism in Action since the 1960s*, Penguin, London 1990.

Michael Ernest Sadler, *Selections from Michael Sadler, Studies in World Citizenship*, compiled by Dr. J.H. Higginson, Leeds University Press, Leeds 1979.

Edward Said, *Orientalism*, Penguin, London 1980.

Edward Said, *Culture and Imperialism*, Chatto, London 1993.

Drusilla Scott, *A.D. Lindsay*, Blackwell, Oxford 1971.

Peter Searby & the Editors, 'Edward Thompson as a teacher: Yorkshire and Warwick' in *Protest and Survival, the Historical Experience, Essays for E. P. Thompson*, John Rule and Robert Malcolmson, (eds), London 1994.

H. C. Sherwood, 'The Teaching of Literature', *Tutors' Bulletin*, no. 22 April 1939, p23.

Brian Simon, (ed), *The Search for Enlightenment: the Working Class and Adult Education in the Twentieth Century*, Lawrence and Wishart, London 1990.

Kate Soper, 'Socialist Humanism' in Kaye and McClelland, *E.P. Thompson, Critical Perspectives, op. cit.*, pp204-232.

W.J.H. Sprott, 'Review of Karl Mannheim's, *Ideology and Utopia*', in *Tutors' Bulletin*, no. 20 Feb. 1938, pp23-26.

Gareth Stedman Jones, *Languages of Class*, Routledge, London 1980.

Tom Steele, *Alfred Orage and the Leeds Arts Club 1893-1923*, Scolar, Aldershot 1990.

Tom Steele, 'Class Consciousness to Cultural Studies: the WEA in West Yorkshire 1914-1950', in *Studies in the Education of Adults*, vol. 19, no 2, Autumn, 1987, pp109-126.

Tom Steele, 'Metropolitan Extensions: Comparison of two moments in the export of British university adult education', in Martha Friedenthal-Haase, Barry J. Hake, Stuart Marriott, (eds), *British-Dutch-German Relationships in Adult Education*, Leeds Studies in the Education of Adults, Leeds 1992, pp. 73-99

Tom Steele, 'Arnold Hauser in England, Sociology in a Cold Climate', in D. Wallace and Jery Zaslove, (eds), *Arnold Hauser and the Social History of Art: Modernism and Modernity*, Vancouver, forthcoming.

Noel Stock, *The Life of Ezra Pound*, Penguin, London 1974.

W.E. Styler, *Yorkshire and Yorkshire North, the history of the Yorkshire North District of the Workers' Educational Association 1914-1964*, WEA Yorkshire (North) District, Leeds 1964.

Julia Swindells and Lisa Jardine, *What's Left, Women in Culture and the Labour Movement*, Routledge, London 1990.

Göran Therborn, 'The Life and Times of Socialism', *New Left Review* 194, July/August 1992, pp17-32.

Bibliography

E.P. Thompson, 'A Cultural Policy', *Tutors' Bulletin*, Summer 1950, 7-12.

E.P. Thompson, 'Against "University" Standards', University of Leeds Department of Extra-Mural Studies, Adult Education Papers, vol. 1, no. 4, 1950.

E.P. Thompson, 'William Morris and the Moral Issues Today' in *The American Threat to British Culture*, Arena Publications, London 1951, pp25-30.

E.P. Thompson, 'Homage to Tom Maguire' in Asa Briggs and John Saville, (eds), *Essays in Labour History*, Macmillan, London 1960.

E.P. Thompson, 'Review of The Long Revolution – II', *New Left Review*, no. 10 1961, pp34-9.

E.P. Thompson, 'Education and Experience', University of Leeds, Department of Adult Continuing Education, Albert Mansbridge Lecture 1968.

E.P. Thompson, *The Making of the English Working Class*, Pelican, London 1968.

E.P. Thompson, *William Morris: Romantic to Revolutionary*, Merlin, London (2nd edition) 1977.

E.P. Thompson, 'Caudwell' in J. Saville and R. Miliband, (eds), *Socialist Register 1977*, Merlin, London 1977, pp228-276.

E.P. Thompson, 'Outside the Whale' reprinted in *The Poverty of Theory and Other Essays*, Merlin, London 1978.

E.P. Thompson, 'The Politics of Theory', in R. Samuel, (ed), *People's History and Socialist Theory*, Routledge & Kegan Paul, London 1981.

E.P. Thompson, *The Heavy Dancers*, Pantheon, New York 1985.

E.P. Thompson, *Customs in Common*, Penguin, London 1993.

G. H. Thompson, *The Field of Study for WEA Classes*, Workers' Educational Association, London 1938.

G. H. Thompson, 'Beehive Incident', *Highway*, Dec. 1939.

G.H. Thompson, 'Views on Literature' York's North Record supplement to *Highway*, April 1939, n.p.

G.H. Thompson, 'What Sails shall be Set?', *Highway*, Feb. 1940, pp111-13.

G.H. Thompson, 'Progress and Aims in Adult Education', *Tutors' Bulletin*, April 1945.

George Thomson, 'Our National Cultural Heritage' in *Britain's Cultural Heritage*, Arena Publications, London 1952, pp3-19.

Colin Titmus and Tom Steele, *Adult Education for Independence, Adult Education in British Tropical Africa*, Leeds Studies in Continuing Education, Leeds 1995.

C. E. Trevelyan, *On the Education of the People of India*, London 1838.

Graeme Turner, *British Cultural Studies, an Introduction*, Routledge, London 1990

Gauri Viswanathan, *Masks of Conquest*, Columbia University Press, New York 1990.

K. C. Vyas, *The Development of National Education in India*, Bombay 1954.

Morris Watnick, 'Relativism and Class Consciousness: Georg Lukács' in Leopold Labedz, (ed), *Revisionism: Essays on the History of Marxist Ideas*, 1962, pp142-165.

Raymond Williams, 'A Note on Mr. Hoggart's Appendices', Adult Education, XXI, 2 1948, pp96-8.

Raymond Williams, 'Some Experiments in Literature Teaching', Rewley House Papers, II, X 1949-50, pp9-15.

Raymond Williams, 'Books for Teaching "Culture and Environment"', *The Use of English*, 1, 3, 1950, pp134-40.

Raymond Williams, 'Going on Learning', *New Statesman*, 30 May 1959.

Raymond Williams, *The Long Revolution*, Pelican, London 1961.

Bibliography

Raymond Williams, 'An Open Letter to WEA Tutors', Workers' Educational Association, London 1961.

Raymond Williams, 'The Common Good', Adult Education XXXIV, 4, November 1961, pp192-9.

Raymond Williams, *Television Technology and Cultural Form*, Fontana/Collins, London 1974.

Raymond Williams, *Politics and Letters*, Verso, London 1979.

Raymond Williams, *Towards 2000*, Pelican, London 1985.

Raymond Williams, 'The Future of Cultural Studies', in *The Politics of Modernism*, Verso, London 1989.

Raymond Williams, 'Adult Education and Social Change' in Neil Belton, Francis Mulhern and Jenny Taylor, (eds), *What I Came to Say*, Hutchinson, London 1990, pp157-166.

W.E. Williams, 'Reply', *Highway*, Dec. 1939, p55.

W.E. Williams, 'The Limitations of Literacy', *Tutors' Bulletin*, no. 8, April 1933, pp4-6.

Henk E. S. Woldring, *Karl Mannheim, The Development of his Thought*, Van Gorcum, Assen/Maastricht 1986.

A.W. Wright, *G.D.H. Cole and Socialist Democracy*, Clarendon Press, Oxford 1979.

Patrick Wright, *On Living in an Old Country*, Verso, London 1985.

Stephen Yeo, 'Notes on three socialisms – collectivism, statism, associationism – mainly in late-nineteenth- and early-twentieth century Britain' in Carl Levy, (ed), *Socialism and the Intelligentsia*, 1987, pp219-270.

INDEX

A

Adorno, Theodore, 106, 107, 114
Adult Education, 132
Africa, 42, 145
Althusser, Louis, 21, 169, 198, 205
Amis, Kingsley, 66
Amsterdam, 106
Anderson, Perry, 3, 140, 203
Angell, Norman, 194
Anglicism, 55
Antwerp, 106
Arena, 168
Army Bureau of Current
Affairs (ABCA), 5, 73, 129, 131, 132, 145, 177
Arnold, Matthew, 44, 50, 51-52, 61, 68, 69, 76, 86, 195
Arts Club, 5
Arts Council, 20, 74, 134, 170, 203
Attlee, Clement, 27, 34
Auden, W.H., 72, 132
Austria, 145

B

Bacon, Francis, 56
Bacup, Derbys, 36
Baker, Bill, 153, 154
Bakhtin, Mikhail, 153
Baldick, Chris, 44, 50
Balliol College, Oxford, 5, 75, 99, 108
Bantock, Geoffrey, 195
Barrett, T.K., 86
Baudrillard, Jean, 207
BBC, 137-138, 139
Beales, H.L., 15
Beeching, Dr, 205
Bell, Bishop, 109
Benedict, Ruth, 87, 196
Bengal, 54
Benjamin, Walter, 107, 153
Beresford, Maurice, 127
Bertram, Anthony, 78
Besant, Annie, 75
Bethnal Green, 27
Betjeman, John, 130
Beveridge Report 1942, 132
Beveridge, William, 106
Binni, Professor, 130-131
Birmingham, 50
Birmingham Centre for
Contemporary Cultural Studies
(BCCCS), 3, 6, 29, 30, 74, 118, 139, 205

Birmingham, University of, 60, 62, 138
Blake, William, 45, 161, 162
Blatchford, Robert, 45
Bloomsbury Set, 17, 167
Board of Education, 76
Bolshevik Revolution, 64, 67
Bolshevism, 38, 65, 66-67
Bonhoeffer, Dietrich, 109
Bosanquet, Bernard, 108
Bourne, George, 195
Bourdieu, P, 198, 207
Bown, Lalage, 21
Bradford, 153, 158
Bradley, F.H., 108
Brahmin, 53
Braine, John, 153
Brecht, Berthold, 153
Brett, R.L., 133
Briggs, Asa, 15, 153
British Institute of Adult Education, 73
Brook, Dryden, 88, 89
Brown, Ivor, 72, 80
Buber, Martin, 106
Budapest, 14, 98, 107
Bulgaria, 144, 145
Bureau of Current Affairs, 73
Bureau of Education for the British Empire, 58
Burke, Edmund, 54, 59
Burns, Emile, 167
Burns, Robert, 45
Butler, R.A.B., 30, 132, 204
Byron, Lord, 162

C

Calcutta University Commission, 58
Cambridge, University of, 7, 19, 20, 22, 23, 42, 49, 59, 82, 100, 126, 144, 148-149, 177, 187, 192, 197, 205
Cambridge University Press, 86
Cameron, J.M., 20, 77, 134
Campaign for Nuclear Disarmament (CND), 205
Campbell, Beatrix, 140
Carlyle, Thomas, 51, 61, 130, 160, 184
Carpenter, Edward, 42, 45, 75
Caudwell, Christopher, 153, 162, 168, 169, 195-196
Cecil, Lord David, 153
Chapman, Guy, 72, 78, 90, 91, 148
Charter Act 1813, 54
Chartism, 34, 150
Chatham House, 111
Chaucer, Geoffrey, 162
Chesterton, G.K., 82
Chichester, 109
Chinese Revolution, 167
Christian Socialism, 5, 99, 109, 114
Christian Socialist Moot, 107-113, 114
Christminster, 177
Church of England, 57
Churton Collins, John, 50, 60-61, 62, 136
Clarke, Fred, 112
Clay, Harold, 76
Cleckheaton, 153

Cleveland, 40

Cobbett, William, 180

Cockburn Grammar School, 118, 127

Cold War, 6, 11, 20, 73, 119, 120, 123, 133, 147, 164, 167, 179, 182, 203

Cole, G.D.H., 3, 12-13, 15, 20, 26, 72, 75, 90, 91, 92, 99, 108, 112, 114, 130, 150, 160, 181, 196

Colebrook, Henry, 55

Coleridge, Samuel Taylor, 110, 130

Collins, Clifford, 187, 194

Collins, Henry, 21, 23, 179

Colonial Service, 179

Communism, 95, 106, 161, 171

Communist Party of Great Britain, 20, 21, 23-25, 27, 101-102, 134, 146, 163, 164, 166, 177 196

Communist Party Historians' Group, 3, 21

Connolly, Cyril, 130

Conrad, Joseph 125

Conservative Party, 148

Cornwallis, Lord, 55

Council for the Encouragement of Music and Drama (CEMA), 73-74

Cowper, William, 56

Cresset Press, 132

The Critic, 23, 123, 187

Croce, Benedetto, 131

Croft, Andy, 153, 166-167

D

Daily Express, 187

Daily Herald, 83, 187

Daily Mail, 83, 187

Daily Mirror, 130, 187

Daily Telegraph, 187

Daily Worker, 187

Dante Alighieri, 63

Davies, Ioan, 14

Dawson, Christopher, 195

Deherme, Georges, 120

Denby, Elizabeth, 78

Dent, Joseph, 74

Derbyshire, 36-37

Dickens, Charles, 44, 51, 83, 125, 186

Dickinson, H.D., 88-89

Disraeli, Benjamin, 35

Dixon, John, 50

Dobb, Maurice, 149

Dobrée, Bonamy, 5, 20, 119, 124, 126, 127-129, 131-132

Donald, James, 51

Dover Wilson, John, 63, 67, 69, 76, 86-87, 195

Doyle, Brian, 4, 50-52, 54, 65-66

Duff, Alexander, 56

Durham, University of, 205

Dyson, Constance, 87

E

Eagleton, Terry, 49, 50, 198-199

Easthope, Anthony, 30

East India Company, 53, 57, 60

Education Act 1870, 2

Education Act 1944, 30, 132

Elias, Norbert, 92, 107

Eliot, George, 44

Eliot, T.S., 12, 82, 86, 87, 99, 108, 110, 128, 131, 166, 183, 195, 197
Empson, W.E., 188, 194
Elvin, H.L., 83
Engels, Friedrich, 159
English Association, 64
Ensor, James, 111
Epstein, Jacob, 130
Evans, Ifor, 91
Extension Committee, 10

F

Faber and Faber, 137
Fabianism, 67
Fabian Society, 38, 108, 149
Fascism, 20, 95
Fieldhouse, Roger, 11, 13, 123, 178
Fields, G.C., 27
Figgis, Neville, 75
First World War, see World War One
Forster, E.M., 121, 153
Fox, Ralph, 153, 197
Foucault, Michel, 51, 201
France, 128
Frankfurt, 106, 107, 109, 114, 116
Frankfurt Institute, 106
Frazer, J.G., 87
Free Church Institution, 56

G

Galsworthy, John, 83, 186
Gandhi, Mahatma, 75
Gay, John, 168,
General Strike, 46
Germany, 108, 109, 110
Giddens, John, 207
Ginsburg, Morris, 98, 106

Giotto, 127
Gissing, George, 125, 186
Golden Dawn, 75
Goldman, Lucien, 198
Goode, John, 153, 162, 163
Gorky, Maxim, 168
Gosse, Edmund, 130
Gramsci, Antonio, 38, 39, 131, 153, 161, 167, 169, 171, 198
Grant, Arthur, 42
Gray, Robert, 171
Grayson, Victor, 75
Green, Ernest, 10, 146, 178
Green, Michael, 14
Green, T.H., 108
Greene, Graham, 133
Greenwood, Arthur, 76
Groningen, 106
Guild Socialism, 75, 108
Gulf War, 207
Gurvitch, George, 106

H

Habermas, Jürgen, 185, 198, 207
Hackney, 202
Halifax, 151
Hall, Stuart, 15, 105, 126, 139, 140, 205
Hammonds, The, 196
Hardie, Kier, 41
Hardy, Thomas, 178
Harrison, J.F.C., 10, 14, 20, 75, 123, 134, 151
Harrison, Tony, 29
Harrogate, 21
Harvey, David, 207
Hastings, 178
Hastings Trade Council, 191-192

Hastings, Warren, 55-56, 67
Hauser, Arnold, 92, 98, 111
Hawkes, Terence, 67, 69
Hegelianism, 108
Heine, Heinrich, 44
Highway, 11, 17, 72, 78-79, 81, 88, 90, 120, 180
Hill, Christopher, 21, 149, 150, 167, 186
His Majesty's Inspector of Schools (HMI), 27, 68, 76, 178
History Workshop, 3, 21
Hitler, Adolf, 109
Hobsbawm, Eric, 3, 21, 23, 33-34, 35, 39, 45, 46
Hodgkin, Thomas, 1, 10, 11, 73, 179, 180, 188
Hoggart, Richard, 1, 3, 5, 14-18, 20, 21, 23, 27-30, 38, 40, 43, 62, 74-75, 82, 118-141, 164, 181, 182-183, 184, 188, 189, 205, 206
Holderness, Graham, 210
Holland, 106
Hollywood, 163, 164
Horizon,130, 133
Horkheimer, Max, 106, 107
House of Lords, 179
Huddersfield, 154
Hull, 40, 134
Hull, University of, 11, 20, 21, 28, 118, 119, 132, 133
Hunslet, 5, 16, 129
Hunter, Ian, 50, 51, 68
Huxley, Aldous, 81, 82

I

Ibsen, Henrik, 44
Independent Labour Party, 43, 75, 158
India, 4, 53-58, 60, 66, 145
India Act 1853, 57
Indian Civil Service, 58
Industrial Revolution, 66, 94-95, 149, 159
'Industrial Trainers', 183, 184
Inglis, Fred, 158, 204
Institute for Social Research, 107
Institute of Directors, 74
International Library for Sociology and Social Reconstruction, 111
International Relations, 187
Italian Popular Universities, 38
Italy, 5, 145

J

Jackson, Brian, 140-141
Jackson, Tommy, 168
Jacques, Frank, 144-148, 150, 177
Jameson, Frederic, 207
Jameson, Storm, 72, 81, 130
Jardine, Lisa, 140, 141
Jessop, Frank, 180
Johnson, Samuel, 59
Joint Committee for Extension Lectures and Tutorial Classes, 10
Jones, W. , 55
Jonson, Ben, 154
Jowett, Benjamin, 61, 159

K

Kearney, Anthony, 61
Keble College, Oxford, 64
Keele, University of, 112

Kegan Paul Publishers, 111
Kettle, Arnold, 26, 153
Klingender, Francis, 21, 28, 137
Knights, Lionel C, 27, 80, 81, 83, 186, 187, 194
Koestler, Arthur, 133
Korean War, 21, 164
Kracauer, Siegfried, 194
Kramer, Jacob, 127
Kropotkin, Peter, 122

L

Labour Colleges, 9, 13, 202
Labourism, 27
Labour Party, 6, 13, 20, 24-25, 34, 43, 46, 69, 75, 76, 77, 90, 94, 102, 132, 137, 151, 157, 159, 163, 170, 185
Laing, Stuart, 14, 181, 185
Lancashire, 34
Lane, Allen, 74
Langland, William, 162
Laski, Harold, 72, 99, 106
Lawrence and Wishart, 153, 167
Lawrence, D.H., 17, 30, 81-82, 122, 128, 164, 195
Leavis, F.R., 5, 14, 16, 17, 19, 20, 22, 24, 29, 30, 69, 81-84, 119, 124, 126, 140, 141, 152-153, 164, 167, 183, 186, 187, 188, 190, 193, 194, 195, 197
Leavis, Q.D., 5, 16, 17, 22, 27-28, 119, 125, 126, 136, 137, 153, 188, 190, 194
Leavisism, 2, 6, 9, 14, 16, 23, 24, 49, 81-85, 91, 92, 119, 120, 122, 123, 125, 128, 129, 170, 176, 185, 186, 192, 193, 197, 203, 207

Leeds, 3, 5, 18, 29, 50, 51, 118, 127, 131, 151, 159, 209
Leeds Arts Club, 89, 131
Leeds, University of, 5, 10, 11, 20, 21, 27, 42, 62, 77, 88, 90, 105, 108, 118, 119, 123, 127, 130, 134, 144, 153, 156, 163, 178, 179, 180, 202
Left Book Club, 20, 90
Leicester, University of, 138
Leiden, 106
Lenin, V.I., 67, 168
Lerner, Laurence, 21
Levitas, Ruth, 207
Levy, Carl, 39-40
Lewis, C.S., 28, 137
Lindsay, A.D., 1, 5, 99, 107-114
Lindsay, Jack, 197
Liverpool, 50
Local Education Authorities, 67
London, 17, 36, 43, 106
London Institute of Education, 112
London School of Economics, 98, 102, 106
London, University of, 42, 59, 73, 82
Long Revolution, 6
Löwe, Adolph, 92, 99, 107, 109, 112-113
Lukács, Georg, 14, 99, 107, 115, 116, 153, 167
Lynd, R.S. and H.M., 195
Lyotard, Francois, 166

M

MacAulay, Thomas, 52-53, 56
MacColl, D.S., 58

MacDonald, Ramsay, 102
MacNiece, Louis, 130
Maguire, Tom, 40
de Man, Henrick, 107
Manchester, 27, 50, 112
Manchester, University of, 27, 73
Mannheim, Karl, 1, 2, 5, 14, 92-93, 98-116, 122, 135, 160, 171, 184, 196, 203
Mankowitz, Wolf, 22-23, 123, 187
Mao Tse Tung, 167
Marcuse, Herbert, 106, 107
Marlowe, Christopher, 162
Marsden, Denis, 141
Martin, Kingsley, 194
Marvell, Andrew, 162
Marx, Karl, 41, 162
Marxism, 4, 6, 9, 13, 14, 27, 41, 85, 91, 93, 98, 99, 107, 111, 115, 116, 140-141, 148, 149, 150, 160-163, 165, 166, 167, 168, 176, 179, 187, 190, 193, 196, 197, 198, 201, 203, 205
Mayer, William, 194
Mayfield, Percy, 132, 134
McCabe, Colin, 49
McGill, Donald, 28
McGuigan, Jim, 206, 207
McLean, Tony, 21, 179, 180
McMillan, Margaret, 52
Meiskins Wood, Ellen, 45, 165
Mennicke, Carl, 106, 107
Merton Chair in English Language and Literature, Oxford University, 62
Middlesbrough, 21, 63, 132, 134, 137, 152
Milner, Alfred, 185, 197-198
Milton, John, 44, 56, 89, 162
Milverton, Lord, 179
Ministry of Education, 178, 191
Mitchell, Juliet, 205
Modern Quarterly, 168
Moore, T.S., 128
Moorman, Frederic, 42, 59-60, 62, 64, 127, 136
Moot, see Christian Socialist Moot
Morley, 159
Morris, William, 26, 45, 79, 87, 114, 153, 160, 163, 169, 171, 196, 207
Morton, A.L., 90, 153
Mosley College of Aligargh, 58
Moulton, Charles, 60, 61
Muggletonianism, 161
Muir, Kenneth, 26, 153, 194
Mumford, Lewis, 195
Murray, Gilbert, 148, 188
Murry, Middleton, 133
Mussolini, Benito, 131

N

Naples, 130, 131
National Arts Collection Fund, 74
National Cultural Committee, 167
National Gallery, 74
National Union of Teachers, 184
Nazism, 108, 167, 203
Netherlands, see Holland
Newbolt Committee, 64, 76
Newbolt Report 1920, 4, 52, 63,

64-66, 67, 68, 69, 203
Newcastle-upon-Tyne, 60
New Forest, 130
New Left, 1, 3, 6, 13, 15, 25, 30, 99, 106, 115, 116, 161, 176, 204, 205, 206
New Left Review, 24, 126, 139, 205
New Life Movement, 75
New Reasoner, 166
New Universities Movement, 42, 112
Nietzscheanism, 75
North Staffordshire, 112, 178, 179
Nottingham, University of, 11

O

Oakshott, Michael, 108
O'Connor, Alan, 188
Oldham, J.H., 108, 109, 110
'Old Humanists', 183, 184
Open University, 185, 206
Orage, Alfred, 59, 75, 89, 100, 130, 131, 187
Order of the Knights Geruda, 75
Orientalism, 55-56, 58, 67
Orwell, George, 5, 28, 72, 125, 126, 130, 137, 140, 166, 171, 194
Our Time, 130
Oxford, 3, 109
Oxford Delegacy, 5, 10, 11, 12, 20, 23, 25, 57, 58, 59, 62, 93, 99, 127, 135, 147, 178-180, 187, 192, 205
Oxford House, 64
Oxford Tutorial Classes

Committee, 147
Oxford, University of, 21, 42, 59, 65, 91, 100, 108, 178-180

P

Paine, Thomas, 45, 59
Pelican Books, 30, 74
Pels, Dick, 107, 110
Penguin Books, 74, 132, 184
Plato, 10
Playfair, Lord, 44
Plebs League, 13
Plessner, Helmuth, 106
Polanyi, Karl, 1, 92-93, 95, 101, 109, 181, 184, 196
Politics and Letters, 21, 23, 24, 187, 196
Pollitt, Harry, 147
Pollock, Channing, 56
Poole, H.E., 83
Pope, Alexander, 162
Popular Front, 20
Postgate, Raymond, 90
Pound, Ezra, 86, 137
Powys, J.C., 81, 82
Pritchett, V.S., 130
'Public Educator', 184
Pudney, John, 130

Q

Queen Mary College, London, 91
Queen's College Trade Union School, 147

R

Race, Mrs, 152
Rancière, Jacques, 37
Raybould, Sidney, 1, 10, 11, 77, 91, 123, 134, 144-148, 150-155,

158, 178, 180, 188
Read, Herbert, 62, 72, 122, 127, 128
Reasoner Group, 140
Redcar, 124
Rée, Jonathan, 37
Reizler, Kurt, 107
Révèsz, 106
Rex, John, 20, 105, 205
Richards, I.A., 68, 81, 82, 153, 186, 188
Rilke, Rainer, 130
Robbins Report on Universities 1963, 30, 204
Rockefeller Foundation, 106
Rosicrucians, 75
Rotha, P, 194
Rousseau, Jean-Jacques, 161
Rowbotham, Sheila, 3, 40, 140, 202
Rowse, A.L., 149
Ruskin College, Oxford, 3, 22
Ruskin, John, 40-41, 51, 114, 127, 160

S

Sadler, Michael, 42, 57-60, 64, 68, 74, 108, 127, 178
Said, Edward, 4
Salisbury Plain, 148
Samuel, Raphael, 21
Saville, John, 21, 150
Scrutiny, 2, 16, 27, 81, 164, 183, 186, 194
Second World War, see World War Two
Sedgwick, Fred, 147, 150, 152
Shakespeare, William, 44, 56,

59, 60, 63, 65, 74, 76, 84, 169
Shaw, George Bernard, 45, 186
Shaw, Roy, 20, 27, 123, 134, 155
Sheffield, 50, 209
Shelley, Percy Bysshe, 45, 162
Shepley, 154, 155, 160
Sherwood, H.C., 83
Simon, Brian, 50
Simon, Lady, 188
Soames, Janet, 194
Social Democrats, 67
Social Revolutionary Party, 67
Socrates, 10
Soper, Kate, 165
Sorel, Georges, 59
Soviet Union, 106, 164, 196
Sprott, W.J.H., 100-101
Stebbing, Susan, 192, 193
Stedman Jones, Gareth, 43, 50
Stein, Walter, 20, 27
St Patrick, 18
Stuart, James, 42
Swindells, Susan, 140-141

T

Tagore, Rabindranath, 58
Tawney, R.H., 2, 3, 15, 72, 77, 79, 90, 99, 105, 108, 111, 112, 114, 138, 160, 181, 195, 196
Technical Education Act 1889, 60
Technical Education Centres, 61
Temperance Movement, 184
Temple, Archbishop, 108
Tennyson, Alfred Lord, 60
Thatcherism, 141, 200
Theosophy, 75
Therborn, Göran, 35-36
Thinkers' Library, 188

Thompson, Denys, 16, 27, 81, 118

Thompson, Dorothy, 21, 160

Thompson, Edward Snr., 91, 144

Thompson, E.P., 3, 5, 6, 13, 14, 15, 16, 20, 21-27, 29, 30, 33, 34, 38, 82, 88, 91, 116, 125, 126, 128, 134, 136, 139, 140, 144-172, 176, 177, 178, 180, 188, 193, 194, 196, 202, 204, 205, 206, 207

Thompson, G.H., 1, 10, 12, 17-19, 26, 43, 64, 73-80, 84, 85, 88, 89, 90-91, 120, 150, 151, 155, 156, 170, 180, 181, 186, 188

Thomson, George, 168, 169, 196

Thornton, Joe, 159

Thouless, Robert, 192, 193

Three Arts Club, 131

The Times, 73, 187

Todmorden, 152

Tolstoy, Lev, 44, 84

Tönnies, Ferdinand, 195

Torr, Donna, 167

Toynbee, Arnold, 108, 120-121, 133

Toynbee Hall, 64

Trade Union Congress (TUC), 147

Tressell, Robert, 125, 178

Trevelyan, Charles, 53, 57

Trevelyan, G.M., 149

Trilling, Lionel, 133

Tribune, 137

Trotskyism, 27

Turner, Graeme, 14

Tutors' Association, 11, 23, 72, 99, 102, 114

Tutors' Bulletin, 11, 14, 72-73, 81, 83, 100, 102, 120, 123, 169

Tweedale, Marquise of, 57

U

UNESCO, 118

Union of Soviet Socialist Republics (USSR), see Soviet Union

United States of America, 106, 144, 145

Universités Populaire, 38, 138

Utrecht, 106

V

Vansittart, Lord, 179

Vaughan, Charles, 59

Vickers, John, 123, 147

Vienna, 98

Virgil, 63

Viswanathan, Gauri, 53-54

W

Wales, 17, 127, 187

Warwick, University of, 205

Watnick, Morris, 116

Webb, Beatrice, 36, 37, 102, 150

Weber, Max, 138, 195, 196

Weberianism, 98, 99, 107, 122

Wedgwood Memorial College, 123, 146, 147

Wells, H.G., 122

West Africa, 11, 179

West, Alick, 197

Weston, Jessie L., 87

West Riding, 6, 21, 74, 127, 136, 150, 151, 154, 157, 158, 178, 204

Whitman, Walt, 45

Wicksteed, P.H., 62

Williams, J.R., 80-81
Williams, Raymond, 1, 3, 5, 6, 7,
11-16, 20, 22-31, 38, 51, 74, 77-
78, 82, 91, 105, 123, 125-127, 129,
135, 140, 158, 160, 161, 162, 176-
198, 204, 205, 207, 208, 210
Williams, W.E., 72-75, 77-78, 79,
80-81, 82, 88, 90, 91, 120, 131,
170
Willis, Paul, 29
Wilson, Amrit, 209
Wilson, Harold, 185
Wilson, Horace, 55
Wiltshire, Harold, 11
Wisconsin, University of, 106
Woldring, H.E.S., 109
Wordsworth, William, 59, 162
Working Men's Colleges, 44, 50
Working Men's Institutes, 166
World War One, 46, 64, 100
World War Two, 9, 19, 49, 118,
120
Wright Mills, C., 160-165
Writers' Group, 167

Y

Yorkshire, 10, 17, 19, 26, 41, 43,
62, 63, 67, 75-76, 78, 80, 89, 136,
151, 204
Young, Michael, 206
Yugoslavia, 144, 145

Z

Zimmern, Alfred, 108